TO MY WIFE

תנו לה מפרי ידיה

PREFACE

Asked to define the meaning of the term *Shekinah*, Rabbi Sherira Gaon, the famous head of the celebrated Academy of Pumbedita, Babylonia, wrote: "Know, that the Shekinah is to be found among the scholars of the Academy, it is the light of God abiding among them." Divested of its metaphorical expression, this remark of the great leader of Judaism in the second half of the tenth century contains a profound truth, that the spiritual and intellectual life of the Jews always had its center of gravity in the Talmud Academies, or Yeshibot. A knowledge of the life of the Yeshibah will therefore bring us closer to an understanding of the history of the Jews in the last two thousand years.

The lectures presented to the public in this volume, though delivered at long intervals and called forth by certain occasions, form a unified collection. They all have the same purpose, to give the reader some insight into the cultural life of the Jew, by making him acquainted with the bearers of this culture. It was in the Talmud Academies that the spiritual life of the people pulsated, and hence a closer acquaintance with the ideas and ideals of the talmudic scholar will lead to a better knowledge of that life.

The talmudic scholar is the normal type of Jew by which Rabbinic Judaism is to be judged, though, it is true, the normal Jew must not be confounded with the average one. The average Jew was not a talmudic scholar, but the normal one was. The development, however, of the average to the normal is one of the most interesting features of the history of the Jews. By the seventeenth century the average Jew, at least in Eastern Europe, was a talmudic scholar.

Since the loss of political independence Jewish public life found its main outlet in educational activity and the talmudic scholar was the cultural ideal. The first essay, "The Jewish Primary School", attempts to sketch how this ideal dominated elementary education.

Scribes, Pharisees and similar names are often used as devices for saving one the trouble of studying the lives of those so designated. The unbiased reader of the second, third and fourth essays, "The Disciple of the Wise", "The Rabbinical Student", and "The Religion of the Pharisee," will have no difficulty in distinguishing the true picture of the Pharisee from his caricature.

The main study of the Talmudist centered in the Halakah, and accordingly I have placed at the end of the first part of this group of lectures the one on "Jewish Thought as Reflected in the Halakah." I hope that I have not entirely failed in my attempt at showing the permanent importance of the Halakah for an adequate understanding of Judaism.

The second part of the volume, consisting of six biographical sketches of modern Talmudists, stands in close relation to the first part. I have often been struck by the very strange phenomenon that the historians who are immensely interested in the history of the Jew of two thousand years ago or more are entirely indifferent towards the later development of the Jewish people. And yet it is only that period of history which is nearest to us that we can claim to know with some measure of certainty.

It has been well said, that the first duty of the historian is to forget his own time and country and become the sympathetic and interested contemporary of the things and events he treats. But if it be very difficult for a modern man to transform himself into a monk or a rabbi of the twelfth century, it is well-nigh impossible for one of today to penetrate into the soul of a Pharisee of two thousand years ago. The approach we have to the understanding of a personality like Hillel or R. Johanan ben Zakkai is not through Philo or Paul, that would be an attempt to explain that which is unknown by that which is equally unknown, but through men like R. Elijah Wilna or R. Israel Salanter. These great Talmudists and Saints of modern times well known to us, show how the devotion to the Torah and the extreme rigorism in the observance of its precepts, far from developing a legalistic and external piety, were the main motives in producing holy men, whose lives were a protracted service of God.

The sixth and seventh essays, "The Gaon, R. Elijah Wilna," and "R. Israel Salanter" will prove, I trust, to be helpful not only to an understanding of the Judaism of their own times, but also toward that of the early Rabbis.

The vitality of an organism is shown in its power of adaptation. Judaism in modern times, especially in Middle and Western Europe, was confronted with the almost insurmountable difficulty of adapting itself to modern thought. The task that Judaism had to solve was by far more difficult than that of any other religious system. Judaism passed from the fifteenth century into the nineteenth, and this could not take place without a formidable shock. That it withstood this shock is the best proof of the power and energy inherent in Judaism.

The eighth, ninth, tenth and eleventh essays, Zechariah Frankel, Isaac Hirsch Weiss, Solomon Schechter and David Hoffmann, sketch the activities of these great men, who at critical moments in Jewish history understood how to combine harmoniously the old with the new.

The biographical essays were written on particular occasions, the death of one or the anniversary of the birth or death of another. These consist chiefly of praise, but I was glad of the chance to praise great men. It is not always a sign of superior critical judgment to exercise moderation in praise.

The notes at the end of the volume contain the authorities used for the various essays as well as biographical and bibliographical notices. I trust that not only the general reader but also the student will find the notes, at least some of them, useful.

The title "Students, Scholars and Saints," which I have chosen for the volume, is indicative of the message it attempts to convey. It is a plea for the better appreciation of Talmudic Judaism and a closer connection between the past and the present.

NEW YORK, March 30, 1928.

LOUIS GINZBERG

CONTENTS

I

THE JEWISH PRIMARY SCHOOL

The development of the intellect is the development of man, says Auguste Comte, one of the profoundest thinkers of modern times. He does not fail to recognize the momentous influence exerted by factors other than mind in the evolution of society, but he wished to emphasize this point, that whether a single nation is to be appraised or an epoch in the history of mankind as a whole, it is in every case intellectual attainment by which the degree of development must be gauged. In point of fact, it is, as Comte says, "the heart that propounds all questions; to solve them is the part of the intellect." An old Palestinian saying quoted in the Talmud[1] puts the same idea in empiric form: "He who has knowledge, has everything; he who lacks knowledge, lacks everything." And this proverb in turn is an epigrammatic summing up of the biblical notion of the Hakam, "the wise," "the knowing one," who is at the same time the good and pious man, the just. the God-fearing, the truthful, and the pure.

Because writers take too little account of this general historical principle set up by Comte and at the same time are blind to the peculiarity of Jewish history in particular, a misunderstanding has arisen regarding the nature of the transition from the Prophets to the Scribes, from biblical Judaism to rabbinical Judaism.

1

The intellectual endeavors of the Scribes are apt to be considered as a degeneration and decline from the idealism which pervades the conception of life laid down in the Scriptures. The truth is that the Scribes succeeded where the Prophets had failed. Through them the teachings proclaimed in the schools of the Prophets became the common property of the whole people.

The eradication of paganism, against which the prophets fought in vain, among the Jews, together with the immorality that accompanied it, is essentially the achievement of the first great Scribe, Ezra, and of his associates. And again, if three centuries after Ezra the defeat of degenerate Hellenism by the Maccabees was a possibility, it was only because the Scribes, by their constant devotion, had inspired a whole nation with the lofty ideals of the Torah and the Prophets.

In spite of the many vicissitudes to which the Jewish people has been subjected during nearly twenty centuries of dispersion, its intellectual development has suffered no interruption. Under the leadership of the Scribes, the masses of the people were ready to defend the prophetic ideals at every cost and hazard— the same people that had assumed an indifferent, if not a hostile, attitude toward the living words of the Prophets. It must be confessed that the victory of the intellect was not gained at a single blow. The 'Am ha-Arez[2] continued to be a common figure in Jewish life even at the time when the Talmudist stood at his zenith. Theoretically the 'Am ha-Arez submitted himself entirely to the teachings of the rabbis. But in the ordinary course of his life he was little influenced by them; sometimes he was even filled with deadly hatred for the exponents of Jewish learning. The deep veneration shown the scholar among the Jews of the Middle Ages and the extraordinary respect felt for the educated man were phenomena that co-existed and were bound up with a wider spread of knowledge among all classes and with a deepening of religious feeling throughout all the strata of the people. The last link in this long chain of Jewish intellectual development is the *Lamdan*[3] as the dominant figure in Jewish life, especially with the Ashkenazim, and among the Ashkenazim especially in Eastern Europe.

The historical process just described comes out well in the popular sayings of various epochs. To this day many a Jewish woman in Poland and Lithuania soothes her child with the lullaby[4]:

What is the best Sehorah?
My baby will learn Torah,
Seforim he will write for me,
And a pious Jew he'll always be.

In talmudic times words of an entirely different tenor were likely to fall upon the ear of a Jewish child. "O that I had a scholar in my power, how I'd bite him,"[5] were the words often uttered by the lower classes in the early days of the Rabbis. And if we go further back in history, to biblical times, we find the popular characterization of the spiritual leader expressed in such harsh words as "The prophet is a fool, the man that hath a spirit is mad." These extreme epochs of Jewish development lie worlds apart. But even two adjoining periods, the modern and the mediaeval, display a striking contrast. It is a far cry from the time in which the Jewish scholar was a merchant or an artisan to the time in which the Jewish merchant or artisan was a scholar. In the Middle Ages there was no learned estate among the Jews, because the number of scholars was not large enough to constitute a separate class. In Poland and Lithuania later on, when they became the centers of Jewish culture, there was again no learned estate because the people itself was a nation of students. Every Jew was either a teacher or a pupil, or both at the same time. The Lamdan did not belong to a distinct class; he was the representative *par excellence* of the people as a whole.

The many centuries lying between the Prophet and the Lamdan are marked by two apparently incongruous phenomena. The suffering of the Jews was indescribable, yet their intellectual development proceeded apace without interruption. They are the enigma of history, contradicting by their existence the principle *mens sana in corpore sano*, true of nations as well as individuals. Their enslavement by the Persians, the tyrannous oppression of the Greek rulers, the cruelty of the Romans and, finally, the persecutions set afoot by Holy Mother Church, who was so concerned about the salvation of the soul of the Jew that she was ever ready to purchase it with his body—such conditions make one exclaim in wonderment, not at the survival of the Jew, but at his survival unstunted.

Our sages clothed the solution of the riddle in the form peculiar to them. Once upon a time, they say, the heathen philosopher, Oenomaos of Gadara, was asked, "How can we make away with this people?" His answer was: "Go about and observe their schools and academies. So long as the clear voices of children ring forth from them, you will not be able to touch a hair of their head. For thus have the Jews been promised by the father of their race: 'The voice is the voice of Jacob, but the hands are the hands of Esau.' While the voice of Jacob resounds in the schools and the academies, the hands of Esau have no power over him."[6]

We have here more than a suggestive interpretation of a Bible text. It is a subtle comment on an historic fact. The school is the most original institution created by post-biblical Judaism—a magnificent institution, a veritable fortress unshaken by the storms of the ages. To borrow a simile from the Midrash, the school was the heart that kept watch while the other organs slept. Ideals pass into great historical forces by embodying themselves into institutions, and the Jewish ideal of knowledge became a great historical force by embodying itself in the Jewish school.

Like the beginning of all genuine life, the beginning of the Jewish school is lost in the mist of ancient days. There can be no doubt, however, that the higher school for adults, the Bet ha-Midrash, or house of study, is of earlier origin than the Bet ha-Sefer, the elementary school. The Bet ha-Midrash was the sphere in which the *Soferim*, the Scribes, displayed their activity. They were the guardians of literature and culture, who made the *Midrash*, the interpretation of the Scripture, their special care and object, and hence their name, Soferim, "Men of the Book." For it must be borne in mind that the trend of the times was toward religion. Literary interest was determined by the sacred traditions. To the Soferim, however, was entrusted not only the higher education of young and old, but also the dispensation of justice and the leadership of the community—in short, the guidance of the entire spiritual and intellectual life of the people. Nothing perhaps better illustrates the position of the Scribe than the following lines of Ben Sira, who lived at the time when the Soferim had reached their zenith. Ben Sira's description of the Scribes reads:[7]

Not so he that applieth himself to the fear of God,
   And to set his mind upon the Law of the Most High;
Who searcheth out the wisdom of all the ancients,
   And is occupied with the prophets of old;
Who heedeth the discourses of men of renown,
   And entereth into the deep things of parables;
Searcheth out the hidden meaning of proverbs,
   And is conversant with the dark sayings of parables;
Who serveth among great men,
   And appeareth before princes;
Who travelleth through the lands of the peoples,
   Testeth good and evil among men;
Who is careful to seek unto his Maker,
   And before the Most High entreateth mercy;
Who openeth his mouth in prayer,
   And maketh supplication for his sins.
If it seem good to God Most High,
   He shall be filled with the spirit of understanding.

He himself poureth forth wise sayings in double measure,
  And giveth thanks unto the Lord in prayer.
He himself directeth counsel and knowledge,
  And setteth his mind on their secrets.
He himself declareth wise instruction,
  And glorieth in the law of the Lord.
His understanding many do praise,
  And never shall his name be blotted out:
His memory shall not cease,
  And his name shall live from generation to generation.
His wisdom doth the congregation tell forth,
  And his praise the assembly publisheth.
If he live long, he shall be accounted happy more than a thousand;
  And when he cometh to an end, his name sufficeth.

The wisdom of the Scribe is culture, and Jewish culture is primarily religious. The Scribe was not a hermit; "He serveth among great men and appeareth before princes," yet his "Mind was set upon the Law of the Most High." Though the exponent of culture, he "Openeth his mouth in prayer and maketh supplication for his sins."

By the side of the Soferim were the *Hakamim*, "the sages," in their *Yeshibot*, their conventicles. Their knowledge was based on experience and practical observation. It was secular rather than religious. The distinction between the two classes soon disappeared as they were merged into one, that of the scholars, who were now called the Hakamim. That happened when the study of the Torah was enlarged to include every department of human intellectual endeavor. By the time of the Hasmoneans, Hakamim had become the accepted designation of the masters in the knowledge of the Torah, the legitimate leaders of the people.[8]

It was characteristic of the time of the Men of the Great Assembly, a favored name for the leaders of the early Soferim in rabbinic sources, that they urged the duty of "raising up many disciples." Once this idea of higher education had taken root and the system of higher schools had spread as a network over the whole country, the next step could be taken, namely the consideration of the problem of elementary instruction. A well-authenticated talmudic tradition has this to say upon the subject: "In the ancient days every father taught his own son. The fatherless boy (and, it should be added, the child of an ignorant father) was given no instruction. Later, schools were erected in Jerusalem, where the boys were sent from all over the country. But these were inadequate. The fatherless were still left without teaching. Thereupon schools were opened in the largest town of every district, to which youths of sixteen or seventeen, who could do without the care of their parents, were sent. But it was soon apparent that school discipline had no effect upon young men who had come in as adolescents. Then, finally, schools were instituted in every city and town for children of six or seven."[9]

The large, bold strokes in this outline sketch of the history of Jewish education mark out the progress made during a period of two centuries, roughly speaking, from the time of the Soferim (about three hundred before the common era) to the time of the Pharisees (about one hundred before the common era). It is a highly significant fact that the man who deserves the title "Father of the Jewish School," was a great leader of the Pharisee party, Simeon ben Shatah (about seventy A. C. E.). Of the results achieved by the work inaugurated by Simeon, we can gain a good idea from Josephus, who proudly points them out to the Greeks one hundred and fifty years later. "Our principal care of all is this," he says, "to educate our children well," . . . "and if anybody do but ask any one of them (the Jews) about our laws, he will more readily tell them all than he will tell his own name, and this is in consequence of our having learned them immediately, as soon as ever we become sensible of any thing, and of our having them, as it were, engraven on our souls."[10]

It cannot be denied that the ratio of rhetoric to truth in Josephus' writings is sometimes very high. Yet, after his statements are stripped of exaggerations, there still remains a residuum of facts sufficient to certify to the important place assigned to elementary education in his day. However, we must not fail to take into account that Josephus was conversant chiefly with conditions as they existed among the dwellers in cities. The country folk, constituting perhaps the majority of the Jewish people at that time, were still debarred from the blessings of education.

The catastrophes that overwhelmed the Jewish nation in the year seventy and in the year one hundred and thirty-three, and reduced flourishing cities and populous villages to ruins, gave a set-back to the cause of primary education. Accordingly, in the third century of the common era, the leading intellects among the Jews were constrained to devote their attention to the rehabilitation of elementary schools and teaching.[11]

Political and economic conditions went on growing worse for the Jews in Palestine. In spite of all the efforts put forth to promote and develop educational work, the Holy Land ceased to be the spiritual center of Judaism. It was replaced by Babylonia. There the work had to be started anew, for the Jews of the Persian empire occupied a very low intellectual plane, and generations passed by until the Palestinian spirit began to take root and flourish on the banks of the Euphrates.[12] And yet, comparatively speaking, it cannot be said that a long time elapsed before a Jewish culture had established itself in Babylonia. The political and economic conditions of the Jews living there in the third century were very favorable. Under the Sassanids they formed an all but autonomous body. Influenced by great intellectual leaders, the exilarchs and the communal authorities fairly vied with each other in fostering and promoting Jewish studies and culture. Scholars were exempt from the poll tax, from communal tributes and similar imposts. They were permitted to settle wheresoever they would, a great advantage to them if they engaged in business or trades, which as a rule were subjected to restrictions protecting residents against a much-feared competition.[13] Education and knowledge in the course of time became actual marketable possessions, instead of being, as at first, ideal acquisitions—the best standard by which to measure the degree of idealism prevailing in a nation. Where education and intellectual attainments are considered a material asset, idealism must be the attribute of large classes of the people. The natural features of the Babylonian country were another propitious factor. The earth there yielded its products without demanding more than a minimum of human labor. The poorest were in a position to devote several hours of daily leisure to study, and without a great sacrifice they could forego the assistance of their minor children, who thus were permitted to enjoy a schooling of many years' duration.[14]

The wide spread of culture among the Babylonian Jews appears strikingly in the definition of the 'Am ha-Arez found in the Babylonian Talmud. They applied the harsh term to one who, though he had mastered the Bible and the Mishnah, had not penetrated more profoundly into Jewish lore. Contrast this with what the Palestinians called an ignoramus, and the vast progress made in two centuries, more or less, will be apparent. To the Palestinian, the man who could not recite the *Shema'* was an ignoramus; one who knew the Bible, let alone the Mishnah, was if not a scholar, surely an educated man.[15]

In spite of the important place occupied by the school in the intellectual life of Babylonian Jewry, the material dealing with educational work and facilities preserved in the Talmud is so sparse that there is little hope of our ever being able to reconstruct the educational edifice of the time with any degree of completeness. But there is more than enough to warrant the general impression that the school went on increasing in influence under the Babylonian Jews, and the later development of the Jewish educational system in all the lands of the Dispersion is directly traceable to these vigorous Babylonian beginnings.

Unfortunately, the talmudic time is not the only period in Jewish educational history of which we are ignorant. We are in no better position to attempt a presentation of educational conditions among the Jews in a time much nearer our own, namely the Middle Ages which, to quote Zunz, extended for the Jews to very recent times. At most we might venture to deal with the higher institutions of learning. For the primary schools our information is too meager by far. Our reports do not become full and detailed enough to justify an attempt at description until we reach the elementary school of the so-called Polish Jews, the word Polish being here used as a generic term for Slavic countries and Lithuania. We must, therefore, limit ourselves to an attempt at gaining some glimpses of the intellectual and spiritual life nursed and developed in the elementary schools of the Polish Jews.

Jews had been living in Poland for centuries before anything was heard of them, certainly before anything was heard about their intellectual life.[16] The persecutions of the Jews in Germany that extended in unbroken sequence from the First Crusade to the Age of the Reformation cast large numbers of them into Poland, whither they carried their talmudic learning and piety; for it must not be forgotten that there was a time when the Jews of Germany excelled all others in strength of faith and rigorous observance of the Torah. In these times of the almost superhuman suffering of the German Jew, we meet with his long-enduring march to the East of Europe, especially to Poland, the country which, according to a well-known Latin saying[17], is "the heaven of the nobleman, the purgatory of the citizen, the hell of the peasant, and the paradise of the Jew"—such a paradise as the Christian love of those days was likely to concede to him. We may be sure that the narrow-minded town guilds and the fanatical clergy took care not to rob the Jew of his hope of a real Paradise. The economic conditions were far from brilliant even in the sixteenth century, when Polish Jewish prosperity was at its height. In the middle of that century, Rabbi Moses Isserles wrote to a friend in Germany: "Thou hadst been better off in Poland, if only on dry bread, but that at least without anxiety of mind[18]." Of rich Jews, like Simeon Günzburg[19] in Germany, for instance, there were none in Poland. But that is not altogether regrettable. The salvation of the Jews was never wrought by the rich among them. What gave Poland its pre-eminence was the circumstance that it offered means of subsistence, however wretched, to the middle class, by permitting the Jews to enter many branches of business, while in the rest of Europe they were confined to petty trading and money-lending.

Such economic conditions sufficed to give an impetus toward a new Jewish culture, and with an external impulse superadded it resulted in an irresistible movement. The outer force that came to aid the inner was the invention of printing, which made knowledge a common possession of the people. The first notable Jewish scholar in Poland of whom we hear, lived and

worked at the end of the fifteenth century[20]. Scarcely
a generation after the pioneers, the Jews of Poland had
leapt into the forefront of Jewish learning, a sovereign
position from which they have not yet been dislodged.
The significant fact is that the publication of the first
editions of the two Talmudim and of other classical
works of Jewish literature fell in the interval that
elapsed between the time when Poland had but one
scholar of eminence, Rabbi Jacob Pollak, and the time
when it produced Rabbi Solomon Loria, the most
eminent Talmudist of his day[21].

Hand in hand with the development of the higher
education went the education of the Jewish child,
which began at home before he was sent to school,
quite in agreement with the principle of one of the
greatest educators of modern times, who holds that
education is the concern of the family; from the family
it proceeds, and to the family for the most part it
returns. Of Jewish pedagogy the characteristic feature
was that the three chief ends of education were subserved as a unity at one and the same time. The
earliest instruction kept in view at once the intellectual,
the moral, and the religious training of the child. As
soon as he was able to speak, he was taught Hebrew
words and sentences, bringing into play his memory
and his perceptive faculties, and the sentences were
always of religious bearing. They were mainly *Berakot*,
blessings, especially those that form part of the morning and evening prayers and of the grace after meals.
"Blessed be the All-Merciful, the Lord of bread,
blessed be He, who giveth food to all beings," is to-day,

as it was four hundred years ago, the form of grace used by the Jewish children in Poland.[22] The morning devotion consisted of two biblical verses: "Hear, O Israel, the Lord is our God, the Lord is One," and "Moses commanded us the Torah as the inheritance of the congregation of Jacob", to which the rhymed couplet was added: "To the Torah I shall ever faithful be; For this may God Almighty grant His help to me." As the child rose from bed with the Shema' upon his lips, so he went to bed proclaiming his belief in the One God. To the recital of the Shema' before retiring was added the following verse from Psalm thirty-one: "Into Thine hand I commend my spirit; Thou hast redeemed me, O Lord, Thou God of Truth."

A child of three or four years cannot be expected to understand the import of prayers, even when couched in the vernacular. Religious feeling comes into play much later in life. It was an advantage from this point of view that the prayers were put into Hebrew, a language removed from daily concerns. In this somewhat strange guise they appeal to the intellect of the child as well as to his fancy. The alien garb makes them sink into the child's mind as a concrete, almost tangible entity, a vessel to be retained until the proper content comes to hand to be poured into it. The language of familiar intercourse is too fluid to fulfil this pedagogic purpose. For the same reason Hebrew was used for the civil speeches of polite society first impressed upon a child. *Berukim ha-Yoshebim*, "Blessed be ye who are present here," was the greeting extended by a child entering a room in which the company was seated at the table, and on leaving he was expected to say, *Bireshutekem*, "with your permission."[23]

The ceremonials of the Jewish religion early caught the fancy of the impressionable child, and kept him fascinated. Having outgrown his baby clothes, the little fellow was given the "prayer-square," the *Arba'-Kanfot*, as part of his first boy's suit. With two such tangible reminders he was in no danger of forgetting his double dignity as a lord of creation and a son of the chosen people. "Shaking" the Lulab on Sukkot, waving little flags on Simhat Torah, filching the *Afikomen* from the Seder table, and, last but not least, the consumption of delicate butter cookies on Shebuot—these and many others of the lighter ceremonial acts and customs prepared the child admirably for the more serious instruction in the *Heder*, which was begun when he was five years old.

The Heder! In the face of the misunderstandings with which friend and foe alike have treated it in modern times, it is difficult to speak calmly of this, one of the greatest institutions of post-biblical Judaism. Surely a defense is out of place when applied to a system still in use now, though its beginnings are lost in the obscurity of the days when Rome was a tiny Italian republic and Alexandria not yet founded. It is also obvious that a creation of the epoch of the Scribes in Palestine could not persist unchanged in Spain in the heyday of Greek-Arabic culture, and to expect the New York of the twentieth century to accept without change the Lublin Heder of the sixteenth would be as

irrational as to judge the Polish Heder at its best by
the form and constitution it has adopted in our day.
It is one thing to judge a system or institution in its
corruption and quite another thing to measure the
worth and true design of its first founders. All educational institutions must die which do not directly and
conspicuously promote either the spiritual or material
interests of men. Without an inspiring idea and aim,
an institution is dying, if not dead, though to the eye
of sense it may seem still to live. Evolution is not the
only factor that enters into an estimate of historical
development. Degeneration is an equally important
aspect, especially with a people like the Jews, whose
fortunes have often been forced into unnatural channels
by the violent hands of an unsympathetic world. All
human works are exposed to vicissitude and decay,
and the Heder in the lapse of more than two thousand
years has furnished many an instance of that general
law.

The Heder in Poland at the period in which Jewish
culture was at its height was neither a public nor a
private school. It was an institution supervised by the
communal authorities, but managed in detail by private
individuals. The choice of the teacher lay with the
parents, and the teacher was at liberty to accept and
reject pupils as he saw fit, but the community reserved
the right to pass upon the number of pupils, the
curriculum, the schedule, and other particulars regarding the plan of instruction. The school regulations in
force in the Jewish community of Cracow in 1551, the
oldest of their kind known, contain various points of

interest[24]. A teacher of elementary pupils was not permitted to have more than forty children in his class, and a teacher of Talmud not more than twenty, and for these numbers each of them was required to employ two assistants.

A generation later, the same community adopted rules fixing the salary of the teachers, because, it is said, "their demands are so exorbitant that many are not able to satisfy them[25]." To understand this, it must be borne in mind that though the community maintained a free school, the Talmud Torah, parents availed themselves of it only in extreme cases of poverty. "Though you have to secure the means by begging, be sure to provide for the instruction of your sons and daughters in the Torah," is a dying father's admonition to his children in his last will and testament dated 1357[26]. The poorest of the poor sent their children to the free Talmud Torah; the average poor denied themselves food and raiment and paid for the schooling of their boys and girls. This explains why communal ordinances as well as decisions by eminent rabbis concern themselves with the times when tuition fees fell due. Rabbi Solomon Loria decides that half the stipulated remuneration must be paid the teacher in advance, to enable him to maintain his establishment decently[27]. In spite of the authority of Loria, his view does not seem to have prevailed, for the teachers, it appears, were paid at the end of the month[28]. By this arrangement the New Moon Day was a holiday, not only for the pupils, who were not required to return to the Heder for the afternoon session, but also for the teachers who, in addition to their salaries, would sometimes receive "Rosh Hodesh money," a small free-will offering, from their patrons.[29] To prevent sordid competition among teachers, which might have left some of them without school and pupils at the end of a month, it was strictly prohibited to change teachers during the term, and teachers, on the other hand, were not permitted to go about seeking patronage between terms. Parents were expected to decide upon their future action regarding the placing of their children uninfluenced by those financially interested in their decision.[30]

The child's first day at Heder may be said to have been the most impressive one in his life, and the ceremonies introducing the boy to school are very significant of the Jewish attitude toward education in general and religious education in particular.

On Pentecost, the feast commemorative of the giving of the Torah on Sinai, the boy of five began his career at school. Neatly attired, he was put in the care of a member of the community distinguished for piety and scholarship, with whom he went to the synagogue at break of day. There he was met by the teacher, who took him in his charge and began to instruct him. He was handed a slate on which the Hebrew alphabet was written forward and backward, and, besides, the following three verses: "The law commanded us by Moses is the inheritance of the Congregation of Jacob", "And the Lord called unto Moses, and spake unto him out of the tent of meeting, saying," and "May the Torah be my daily calling, and God Almighty my helper," the last from the prayers for children. The first lesson consisted in making the pupil repeat the names of the letters after the teacher. The slate was smeared with honey, which the child licked from the letters, to taste the sweetness of the Torah, as it were. Then the boy was given a cake baked by the innocent hands of a virgin, on which several verses from the Prophets and Psalms were traced: "And He said unto me, Son of man, cause thy belly to eat, and fill thy bowels with this roll that I give thee. Then did I eat it; and it was in my mouth as honey for sweetness;" "The Lord God hath given me the tongue of them that are taught, that I should know how to sustain with words him that is weary; He wakeneth morning by morning, He wakeneth mine ear to hear as they that are taught. The Lord God hath opened mine ear, and I was not rebellious, neither turned away backward." Moreover the cake bore eight verses from Psalm one hundred and nineteen, all of them proclaiming the praise of the Torah. The following verses were inscribed on an egg: "From all my teachers have I learned wisdom" and "How sweet are Thy words unto my taste! Yea, sweeter than honey to my mouth!" All these verses on the cake and on the egg the teacher read and the young neophyte pronounced them after him, and at the end of the lesson the boy was given the cake and the egg, and apples and other fruit besides. Then he was taken on a walk along the banks of a stream, because the Torah is likened unto water: "As water rests not in elevated places, but flows downward and gathers in the lowlands, so the Torah resides only with the humble and modest, not with the proud and presumptuous."

The final ceremonies took place in the house of the parents of the boy. In his honor they prepared a banquet, at which he was greeted by the assembled guests with the words: "May God enlighten thine eyes with His Torah[31]."

Peculiar as these customs may seem, they reveal clearly what the ideals were that filled the mind of the father at the moment of devoting his son to the service of the Lord. It was not the yoke of the law that he sought to impose upon the lad. He endeavored to inspire him with the conviction that the Law of God is lovely, so that when he attained to discretion, he would keep it and observe it with all his heart. Primary instruction was therefore arranged with a view to giving the child a knowledge of the Hebrew text of the Bible and of the prayers, together with their translation into the vernacular. The Bible itself was put into the hands of the Jewish child, and it was the Bible that shaped and moulded his heart and mind.

Hebrew reading was the earliest subject in the course of study in the Heder. The alphabet was put on large charts, first in the usual order, from Alef to Taw, and again in the reverse order, from Taw to Alef; then with vowels and again without vowels. The charts contained also a few Bible verses. To enliven the drudgery of alphabet learning, the children were taught not merely the names of the letters, but also the meaning of the names, of their form, and their position, a method not unlike that of the modern picture book. This practical way of teaching appealed both to the fancy and the intellect. Alef-Bet—the child was told—means, "learn wisdom" (the Hebrew for learn is *Alef* and Bet reminds one of *Binah* "wisdom"); Gimel-Dalet, "be kind" (*Gomel* in Hebrew to be kind) "to the poor" (*Dal*). In a similar manner the forms of the letters were made to live in the fancy of the child. The foot of the Gimel, he was taught, is turned in the direction of the following letter, Dalet, to remind us that one should be kind-hearted and look for the needy to render them assistance. The Tet has its head hidden—turned inside—and a crown thereon so that we may know that the charitable hand must not be seen if we aspire to receive the crown of glory from God for our kind actions. The Shin has three branches but no root to indicate that falsehood—in Hebrew *Sheker*, the initial letter of which is Shin—never takes root. One leg of the Taw is broken to teach us that he who desires to devote himself to the study of the Torah—which word begins with a Taw—must be ready to have his feet bruised by his wanderings to the houses of study. And finally, as the leg of this letter is bent, so must the student of the Torah bend his pride[32]. Other explanations of the alphabet aim to make the child remember the sounds. "Tell the child," says an author of the sixteenth century[33], "that the Bet has its mouth open, and the Pe—mouth in Hebrew—has its mouth closed." The pedagogue thus conveyed to the learner not only the difference in the appearance of these two letters, but also the difference in the position of the lips in pronouncing them, and to this day the Kamez, the long a, is described in the Heder as the Patah with a beard.

The next step was to the prayer-book, which became the text-book for reading as soon as the boy was able to put letters together into words. As it was a cherished purpose to have the child say the prayers by himself as soon as possible, no attention was paid to their meaning, until he could read them fluently, on the principle that a child was first to be religiously active, and religious thinking would follow as his intelligence developed with years. Moreover, the prayers not being composed in the classical Hebrew, it was thought advisable to defer effective instruction in the Hebrew language until the study of the Bible could be begun. The third Book of Moses was chosen as the first subject of instruction in the Bible—the principle here being, the law of Israel before the history of Israel.[34] After a part of Leviticus had been taken, the instructor devoted himself to teaching as much of each week's Pentateuch portion as the pupil's time and capacity permitted. The disadvantage of this practice was that the beginner, unable to manage the whole portion, acquired the Pentateuch in fragments. On the other hand, it must be remembered that to teach Hebrew grammar was at this stage as little the intention as to convey the historical content of the Scriptures or their theological interpretation. The aim for the moment was to enable the learner to acquire an extensive Hebrew vocabulary. With only this in view, it was not long before a boy of even average ability could easily be made to go through the week's portion in season.

A clear notion of the methods of Bible instruction in vogue in the sixteenth and seventeenth centuries may be gained from two works entitled, *Baër* (or *Beër*) *Mosheh*, and *Lekah Tob*, composed by Rabbi Moses Saertels, and printed at Prague in 1604-5. The author himself tells us that it was his purpose to perpetuate in print the traditional translation and explanation of the Bible. This being the case, it does not astonish us to find the regulations of the Jewish community of Cracow[35] making it obligatory upon teachers to use Rabbi Moses Saertels' books. From a comparison with the Bible Commentary by Rashi it appears that they depend upon it throughout. Virtually they are an introduction to Rashi, whose Commentary was the text-book given to the pupil after he had mastered a part of the Bible.

Another subject in the primary classes of the Heder was writing, both the square characters and the script, the latter, the so-called Juedisch-Deutsch, being used in correspondence. If we mention, besides, arithmetic from addition to division, and the outlines of Hebrew etymology, we have exhausted the curriculum of the primary Heder or, as the Jewish expression goes, the work of the *Melamed Dardake*, the primary teacher.

At the age of about ten the boy passed from the primary Heder to its higher division, the Talmud Heder, in which all subjects of study gave way to the Talmud, and henceforth he devoted himself to it exclusively. The Melamed Dardake surrendered him to the Talmud teacher, and in his charge he remained until he was able to enter the *Yeshibah*, the talmudic high school.

Different as the course of studies and the method of teaching were in the Heder from those in the modern school, the two institutions depart still further from each other in the life their respective pupils led and still lead. Life in the Heder was arranged with more than due regard for individuality. Not only was the Heder, as we have seen, a private institution in which the parents were given the opportunity of choosing the teacher with a view to their children's needs and gifts, but the teaching also was personal in character. Restricted as the number of pupils was, they were nevertheless divided into *Kitot*, sections.[36] The teacher usually occupied himself with no more than four children at a time. In this way a close personal relation could grow up between master and pupil. It was practically impossible to deceive a teacher by palming off work on him done by others at home. Instruction, especially in the Talmud, was discursive, and the cadence or, better, the sing-song, of a talmudic sentence sufficed to indicate whether or not the little Talmudist understood it. The result was that in many cases the teacher came to take a vital personal interest in the pupils. With pleasure and pride he would observe the progress of his boys, and no greater joy could come to him than to be caught napping by one of them who urged a difficult objection to some talmudic statement, which the teacher was not prepared to answer on the spot. As the whole system purposed the training of the intellect, a "good scholar" in the Heder meant only a mentally well-endowed pupil. Qualities other than intellectual did not count. "A mischievous boy has a good head" is the Jewish way of saying that a bright boy is privileged to indulge in pranks in the Heder.

As a rule the teachers were mild enough in meting out punishment. Some of their gentleness may perhaps be set to the account of self-interest. They may have feared to lose paying pupils through over-great severity. One of the teachers describes the dilemma in which he and his confreres were often placed, in the following graphic words: "When a teacher flogs one of his pupils, he bursts into tears, goes home to his father, and complains tearfully. The father gets angry, and the boy is encouraged to complain to his mother, too. She, in her affection for her son, incites the father against the teacher, who, she says, has come within an ace of killing the boy, and she calls him a fool. Naturally, the father is wrought up against the teacher, and seeks to engage him in a quarrel, etc., etc.[37]"

The Melamed (teacher) was certainly more humane and gentle than most of the masters of the English schools, who till very recently ruled as tyrants. We may be quite sure that he was not the brute pictured by the morbid imagination of certain *Maskilim*, whose animus against the Heder is probably to be sought in a hatred of the deeply Jewish atmosphere that prevailed there, and that too in spite of the lack of explicit religious instruction in the modern sense. The Heder would have refused to tolerate long-winded definitions of the being and existence of God, and the little Talmud pupil would not have suppressed his whence and his what, his *Minna hanne Mille* and his *May ka mashma lan.* The Jewish martyrs and saints were not raised in the hot-house atmosphere of religion spread by the catechism, and it is hardly an accident that the desire for religious text-books did not manifest itself until Judaism was being forced into the four walls of the synagogue. Previous to that time Jewish literature, rich as it was, had no such book to show except a single one composed at the end of the sixteenth century, which is modelled after the catechism used by the Catholic clergy. The author of this book was said to have become a convert to Christianity, which is not true, but it seems as if he laid himself open to such accusations by writing a catechism.[38] The Jewish religion is not a religious arithmetic. It does not permit the idea to usurp the place of the spirit. From the first the Jew has felt that reality is not abstract but individual. Religion to be a vital influence must be lived, not taught, and this condition was fulfilled in the Heder. The whole life there was religiously Jewish, for though the Jewish school aimed first and foremost to cultivate the mind, the other point of view was never lost sight of, that "the fear of God is the beginning of wisdom." The teachings of the Prophets and the lives of the sages were not abstractions to the Heder boys, but flesh and bone realities. Rabbi Akiba's persistence, through which the water carrier became the most celebrated scholar of his day, his devotion to his wife Rachel, and his martyr's death, were not mere incidents in the biography of a hero dead fifteen hundred years. They formed the history of an old and tried

friend whose acts and opinions left an indelible impression upon the child's mind. The Melamed, on the
other hand, was not a critical historian. He did not
differentiate history from fable. The gnat that was
said to have gnawed the brain of Titus was as historical
to him as the destruction of the Temple by the same
Titus. And yet he did more for the preservation of
Jewish nationalism than all the well-turned phrases of
modern orators when, on the day preceding Tish'ah
be-Ab, in a voice choked with tears, he read to his
pupils the *Hurban*, the talmudic narrative recount-
ing the details of the catastrophe that overtook Israel
in the year seventy and again in one hundred and
thirty-three.

As history was disregarded in the Heder, so ethics as
such did not appear in the curriculum. There was no
need to give moral instruction directly. The study of
the Talmud and of rabbinical literature took the place
of the best conceivable manual of ethics. It compelled
the student to think profoundly and assimilate actively
what suited the needs of his nature in the ample
wealth of moral teachings scattered throughout this
literature. The pupil was not called upon to compose
his face solemnly while moral exhortations were poured
down upon his devoted head. In the regular course of
studies the Talmud offered him ethical observations of
fundamental importance, while ostensibly propound-
ing an intricate judicial question which requires fine
dialectical reasoning. The transition from the legal
element to the ethical in the discussion of the Talmud
is almost imperceptible; sometimes the inter-relation

between them is so close that the dividing line cannot
be discerned. Accordingly, the intellectual interest of
the student was not interrupted. "Let thy yea be yea,
and thy nay, nay," for instance, is the last link in a
long chain of complicated discussions on the legal
character of a deposit[39], and the conclusion meant
nothing to the student who had not followed the
devious reasoning understandingly and constructively.

Nor was the imagination of the child left to starve.
How could it, with the numberless stories the Talmud
contains about the life and deeds of the great in Israel!
Take, for example, the very sentence just quoted: "Let
thy yea be yea, and thy nay, nay." As an illustration
of it, we are told concerning Rabbi Safra that he was
negotiating a sale. The would-be purchaser happened
to approach Rabbi Safra and spoke to him about the
transaction at the moment when the rabbi was engaged
in reciting the Shema'. Not noticing that the rabbi was
praying, he made him an offer. Rabbi Safra naturally
would not interrupt his prayer. With a gesture he tried
to convey to the purchaser that he did not wish to be
disturbed. Misunderstanding the import of the gesture,
he offered a higher price. At the end of his devotions
Rabbi Safra accepted the first price. He would not
profit by the other's mistake, for he had silently given
his assent to the lower offer.[40]

Again, could there be a more impressive way of
teaching children the Jewish view of the treatment of
animals than through the suffering of the Patriarch
Rabbi Judah, the compiler of the Mishnah? A calf, the
Talmud tells us, about to be led to the shambles, took

refuge with Rabbi Judah, and hid its head in his mantle, entreating help. "Go," said Rabbi Judah, "for this thou wast created." Thereupon it was said in heaven: "Because he showed no mercy, no mercy shall be shown to him," and suffering was decreed for him. One day his maid-servant wanted to pluck out a nest of young weasels which she found in his house and cast them out to perish. "Leave them in peace," said Rabbi Judah, "it is said of God, 'His tender mercies are over all His works'." Then it was said in heaven: "Because he showed mercy, mercy shall be shown to him," and his pain ceased forthwith.[41] To develop the feeling for which Jewish tenderness more than fifteen hundred years ago coined the significant expression, *Za'ar Ba'ale Hayyim*, this naive story was more effective than many a preachment on our duty to the brute creation. The Heder boy, whose sole aim was to search out and know the teachings of the ancients, derived his ideals from those whose lives interested him in the measure in which he entered into their ideals.

The Heder life must not be thought of as a life of serious tasks only. The boys had more opportunity to play tricks there than in a modern school. Games and youthful merriment were quite compatible with the big Talmud folios. The Heder decidedly had its gay side. On the whole, its life may be said to have been less rule-bound than life in a modern school. To begin with, the chief spur to study was the expectation of reward rather than the fear of punishment. Following in the footsteps of old Jewish authorities of high standing, a popular book of the beginning of the seventeenth century has this to say of the bringing up of children: "One should always teach a child in pleasant ways. First give him fruit, or sugar, or honey cake, and later small coins. Then he should be promised clothes as a present, always making the reward appropriate to his intelligence and his years. Then tell him, if he will study diligently he may expect a large dowry when he marries; and later he should be told that if he will study diligently he will be ordained and will officiate as a rabbi. He must be urged on until the boy himself realizes that he must study because it is the will of God.[42]" The directions to teachers are of similar tenor, and it was the general habit of teachers to attract the children by kindness. To this very day it is the custom, as it was hundreds of years ago, for the teacher to throw sweets or a few coins on the alphabet chart when the child has his first lesson at school, saying at the same time: "An angel has thrown this down for you because you are so good[43]." In some congregations the teachers used to prepare a treat for the children on Hamishah 'Asar be-Shebat, and on Lag ba-'Omer, when no school sessions were held.

The teacher had neither time nor disposition to play games with the children. His place was taken by his assistant, the "Behelfer," who called for the children at their homes and took them back after school hours, and one of whose duties it was to provide for the entertainment and recreation of his charges. The Behelfer was the one who carved the wooden swords for Tish'ah be-Ab and manufactured the flags for Simhat Torah. If the boys were well-behaved, he

allowed them to be present while he made his prepara-
tions for the Purim play, in which he took the part of
Mordecai or Haman or even, at a pinch, of Esther.
The big boys, who had outgrown the services of the
Behelfer, did not scorn to buy his good-will, sometimes
with hard cash. In the first place, it was important to
be in his good graces, else he might betray their pranks
to the teacher. Besides, his active help could not
always be dispensed with. In summer he was the
swimming master, and in winter he taught the boys
how to skate, the two most delightful forms of amuse-
ment known to Heder boys. But even such neutral and
secular interests lying at the periphery of Heder life
did not escape its genuinely Jewish atmosphere. The
boys did not hesitate to call a certain figure on the ice
the *"Wa-Yomer David* run," because it was executed
in the same position as is adopted in the saying of the
prayer in question, with the head resting on the arm.
In addition to all these accomplishments, the Behelfer
was an adept in making the Drehdel[44], and this game,
known to the Greeks, Romans and Germans, was also
given a Jewish aspect. It was played only on Hanukkah, but then most vigorously. The sections of the
class not actively engaged with the teacher played it
in the intervals between lessons during the Hanukkah
days, behind the teacher's back, of course. Its connection with Hanukkah was established by interpreting
the letters on its four sides as the initial letters of the
sentence, *Nes gadol hayah sham*, "A great miracle was
done there."

And, in fact, a great miracle *was* done there! The

wonderful salvation of Israel was wrought *there*, in the
Heder! Goethe advises us "always to oppose the great
masses produced by the historical process of the ages
to the perversities of the fleeting hour as they arise."
According to this, the perversities that result when
individual observations are over-emphasized and eph-
emeral fashions followed, ought to be opposed by the
Jewish school as it was developed in the course of
twenty centuries and more. An important and profound lesson will be derived, which the Talmud expresses in the words: "He who says, Nothing exists for
me but the Jewish religion, not even the Jewish religion
exists for him."[45] Although the Jewish school was the
nursery of all the manifold aspects of the Jewish spirit,
yet it brought forth not only heroes of the intellect, but
religious geniuses as well. If hitherto the Jews have
put no pictures of saints in the synagogue, it has not
been for lack of them, else they might long ago have
resorted to the device of borrowing them from the other
nations. It was because the Jews met their ideal saint
outside of the synagogue as well as inside. He was a
thinking and an acting saint no less than a praying saint.

The most significant truth to be learned from the
long history of Jewish education remains to be mentioned. All true culture issues from a unified *Weltanschauung*, from a decided view of life and men and the
world, and in the last resort the value of culture
depends upon the help it gives us in acquiring and
formulating such a *Weltanschauung*. If Jewish education is to resume its old place and significance in
Jewish life, it must cease to be the supernumerary

adjunct of a person or a cause. It must again be an independent institution, fulfilling its task autonomously. It must be, as it was, the focus of Jewish life, of the Jewish intellect, and of the Jewish religion.

II

THE DISCIPLE OF THE WISE

While "the sword without and terror within" ravaged
Jerusalem, a venerable old teacher quit the walls that
harbored misfortune and fled to the enemy. The Roman general gave the fugitive, no less a personage than
Rabban Johanan ben Zakkai, a friendly reception, and
promised to grant one request that he would prefer.
The rabbi modestly asked that he be allowed to open
a school at Jabneh, where he might teach his pupils.
The imperator had no objection to this harmless desire,[1] for he could not suspect that its consummation
would enable Judaism, apparently so weak, to outlive
Rome, for all its iron strength, by thousands of years.
Our criticism of Vespasian for his shortsightedness
would probably be milder if we took into consideration the fact that at this very day there are people
who reproach the great master for carrying on "aca-
demic discussions" with the arch-enemy of his people
at the moment when the noblest of them were shedding
their blood on the altar of liberty. The last eighteen
hundred years of Jewish history, however, are the best
justification of the wisdom of Rabban Johanan. That
the Jewish nation has survived the downfall of its State
and the destruction of its national sanctuary is above
all due to this great genius, who made of religious study
a new form in which the national existence of the Jews

35

found expression, so that by the side of the history of nearly two thousand years of suffering we can point to an equally extensive history of intellectual effort. Studying and wandering, thinking and enduring, learning and suffering, fill this long period. Thinking is as characteristic a trait of the Jew as suffering or, to be more exact, thinking rendered suffering possible. For it was our thinkers who prevented the wandering nation, this true "wandering Jew," from sinking to the level of brutalized vagrants, of vagabond gypsies.

In Jabneh Rabban Johanan kindled the eternal light of the Torah—the light that was never to be extinguished. Usha took up the work begun at Jabneh, and was in turn replaced by Sepphoris, and after the sun of learning in Palestine had passed its meridian and hastened toward its setting, it appeared in the sky of the East. Nehardea, Sura, and Pumbedita for eight hundred years radiated a brilliant light, and their lustre rivalled that of Jabneh and Sepphoris. When, toward the beginning of the eleventh century, darkness spread its wings over the Babylonian Jews, bright day dawned in European countries. Cordova, Gerona, and Barcelona in Spain; Mayence, Worms, and Speyer in Germany; Lunel, Montpellier, and Narbonne in Provence; and Troyes, Rameru, and Dampierre in Champagne are stars of the first magnitude in the heaven of Jewish learning.

The dawning light of modern times did not shine upon the Jews of Western and Central Europe. During this time it was chiefly the Slavic lands that

offered a refuge for Jewish learning. Posen, Lublin,
and Cracow in Poland; Brest-Litovsk, Wilna, and
Grodno in Lithuania began in the sixteenth century to
assume the position which in the Middle Ages had been
held by the cities on the Rhine and in Provence. A
plant native to Palestine, which flourished by the rivers
of Babylon, blossomed out luxuriantly in Spain, and
bore savory fruit in icy Poland, must indeed have been
tended by the hands of gardeners who combined love
and knowledge in the highest degree. "The vineyards
of the Lord,"² as the Rabbis call the Jewish academies,
were cultivated by the *Talmide Hakamim* or, in English parlance, the Disciples of the Wise. These are the
men out of whose midst the builders of the unique literary monument known as the Talmud arose.

In the lecture which I have the honor to deliver to
you to-night, I shall endeavor to describe the intellectual life, the aims, ideals and achievements of the
makers of the Talmud or, in other words, to give a
short characterization of the Jewish scholar at the time
of the Talmud. I lay special stress upon "scholar" not
upon "Talmud," although to do justice to the subject,
an exact definition of the word "Talmud" would be
necessary. But one lecture would hardly suffice for
that, and so, without more ado, I shall assume that all
present here have travelled the "sea of the Talmud"
and do not need aid to guide them across it. Nevertheless, I cannot refrain from making one remark about
the Talmud. You doubtless know that a learned
Capuchin (Henricus Seynensis) once spoke of "Rabbi
Talmud."³ Less known is the fact that the famous

French theologian, Bossuet, requested the German philosopher, Leibnitz, to procure for him the translation of the Talmud by Monsieur Mishnah. These solecisms in our days of encyclopedias provoke only a pitying smile. The smile, however, disappears when one hears opinions about the Talmud on the same level of ignorance pronounced by persons from whom one might expect a better understanding of Judaism and of Jewish history. It was recently proclaimed "urbi et orbi," that the Talmud or, at least, the greater portion of it, together with rabbinical literature in general, contains nothing but "questions concerning eating and drinking, which things are forbidden and which are allowed, what is clean and what is unclean," and the study of the Talmud was declared to be entirely superfluous in our times, when everything that is pleasant is permitted, everything that is attractive is clean. And what is more, the Talmud has been characterized as a work which "tends rather to produce skepticism," and which must, therefore, be kept at a distance from innocent youth. This advice is not necessary at a time when even our Rabbis do not show any excessive eagerness for the study of the Talmud, nor is it original. During the period of the Reformation, the Catholic clergy forbade the laity to study the Bible on the ground that "it induced skepticism." The only new feature in this most recent declaration of war against rabbinical literature is that while formerly hatred of the Talmud sprang from hatred of the Jew, it was reserved for our glorious generation to invent a hatred of the Talmud that purports to spring from love of the Jew. Well may the Jew exclaim: "God defend me against my friends and I will defend myself against my enemies."

The Talmud, which has survived the stake and the inquisition, will also resist these impotent attacks, which will cease as soon as the understanding of the Talmud shall become the common possession of cultivated men or, at least, of cultivated, intelligent Jews. If ever the saying "by their fruits shall ye know them" was justified, it is in the case of the Talmud; hence the more we know of the makers of the Talmud, the nearer we are to a correct comprehension of the Talmud itself.

Already at the beginning of the common era the *Talmid Hakam*[5] not only was the religious head in whom the Jew reposed unqualified confidence in spiritual matters, but he was also called upon to lead in worldly affairs, and his decision, affecting both individual and general concerns, was accepted with submission. His word carried just as much weight in questions of clean and unclean as in questions of "mine and thine." He supervised the cult as well as the market places, the weights and the measures. He determined the time and the form of prayer and, on the other hand, he regulated the relations between employer and employe, and protected the lower classes from being exploited by rapacious capitalists.

The Talmid Hakam, though the most powerful and important member of the community, was not an official appointed by the latter. This fact naturally provokes the question so difficult to answer: Whence did the Talmid Hakam draw his power? The learned caste among the Jews of antiquity and the Middle Ages is a unique phenomenon in history. The Talmide Hakamim were not priests, for the whole of Israel is a nation of priests; they were not *Seelensorger*, i. e., caretakers of the soul, for our ancestors would not have entrusted their souls even to a "rabbinical conference," nor yet to a board of trustees, much less to a single person. Indeed, the expression "caste" in its real meaning is not applicable to the Talmide Hakamim, since the Tannaim and Amoraim, as well as later the rabbis of the Middle Ages, belonged to various classes of society. More than one hundred scholars mentioned in the Talmud were artisans, a considerable number were tradesmen, and others were physicians or followed various professions.   Hence the source whence the Talmid Hakam drew his power is to be found neither in the existence of a learned class nor in the constitution of the Jewish community. It was rather the personality of the scholar that gave him his prominent position. He was one whose mission was proclaimed by nothing in his apparel, but whose life and words made themselves felt in all hearts and consciences. He was of the people, and the people recognized themselves in him. This explanation possibly is rather awkward for many people, because it lays stress on a manifestation of the Oriental character of the Jews as such. The Oriental is strongly subjective; he judges everything in life from its personal aspect.

In the opinion of the Oriental, a man whose moral make-up is much finer than the average has a right to claim not only esteem, but also authority and obedience. It was not the learning of the Talmid Hakam that gave

him his position, but his ideal life, which taught the
ignorant that knowledge of the Torah is the way that
leads man upward to perfection. The words of Deuteronomy, "And thou shalt love the Lord thy God," were
paraphrased as follows by a rabbi of the fourth century: "Through thy deeds thou shalt cause the Lord
thy God to be beloved and honored of men. Thou shalt
study the oral as well as the written Torah; thou shalt
pursue thine affairs honorably, and deal with thy
neighbor in gentleness. Then will it be said of thee:
Happy he, that he studied the Torah; happy his father,
that he caused him to learn the Torah; happy his
teacher, that he taught him the Torah; woe to them
that have not learned the Torah. Behold him who has
studied the Torah, how beautiful are his ways, how
just his deeds! Of him it is said in the Scriptures:'Thou
art My servant, Israel, in whom I will be glorified.' "6

The learned Capuchin, therefore, who thought the
Talmud was a person, came much nearer the truth than
those who hold a Talmudist to be a sort of thinking
machine, deprived of all personality. No less erroneous
is it to represent the spiritual activity of the Talmid
Hakam as one-sided, and the Talmid Hakam himself as
a learned jurist. The "four ells" of the *Halakah* seem
narrow only to the narrow-minded; as a matter of fact,
they express in concentrated form a comprehensive intellectual activity. It is of the essence of genius that it
strives to find a single comprehensive expression for
all the complex phenomena of the material, as well as
of the spiritual world. Modern culture, which owes its
existence chiefly to the genius of the Hebrews and the

Greeks, originated only through a process of concentration. The æsthetic genius of the Greeks produced not only the Homeric epics, the lyrics of Pindar, the creations of Phidias and Polycletus, but also Platonic and Aristotelian philosophy. It was the aesthetic feeling of the Greeks that in art produced the highest forms of harmony and symmetry, and in the province of thought endeavored to attain the same end through philosophy, which is nothing else than an expression of the harmonious and symmetrical relation of the whole to the individual. Hebrew genius, like no other, conceived the idea of duty in all its depth, and accordingly created the Psalms, in which the deepest expression is given to the relation of man to God. But Hebrew genius created also the Halakah, the profoundest conception of duty both in the relations of man to man and of man to God. The Halakah, "conduct of life," is as broad and deep as life itself, life in its endless variety, and it seeks to regulate life even though it may seek to do it by summing up all of life's complexities under one point of view. The Halakah subordinates everything to the Torah, but in order that the teachers of the Torah might master it, it was necessary that they should learn to know life in its various forms.

Accordingly, the material which the Talmid Hakam was expected to assimilate embraced all branches of human learning. But just as the whole of life was dedicated to religion, so the sciences were drawn into the circle of the intellectual activities pursued by the Talmid Hakam, not as a sort of mental gymnastics, but chiefly to serve the ends of religion, as the Greeks made all things subserve their interest in nature and its phenomena. "The man," says a teacher of the second century, "who understands astronomy and does not pursue the study of it, of that man it is written in Scripture: 'They regard not the work of the Lord, neither have they considered the operation of His hands.' "[7] The observation of nature is in a certain sense held to be a religious duty, leading man to admire the greatness of God and to recognize his own insignificance. At the same time astronomy was of great importance for religious practice, because in ancient times the Jewish calendar was not fixed, and thorough mathematical and astronomic knowledge was needed by the Talmid Hakam in order that he might make calculations for the calendar. Samuel, one of the greatest of the Babylonian teachers, could say of himself: "The streets of the heavens are as familiar to me as the streets of Nehardea."[8] Nehardea was his birthplace and the city in which he lived. The result is that one of the greatest authorities in the history of the calendar, could say that the Jewish calendar is the most brilliant achievement of its kind.[9] Comprehensive knowledge of the animal and the plant world was indispensable for one who sought to investigate and become acquainted with the Halakah in its widest extent. There are entire tractates in the Mishnah, the understanding of which presupposes a thorough knowledge of natural history. I have already said that many Talmide Hakamim were professional physicians, and this is probably to be explained by the fact that the anatomy of the human body and the bodies of animals formed an important subject in the scheme of their study, since a comprehension of important precepts was based upon it. In this connection it is interesting to note that the Church Father, Jerome, reproaches severely the Jewish scholars of his age for wasting their time in the laboratories of the physician.[10] He showed thereby of what little use his great classical learning was to him.

Highly characteristic of the culture of the Talmid Hakam is his attitude toward foreign languages. The Hellene looked down with scorn upon every non-Hellene, whom he simply called "barbarian." The *immanitas*, the savagery, the inhumanity of the barbarians constituted the opposite pole to the *humanitas*, the civilization, humanity of the Græco-Roman world. This conception, derived from the classic nations, according to which no culture existed outside their own, became, *mutatis mutandis*, a general idea which obtained throughout the civilized world. Celsus in the second century and Porphyry in the third, despite their many-sided culture, had just as little comprehension of the Bible as a literary production as Voltaire and Diderot had in modern times. The idea of a *Weltliteratur*—universal literature—we owe to Herder, and the phrase comes from Goethe. One expects, therefore, to find in Germany a fine appreciation of the literature of foreign nations. Our old teachers, however, were spared the one-sidedness of their non-Jewish contemporaries, and these so-called dry-as-dust jurists show in their utterances a finer understanding of the peculiarities of foreign languages than did the professional aesthetes of classi-

cal literature. "There are four languages," remarked
a teacher of the third century, "that one ought to use:
Greek for the art of poetry, Latin for the terms of
military command, Aramaic for elegies, and Hebrew
for daily speech,"[11] a statement which in a measure
anticipates what Heine said of the Latin language:
"The speech of the Romans can never disavow its
origin; it is a speech of command for generals."

The translation of the Bible into Greek is characterized by an allusion to the blessing of Noah: "The
beauty of Japhet (the Greek language) shall reside in
the tents of Shem (the Hebrew Bible)."[12] The tenacious hold maintained by the Talmudists upon the
dead language of the Bible sharpened their sense for
linguistic phenomena, and, from this point of view, we
may speak of the old Talmide Hakamim as the first
philologists, since they had to study another language
beside their mother tongue. Many among the authors
of the Talmud were masters not only of two, but of
several languages, such as Persian, Arabic and other
Oriental languages.[13] These, again, subserved the one
aim of the Talmid Hakam. His linguistic knowledge
enabled him to explain many an obscure term in the
Scriptures; and it was not mere chance that Ibn Koreish,
a North African rabbi, should have discovered the law
governing the transmutation of consonants in cognate
Semitic dialects.[14] His knowledge of the Hebrew Bible
and the Aramaic Targum, joined to the knowledge of
his mother tongue, made of the Jewish-Arabic scholar
a master of the chief divisions of the Semitic group of
languages.

Up to this point I have done no more, to use a talmudic expression, than circumscribe the periphery of the circle within which the Talmid Hakam moved. The center from which all the diverse tendencies of his activity radiated was religious study, the doctrine of the law, briefly called the Halakah. I may preface my further remarks by quoting a Roman writer, Cicero, an anti-Semite of Aryan descent (the Semitic species of this genus is a modern product). Cicero says: "I will boldly declare my opinion though the whole world be offended by it. I prefer this little book of the Twelve Tables alone to all the volumes of the philosophers. I find it to be not only of more weight, but also much more useful."[15]

I have quoted these words of a pagan who had hostile feelings toward the Jews because they betray a better understanding of the Law than is shown by some modern theologians, be it of the Jewish or of the Christian persuasion. What Cicero says of the Roman law is even more applicable to the Torah, the highest form for all the relations of life. Although the Talmide Hakamim were well versed in the branches of learning generally pursued in their time, their real occupation was the interpretation of the Scriptures and the study of the Halakah. Like Cicero, the Talmid Hakam preferred the study of the Torah to all other learned pursuits; for, if the Torah was the true and eternal revelation of God, then its statements must find application in all times and in all circumstances; then it must comprehend not only the dogmatic and the ethical in religion; not only the ceremonial law, whose aim is exclusively the maintenance of what is moral and religious, but also everything that man does to preserve himself body and soul. For the Talmid Hakam morality, justice, society, in short, all provinces of culture stood in close inward connection with religion, so that the search in the Torah included this and much more. "Search the Torah carefully; search it again, for everything is contained therein, and swerve not therefrom, for thou canst have no greater excellency than this."[16]

These are the words of a teacher of the first century, and they clearly express what the study of the Torah was to the Talmid Hakam. The law that manifests itself to the eyes of man everywhere—in the blade of grass which completes its course in unfolding and withering, in the stone that falls to earth, in the track of the stars far above us—this same law rules the life of man, and the same God whose law is obeyed by the entire universe in its tiniest parts, gave also to man the law of his life. It is to such an ideal conception of the Torah that we owe true Jewish piety, which was too earnest and too tenacious to resort to sacraments as the lame resort to crutches and hypochondriacs to quack medicines.

After preparation in the elementary and secondary schools the Talmid Hakam received his education in the *Bet ha-Midrash* (house of research). Although nothing is known concerning the origin of these Jewish academies, we shall probably not be far from right if we suppose them to have been established in the time of the early Scribes. The author of the apocryphal book "Ecclesiasticus" knows the institution as well as its name,[17] but we learn little from him concerning its characteristics. Typical of the school is the name given it in ancient times,[18] *Bet Wa'ad la-Hakamim,* "the house of assembly of the wise." In contrast to our universities, in which there are only instructors and pupils, the *Bet Wa'ad* was the place that brought together scholars and disciples—scholars who exchanged views and opinions with one another; disciples who were not only allowed the right to put questions, but might also express their opinion though, of course, in modest fashion. One must not forget, then, that the Talmid Hakam of old ever remained a student, and was at all times ready to sit at the feet of a master if only he found one. The difference between teacher and disciple was thus in many cases not a distinction of age but of learning.

There were academies in ancient times in every large city, and even in small places where a prominent scholar happened to have his home. Before the destruction of the Temple, as long as Jerusalem constituted the spiritual center of the Jews, the most important schools were in that city. In Jerusalem the great Hillel sat at the feet of his masters Shemayah and Abtalion; here later he himself gathered large numbers of pupils about him; and here too during a fairly long period of time, his favorite pupil, Rabban Johanan ben Zakkai, continued his activity as a teacher until the destruction of the Temple transferred the center of Jewish learning from Jerusalem to other places. As has been pointed out above, it was this master who rendered a service never to be forgotten—the establishment of a

spiritual center for Judaism outside of the holy city
and independent of the sanctuary at Jerusalem. And
this was accomplished by the academy founded by
him at Jabneh. As Josephus remarks in a work written
by him soon after the destruction of the Temple, "For
though we be deprived of our wealth, of our cities
or of the other advantages we have, our Law continues
immortal."[19]

Occupation with the Law or, in other words, the study
of the Torah became much more intensive after the
destruction of the Temple than it had been before,
since from this time on it was the one outlet open to
the energy and genius of the Jewish nation. As a result, toward the end of the first century we find alongside of the academy at Jabneh, which was presided
over by the Patriarch, similar important institutions
in Pekiin, Lydda, Bene-Barak and a number of other
places.[20] And the powerful influence of these schools
upon the people may be best judged from the fact that
the religious persecution of Hadrian was able to deci-
mate the Jews, but was impotent to annihilate Judaism,
which came forth from the glorious struggle fresh and
powerful. At the end of the second century the academies stood upon heights hitherto unattained, so that
the effects of the bloody wars and the still bloodier
persecutions can scarcely be detected in them.

At this time a new, pulsating, intellectual life began
for the Jews of Babylonia under the leadership of Abba
Arika and Samuel, and the turning point is marked by
the foundation of the academy at Sura by Abba Arika
and the reorganization of the old academy at Nehardea

by Samuel. While the former school flourished for nearly one thousand years, the ancient Jewish city of Nehardea was destroyed a few years after the death of Samuel. But the traditions of that school were continued in Pumbedita, which was still a seat of Jewish learning near the middle of the eleventh century.[21]

I must refrain from giving a detailed description of these academies, because it does not belong to the subject under discussion, and shall limit myself to a few points which will characterize them and at the same time throw some light upon the personality of the Talmid Hakam. What especially attracts one to these Jewish academies is their democratic character. Culture, religious as well as secular, is a power, and so originally a privilege of the ruling classes. The general impression prevailing nowadays that theological studies are good enough for persons who cannot do anything better is exactly the opposite of what our ancestors of old thought. They were not content to have had scholarly grandfathers; they desired that their grandchildren should partake of the same honor. We see, then, that there was a time among the ancient Jews, as among all other nations of old, when the school doors stood open only to the aristocratic and the rich.[22] These aristocratic privileges, however, disappeared very quickly, and the Bet ha-Midrash more and more developed into an institution eminently successful in fostering the democratic spirit. "Take heed of the children of the poor, for from them will come forth the word of God," is a favorite saying of the Talmudists.[23] The Patriarch and president of the academy at

Jabneh, Rabban Gamaliel II, undoubtedly the most aristocratic Jew of his time, shared the dignity of his office with the poor smith, Rabbi Joshua,[24] who held the post of *Ab Bet Din*, vice-president. A generation later Rabban Simeon, the son of Rabban Gamaliel, who inherited his father's position and honors, had as his two co-regents in the direction of the academy the son of the Exilarch in Babylon, one of the greatest officials of the Persian kingdom, and a poor scribe whose weekly income amounted to three denars, a third of which he gave away to still poorer scholars.[25] In an institution directed by a duke and a smith it is obvious that no distinctions of caste or of class could arise. Peacefully, side by side on the same bench, sat physician and tailor, shoemaker and landed proprietor. In the halls of the Torah all were equal or, in the words of the Rabbis, "only he is free who occupies himself with the study of the Torah."[26]

As a matter of course, this spirit of equality prevailed beyond the doors of the academy as well as within. On the one hand, it must be remembered that the Talmid Hakam spent more time in the Bet ha-Midrash than beyond its walls and, on the other hand, it is no less true that what was learned at the school realized its true purpose only when it was put to practical use in daily life. Consequently, the Bet ha-Midrash contributed more than any other institution of antiquity to cause differences of class and caste to disappear from among the Jews. To sing hymns about the equality of men and then, on leaving the house of God, to snub the beadle, is not the way, according to the Jewish

conception, which leads to democratic sentiment. I
do not wish to be misunderstood. I do not mean to
deny the old Talmide Hakamim class consciousness.
They were aristocrats of the intellect; they belonged
to an aristocracy which carried with it no privileges,
but many duties. They were rather democratic aristocrats than aristocratic democrats. A work bearing
the title "The Conduct of the Wise," preserved from
the period when Jewish learning was in its flower in
Palestine, gave the Talmid Hakam, in brief and crisp
form, a program according to which he was to regulate
his entire life. The first sentence of the work reads:
"The way of the wise is to be modest, humble, alert
and intelligent; to endure injustice, to make himself
beloved of men; to be gracious even in intercourse with
subordinates; to avoid wrongdoing; to judge each man
according to his deeds; to act according to the motto,
'I take no pleasure in the good things of this world,
seeing that life here below is not my portion.' Wrapped
in his mantle he sits at the feet of the wise; no one can
detect anything unseemly in him; he puts pertinent
questions and gives suitable answers."[27]

If we were to inquire of the Talmud—the true reflex
of the intellectual and spiritual activity of the Jews—
what it has to tell us about the life of the men that
built it up, we would get an entirely different picture
from that drawn by the simple Galilean fishermen in
their denunciation of the Scribes. How different was
the true Talmid Hakam from the caricature which
paints him as the man who thanks God for not having
made him like other people. A current saying among

the scholars of Jabneh, which may therefore be regarded as a characterization of Talmudists by the Talmud, runs as follows: "I am God's creature and so is my fellow-man; my vocation is in the city, his is in the field; I go to my work joyfully and he goes to his; as he does not pride himself upon his work, so I do not pride myself upon mine, and should he think that he accomplishes little while I accomplish great things, I would remind him of what we have learned: Whether much, whether little, it is all the same, provided the heart be directed toward Heaven."[28] Instead of the pride usually attributed to the Pharisees, it is precisely the opposite traits, modesty and humility, which are designated as the necessary conditions for being a Talmid Hakam; and the Talmud, as well as the rest of rabbinical literature, is full of examples drawn from the lives of great men in Israel, which best illustrate how their conduct measured up to the standards which they themselves set up. The following is related of Rabbi Meïr, the most distinguished disciple of Rabbi Akiba and the greatest scholar of his time: One Friday evening a woman came home very late because she had attended a lecture of Rabbi Meïr, which he had drawn out to great length. Her husband was furious. He slammed the door in her face and swore he would not let her in until she had spit in the Rabbi's face. When Rabbi Meïr heard of the quarrel, he pretended that he had pain in his eyes and begged the woman to charm away his trouble. The way to do this, according to an old superstition, was to spit on the eyes. The woman did so, and in parting from her after having undergone the pretended treatment, Rabbi Meïr said to her: "Go home now and tell your husband you have done his bidding and have spit in my face."[29]

But the Talmid Hakam could also be proud and aristocratic, especially in the interest of truth and virtue. A rabbi of the third century once preached an impassioned sermon against the Patriarch and his house, who were eager enough to maintain their rights but concerned themselves little about their duties. His bold speech brought him into great danger, and it needed the intercession of prominent scholars to appease the Patriarch. But when the poor rabbi appeared before the prince, who probably expected an apology, the rabbi began to complain of the depravity of the times and ended with the words, "as the garden, so the gardener."[30] By this he wanted to show the Patriarch that he was not justified in putting all the blame upon the people.

The great Amora, Abba Arika, on his return from Palestine to his Babylonian home, was appointed supervisor of the markets by the Exilarch. His duties consisted in inspecting weights and measures and regulating prices. The Exilarch bade him keep prices down and prevent increase in the cost of foodstuffs. But Abba Arika disregarded the command of the Exilarch, although it would have met with the approval of the people because, in his opinion, it was against the law, which had to guard the interests of the tradesmen as well as those of the people at large. His refusal cost him his liberty; he was thrown into prison by the Exilarch.[31]

In general the clashes between the Talmid Hakam and the Jewish secular rulers, the exilarchs and patriarchs, are very typical of the strength of character displayed by the Talmide Hakamim and their strict adherence to principle. Neither threats nor allurements on the part of the authorities had any influence upon them. Unconcerned about their personal interests, they insisted upon what was right and just. It is related of some Talmide Hakamim that they refused to accept gifts or invitations even from the patriarchal house because they wanted to be entirely independent. Once a certain rabbi accepted an invitation to dine with the Patriarch, but he said expressly, in true aristocratic fashion, "I do not want to deprive His Excellency of the honor of my presence."[32]

This independence and freedom, which the Talmid Hakam would not have exchanged for any treasures in the world, were in a measure due to the fact that the frugal needs of the Talmid Hakam were readily satisfied; indeed, he may be said to have been almost without wants. His principle was: "This is the path of the Torah: A morsel of bread with salt shalt thou eat; thou shalt drink water by measure, and shalt sleep upon the ground, and live a life of trouble, the while thou toilest in the Torah. If thou doest thus, happy shalt thou be in this world, and it shall be well with thee in the world to come."[33]

This sentence, however, is not a pious wish. It corresponds to an essential feature in the make-up of the Jewish scholar; and numerous examples occur in the Talmudim and Midrashim that show us how the Tal-

mide Hakamim tried to realize the principle in their
own lives. It is related of Rabbi Eleazar b. Harsum,
the Rothschild of the second century, the owner of a
thousand villages and a thousand ships, that a bag of
flour sufficed for his needs. He carried the bag on his
back and daily journeyed in this fashion from teacher
to teacher in order to pursue the study of the Torah.
Being unknown to his employes, as he never appeared
among them to transact business, he was on one occasion forced by them to do compulsory work. When he
begged them to let him go his way that he might continue his study, they exclaimed: "As surely as our
master, Rabbi Eleazar b. Harsum, lives, we will not
let you go."[34]

A similar story is told of a contemporary of Rabbi
Eleazar, the celebrated Rabbi Tarphon. A keeper of
his garden caught him eating dates which he had found
lying on the ground after the harvest. The keeper,
who did not know him and who had been recently
troubled a good deal by thieves, seized the rabbi,
thrust him into a bag and wanted to throw him into
the water, but the rabbi, nigh to death, cried out:
"Woe unto Tarphon that he must meet with such an
end." These few words were enough to throw the
keeper into a panic, and he set the rabbi free. A colleague of Rabbi Tarphon adds that all his life Rabbi
Tarphon regretted the episode and was wont to exclaim: "Woe is me that I made use of the crown of the
Torah." The fear of deriving any profit from learning
was carried to such an extreme by Rabbi Tarphon that
he could never forgive himself for having made use of

his fame in order to save his life.[35] We may consider this complete renunciation of every feeling of ambition and pride as exaggerated, but we cannot help admiring such heroic sentiments. "Whoever makes use of the crown," said Hillel, "will perish." A younger contemporary of his added the explanation: "Make not of the Torah a crown wherewith to glorify thyself nor a spade wherewith to dig."[36] The Torah is a crown and raises its wearer to the highest rank of society. But the crown of the Torah has value only if the man that wears it joins to it the crown of good deeds.

In conclusion, let me characterize briefly the difference between the Talmid Hakam and the 'Am ha-Arez, a difference which existed among Jews even in very early times, and which to a certain extent continues to exist to this very day.

There are certain theologians who warmly espouse the side of the 'Am ha-Arez, which is all the more astonishing as they themselves are brimful of the very faults, such as self-sufficiency, pride of learning and the like, which they are so fond of describing as "Pharisaic." They are the men who while speaking about the Pharisee, who thanked God for not having made him like other people, do not fail to thank their God for not having made them like the Pharisee. They would do well to study the character and temperament of the Talmid Hakam as they have unfolded themselves before our eyes in our attempt to trace out his history, development and attitude toward life and its concerns.

As we have seen, the Talmid Hakam was a cultivated man; but what counted for more, he was a thoroughly ethical being. Culture, morality and learning were on the side of the Talmid Hakam. It is not lack of learning that stigmatizes one as an 'Am ha-Arez, but lack of morality and culture. We have indeed other standards of culture today; and as for morality, it is not an unusual thing in certain circles to wink at traits not altogether admirable, if only the person to be admitted into so-called good society possesses certain other useful qualities.

Which of the two, then, is guilty of "Pharisaic" hypocrisy, modern society or that of the ancient Jews? The reply to this question I leave to every man of unbiased judgment.

The love and veneration with which the great mass of the people—and by far the greater part of them were 'Amme ha-Arez—clung to the Talmide Hakamim, their guides and teachers, express clearly the people's approval of the ways in which their leaders sought to direct them. The dominating principle of the Talmid Hakam at all times was: *Kol Yisrael Haberim*, "all Israel forms one brotherhood."

III

The Rabbinical Student

The appellation "people of the book," coined for the Jews by one of the greatest men of the Middle Ages[1], characterizes them in more ways than one. Primarily it indicates their devotion to the Bible, the Book of books, the most precious gift conferred upon mankind by Israel, and Israel's most conspicuous contribution to civilization—the Holy Scripture, without which we cannot conceive of a peculiar Jewish people in the past, in the present, or in the future. But the Jews are not "the people of the Holy Book" alone; they are also the people of the book in general. The history of Israel is not a chronicle of the development of political power and greatness; it is the story of a peculiar spiritual development; and the national heroes of Israel are not heroes of the sword but of the pen. Therefore, the loss of political independence did not destroy Israel as an historical entity.

This original character of Jewish history must be patent to the most superficial observer. The fixation of the Canon, the redaction of the Mishnah, the completion of the Talmud, the appearance of the Moreh Nebukim, these are the events that mark off the epochs of Jewish history, while the recital of the external events consists of nothing but monotonous repetitions of long drawn out martyrologies lacking even typical chapter headings. As regards cruelty and inhumanity, the persecutions inflicted in the name of the religion of love are in no measure inferior to those sponsored by the representatives of Hellenic civilization; and the barbarism of the twentieth century cannot lay claim to any refinements in the treatment of the Jews not known and practised by the dark centuries of mediaeval days.

In view of the fact that Jewish history in its essence is the history of a literature and of a culture, it is natural that in many lands its beginnings should coincide with the rise in those places of the study of the Talmud. Jews lived for more than ten centuries in Europe and Northern Africa, and aside from regularly recurring persecutions, we hear nothing about their fate and fortunes during the whole of this long period. Toward the end of the tenth century of the common era, we are told in an old chronicle, four distinguished Jewish scholars while on a sea-voyage were taken captive by a Spanish-Moorish admiral. Their subsequent fortunes carried them, the one to Spain, the second to Northern Africa, the third to Egypt, and the fourth, it seems, as far as Narbonne, each of them becoming the founder of Jewish scholarship in his new home. Recent investigations go to show that this report is more or less legendary[2] but, as in many another case, the legend expresses truth in the form in which it appeals to the imagination of the people. For the fact remains unchallenged that the establishment of Talmud schools toward the end of the tenth century in Spain, France, and Northern Africa introduces a new era in the history of the Jews of these countries. What we are told about them up to the end of the tenth century concerns the fate of the *Jews* living there; after the foundation of the Talmud schools, there begins a history of *Judaism* and of *Jewish culture*. R. Hushiel, R. Moses, and R. Elhanan ben Shemariah are not merely the founders of talmudic learning in the lands of their adoption, they are also the originators of Jewish culture there.

The characterization of the rabbi as architect and exponent of Jewish culture makes it obvious that we are here not concerned with the rabbinical institution of modern times. The rabbi of centuries gone by called himself neither disciple of the prophets, nor successor to the priests, nor pastor, nor aught resembling these epithets. He was anything but what we are at present in the habit of understanding by the term rabbi. He was neither an official of the congregation nor its minister. His modesty forbade the one, his pride the other. He was master over none but himself, and he was servant to none but his God. Still less may we conceive of the rabbi of yore as the preacher, the orator of the synagogue. In the good old times, every Jew considered himself at home in the synagogue, and there was no need to delegate the privilege of speaking to one particular person. For a specialist who says the prayers for the rest of the worshippers there was no sphere of activity at a time in which every single member of the congregation was an eager participant in the divine service. Nor could rabbinic Judaism, which lays particular stress upon the dogma of the

direct communion between God and man, brook the
intervention of a mediator between the Most High
and the meanest of His human creatures. In short,
the rabbinate as a profession is of comparatively
recent growth. In the olden days, rabbis were recruited from all classes of society. State officials and
men in the humblest walks of life, physicians, astrono-
mers, tradesmen, and artisans,—all vied with one
another in the vast audience-chamber of rabbinical
literature, and there they and their opinions all received equal consideration. "The student of the Torah
who devotes himself to its investigation in order to
escape the duty of toil and self-support, desecrates the
honor of God; he disgraces the Torah, extinguishes the
light of faith, brings an evil fate down upon himself,
and forfeits his portion in the world to come."[3] These
expressions are not excerpted from a collection of
ethical sayings, but are quoted from a rabbinical code
of laws, and they explain, from an economic point of
view, why a rabbinical profession could not develop in
former days.

What is it that made the Jewish scholar of the
Middle Ages the important factor he actually was in
the spiritual life of his people? The reply to this
question is of vital interest, and not alone to those of
us to whom Jewish culture is more than an idle word.
Even he who does not see his ideal in the rabbi of the
Middle Ages, will do well to examine his radiant figure
and try to define and grasp its harmonious proportions.
The old rabbinical ideal is in very truth superseded
only when the best it offers can be replaced by some-

thing better. To shove it aside contemptuously is not
to know it. Who knows it cannot but admit how much
is to be learned from it and the instruction will come,
not from an adversary but from a friend, which instruction far from fettering his modernity will but
enhance it.

I have chosen the inner and outer life of the rabbinical student as my subject, because I hold that a
consideration of it will enable us to reply to the
question, what is it that gave the Jewish scholar his
peculiarly important place in the spiritual economy of
his nation?

The first communal duty as well as the highest—
since all others depended upon it—was to provide for
the broadest possible dissemination of a knowledge of
Jewish literature among the members of the community.
It was the conscious purpose to train every Jew to go
to his national literature for draughts of spiritual
refreshment. The boy was led to it; through it the
youth was to develop into maturity; from it the full-
grown man was to derive enlightenment and strength
and courage for his work and his activities; and with
its light as a lamp for his feet, the venerable in years
was to travel the path to the hereafter.

Besides elementary schools, every Jewish community
of size and standing had an intermediate school for the
advanced study of the Bible and the Talmud.

A latter day description of talmudical studies in the
German and Polish Yeshibot is not unlike the sensa-
tions a hungry man experiences while reading the
menu of a French chef. Of what avail the fine names

without the substantial products of his art? Shibboleths like *Pilpul*, dialectics, sophistry, beg the question.
They are weak characterizations of an intellectual
tendency that moulded the greatest Talmudists of the
last four hundred years. Modern historians are lavish
of praise for the well-ordered studies of the Sefardim,
and equally lavish of censure for the topsy-turvy
methods in vogue among the Ashkenazim, which
embarked a ten-year-old lad on the "sea of the Talmud" and kept him there until he became a master
navigator. In view of this attitude, is it not rather
startling to find that since the time of Rabbi Joseph
Caro (d. 1575) the Sefardim cannot show a single
name in the realm of the Talmud comparable with the
distinguished scholars of Poland? Would it not seem
that after all there must have been method in the
methodlessness of the Polish Jew? The principle
underlying the study of the Talmud in Poland was
"non multa sed multum," not quantity but quality.
Whatever was studied was searched out in every detail,
while with the Sefardim the thing that signified was
the extent of the field covered. For the Sefardim
learning was a matter of sentiment, for the Polish Jew
it was an intellectual occupation. The former studied
in order to know how the law would have them act in
given practical cases; the latter in order to analyze the
theory on which the practice was based. The Sefardic
student aimed to become a rabbi who would have to
decide questions of law and custom; the Ashkenazic
student, to become a Lamdan able to control the
decisions of his rabbi and, in case of necessity, show up

their falsity.   The protest made by a number of
prominent Polish scholars of the sixteenth and seventeenth centuries[4] against the dominant practice in the
study of the Talmud, was justified from the point of
view of sentiment.   The dialectic method gradually
secularized Jewish religious knowledge. But it must be
borne in mind that the Lamdan educated in the Heder
does not represent the class of the pious; he is the type
of the educated Jew, and the decried method was the
only one calculated to produce this type. It is incorrect
to think of the Yeshibah as a religious school, as it is
generally assumed to be.   It was more, it was the
institution for general Jewish education.

Errors are transmitted like diseases. The inaccurate
rendering of the Hebrew word "Torah" by "law," for
which we are indebted to our Greek-speaking brethren,
has all along been a barrier in the way of a certain
school of theologians. It has prevented them effectually
from understanding the system of Rabbinism as a
whole, but especially from comprehending the specific
ideal of Rabbinism which is summed up in the term
Talmud Torah, the study of the Torah. The most
deplorable aspect of this lack of comprehension is that
it has not remained without effect upon the Jews
themselves, at least so far as their estimate of the
development of post-talmudic Judaism is concerned.

Torah is not law. It is an expression for the aggre-
gate of Jewish teachings. It comprises every field and
mark of culture—morality, justice, society, education,
etc.   The term aims to gather them all up as a unit
because the Jewish view is that all the nobler mani-

festations of human conduct must be connected with religion. The education of the Jewish child, from the Soferim down to our own day, has been exclusively Jewish, though not exclusively religious, certainly not exclusively legalistic. Paradoxical as it may sound, the education of the Ashkenazic child was more secular than the education of the Sefardic child. The Jewish school of the Sefardim had a more strongly religious character than that of the Ashkenazim, in spite of the fact that the Sefardic child was taught non-Jewish branches of knowledge. Externals do not count. Nine hundred years ago, Mohammedan children sat on the same benches with Jewish children in a synagogue used for school purposes.[5] That was among Sefardim. Nothing like it is thinkable among the Ashkenazim, whose educational system was laid out on Jewish lines exclusively, not because they objected to secular knowledge on principle, but because in Christian countries education of any kind was clerical and, of course, inaccessible to the Jew. The very fact that the Sefardim were often adepts in philosophy and the natural sciences produced the result that Jewish studies among them gradually stiffened into a religious exercise. They cultivated them to satisfy their heart's cravings. For the Sefardic intellect there were other than Jewish sources of gratification. Among the Ashkenazim, Jewish studies offered the sole and only field for the manifestation of their mental activity. As a consequence, even their religious literature was cultivated for educational and intellectual purposes. At the end of about five centuries of parallel development, the two tendencies culminated in the sixteenth century, the one in the Kabbalah of the Orientals, the other in the Pilpul of the Jews of Poland. The process was this: When the Sefardim were expelled from the Pyrenean Peninsula and came to countries in which culture and science were at a low ebb, their intellect had no support; they had to fall back upon their Jewish feeling, and so they lost themselves in mysticism. In Poland, again, where the Jews likewise came in contact with a low stage of cultural development, the same intellectual attitude asserted itself in them which in the twelfth century had brought forth the school of the Tosafists in France. Critics like Rabbi Solomon Loria and Rabbi Joel Sirkes in Poland may fitly be mentioned in the same breath with Rabbi Jacob Tam and Rabbi Isaac ben Samuel in France. The Pilpul, so far from being the result of a process of deterioration, is in reality nothing but the inevitable issue of the intellectual movement inaugurated by the Soferim. From the first the school was raised on a national basis, the only firm foundation for the education of the young, and as religion occupies the most prominent place in the national life of the Jews, the Jewish school was a religious institution as well. So long as the Jews lived in their own land, and could develop their national life without let or hindrance, there was no objection to introducing elements of alien origin into the school. It had no difficulty in transforming them Jewishly and assimilating them.

But when a national life was precluded, the Jewish school perforce had to narrow its compass. This was the only escape from the dangers of absorption by the surrounding cultures which menaced Jewish intellectual life. But even after its aims suffered such contraction, the Jewish school did not fail to reveal the intellectual impulse as the mainspring of the education it afforded. In spite of its one-sidedness in excluding everything non-Jewish, therefore, the Talmud Heder did not cease to be the great national institution for the development of the Jewish intellect.

Student life in the true sense of the term began for the Jewish youth when, at the age of seventeen or eighteen, he left home and fared forth on his journeyings. Poor travelling students were, in fact, a mediaeval institution. One result of this was the production of a large number of tramps who called themselves students and who wandered about over Europe and lived on the charitable. They were little better than sturdy beggars and idle vagabonds, and as such, no small trouble to the towns and villages at which they halted.[6]

Ein fahrender Scholast? Der Casus macht mich lachen, says Faust. The contemplation of the Jewish student during his journeyman years compels not laughter but rather honest admiration. What sacrifices was he not ready to bring, the Jewish youth who trudged afoot from the banks of the Danube to the banks of the Seine, bidding defiance to hunger and cold, only to drink in the words of some far-famed master! How he would wander about, a restless wayfarer, for half a year across ditches and mountains and among brigands on his journey from Cologne to Venice for the sake of the Talmud explanations to be had from an Italian scholar! To follow a school to new abodes was, to be sure, not a novel phenomenon peculiar to the Middle Ages. The Jewish sage of the second century warmly recommends the practice of exiling oneself to a place in which the Torah is taught. But when the Jews had scattered over all the continents, it took on a new meaning. In ancient times the only countries that entered into the Jewish student's itinerary were Palestine and Babylonia, and the number who resorted to them from distant lands was naturally inconsiderable. But when the study of the Talmud began to flourish in Middle and Western Europe, when every country, every province had its distinguished man and boasted famous names, then it became an essential in the education of a Jewish scholar to have enjoyed the personal instruction of renowned masters, and he shrank from no sacrifice, however great, to obtain this privilege.

Of entrance examinations and graduating exercises there were none. The schools made demands upon their pupils without conferring privileges, and therefore such formalities as examinations were entirely out of place. The student merely presented himself before the master whose course of lectures he wished to attend, and a brief conversation sufficed to reveal the extent of his rabbinical attainments. If the teacher was satisfied with the prospective disciple, he was enrolled a member of the Yeshibah, as the Talmud academy was called.

In one respect the Jewish student was the superior of his Christian colleague; as he exceeded him in years when he entered the school for higher learning, so he surpassed him in knowledge.[7] On the average, the candidate for university work in the Middle Ages was a lad of fourteen who had read Aristotle instead of Cicero and disputed about sophisms instead of doing Latin prose composition. When the *Bahur* presented himself in the Yeshibah, he had endured a very much severer intellectual discipline. In the Heder he had gone through the whole or at least the greater part of the Bible, the instruction in the Scriptures being based upon the commentary of Rashi from almost the time of its appearance. If little stress was laid upon Hebrew *grammar*, the implied loss was more than compensated for in that the pupil learned *Hebrew*, the language itself, in the Heder. The commentary of Rashi had peculiar qualities that made it an eminently fit introduction to the study of the Holy Scriptures. A simple, natural system of exegesis which, through the frequent use of the Midrash, was presented with warm, deep feeling, made the Bible a living book to the child student. It enabled him to penetrate to its very recesses. At the same time the study of the Scripture with Rashi was the best possible introduction to rabbinical literature—the Midrash and the Talmud— from which Rashi gives frequent quotations in his Bible commentary, making them intelligible in his unsurpassed way. Instruction in the Talmud was begun at an early age. When the Bahur entered the Yeshibah at the age of seventeen, he could look back upon at least seven years of Talmud study. In the Middle Ages a candidate was allowed to enter the

University of Paris only on condition that "he presented his petition to the rector in Latin, without resort to French words." The Jewish student at a corresponding point in his career, not only was master of the Hebrew language, but also was acquainted with a considerable portion of the post-biblical literature. It is true the Hebrew used by the mediaeval rabbis has been subjected to adverse criticism, but the criticism has, as a rule, proceeded from such as were not able to read the works of the scholars upon whose language they cast aspersions. It is human frailty to throw the blame for our own shortcomings upon others. In this case, however, the fact is undeniable that the idiom which in the Scripture is known to us essentially as the exalted medium of lyric passion was transformed by the rabbis into a pliable, elastic and precise medium for legal discussions and the multifarious needs of a complex civilization. The so-called barbarisms in the rabbinical Hebrew appear chiefly in the coining of new terms from the talmudic language and in the new forms developed from the classical Hebrew, whose coinage and acceptance were due to changed circumstances and demands.

Thus equipped with knowledge that enabled him to follow the advanced lectures on the Talmud, the Bahur entered the Yeshibah. The lectures in the Yeshibah were of a twofold character, differentiated nowadays at the rabbinical seminaries of Germany by the expressions *cursorisch* and *statarisch*. The Jewish terms are *Perush* and *Tosafot*. The former, the Perush, is the simple explanation of the text as it stands; it concerns itself neither with parallel passages in other treatises of the Talmud nor with critical analysis. The model for this method was the Talmud commentary of Rashi, and as long as the correct understanding of the text offered many difficulties, the Perush was the only method of explanation employed. With the development of the study of the Talmud, especially through the activity displayed in this field by the so-called Tosafists—Franco-German scholars of the twelfth and thirteenth centuries—the Yeshibah began to lay great stress upon criticism, the analytical method of study, Pilpul as it was later called. Here the student of Jewish history must be cautioned against a pitfall. The acumen and dialectics of the rabbis are not to be confounded, as they sometimes are, with quibbling and pettifogging. The treatment of the Talmud by the scholars of the Middle Ages remains the standard to this day, and that too in spite of the admission that they shared the defect peculiar to the whole mediaeval world of scholars: very few of them were endowed with a sense of historical criticism. Such snap judgments as "rabbinical subtilizing," and "rabbinical casuistry" are born not of hostile feeling alone; ignorance has its share in their paternity.

It must also be admitted that little attention was paid to philology, so that the great Talmudist often mistook a Greek word for an Aramaic, and, *horribile dictu*, sometimes would not even be able to distinguish Aramaic from Hebrew. But while a little grammar would certainly have been of some use to the mediaeval scholar, a larger portion thereof would as little have made him a Talmudist as it has succeeded in the case of the modern grammarians and philologians.

No less an authority than Nöldeke remarks that "we modern scholars who approach the Talmud as philologists and historians will always remain bunglers in this field of study." This is the expert opinion of the greatest Semitist of modern times, who laid the foundation for the scientific study of the philology of the Talmud. Many profited by Nöldeke's contributions to talmudic philology, but few followed his candid advice not to express opinions about the proper method of the study of the Talmud without knowing it. With all the short-comings of the mediaeval scholars, they knew the Talmud, and their great mastery of this branch of Jewish literature is the best proof that their model of study was essentially the right one.

The two methods of explaining the Talmud previously mentioned were applied successively. First the lecturer confined himself for a considerable time to the mere elucidation of the text, and later the whole of the raw material thus acquired by the pupil was worked over again critically. The lectures were delivered daily with the exception of Sabbaths, holidays, and Fridays. In later times the practice prevailed of reviewing the lessons of the week on Thursdays, and the review frequently required the whole day and the better part of the night. Naturally, a review of this searching sort presupposed intense application on the part of the student. In general, great importance was attached to private study, and every student was granted complete

Lernfreiheit, complete liberty in the matter of atten-
dance upon lectures. The industry of the *Bahurim* was
phenomenal. They knew too well that there are no
short cuts to knowledge. Many of them did not sleep
in a bed except during the night from Friday to the
Sabbath. All other nights of the week they spent in
the Yeshibah, permitting themselves only a short nap
as they sat over their folios.

The needy student received his meals free of charge
in the Students' Refectory, the "Bahurim Room,"
which was maintained by contributions from the local
and outlying communities. Very frequently the rector
of the academy, the *Rosh Yeshibah*, lodged with the
students, permitting his wife and children to live elsewhere, so that he might establish the intimate relations
with his disciples which are a characteristic feature of
Jewish student life.[9] On Friday evening, as a rule, all
the students dined with the rector, each one being
provided with a beaker of wine while the host recited
the *Kiddush*. This Friday evening meal was graced by
the presence of the married students as well as the
others. Those who had already established households
were in the habit of first consecrating the beginning of
the Sabbath at home, in the circle of their families, and
then they would repair to the Bahurim Room for the
common meal.[10] And as the Sabbath was welcomed by
teachers and disciples assembled together, so it was
ushered out in the same way. *Habdalah* was recited
by the rector in the presence of the students, who all
drank from the chalice of the master.[11]

The holidays peculiar to student life were the

eighteenth of Iyyar, *Lag ba-'Omer*, and the days on which the study of a tractate of the Talmud was completed in the academy.[12]   Besides, unusual festivities were connected with the first day of Pentecost and the last day of Passover. On these holidays the rector of the academy gave a banquet, to which not only the whole student body was invited, but also prominent members of the community, dignified *Ba'ale Batim*.[13] But the days of greatest merrymaking were Hanukkah and Purim. On those days the Jewish student ceased to be "cabin'd, cribbed, and confined." For a space rigor and discipline made room for jest and jollity. A distinctive feature of the Hanukkah celebration was formed by the *Ketowes*, while the Purim banquet was signalized by Parodies. By *Ketowes*, a word of uncertain origin, is meant riddles, doggerel rhymes, and all sorts of quips and cranks. Here is an example: The renowned scholar Isserlein, one of the most learned authorities of the fifteenth century, asked his pupil, Yosel by name, whether he knew how many candles are used on Hanukkah. "If thou knowest not," continued Isserlein, "thou canst easily find out— simply remove thy mantle." The explanation is that the numerical equivalent of Yosel's name in Hebrew is fifty-three; and the numerical equivalent of *beged*, mantle, is nine; subtract the one from the other, and the remainder is forty-four, the number of Hanukkah candles, including the candles that serve as "sextons," *Shammashim*, each night.[14]

In connection with the Hanukkah celebration, a Jewish student song, the only one of its kind, has been

preserved. It is a most remarkable circumstance that
this secular song found its way into the prayer-book
of the German Jews, in the guise of a Hanukkah hymn,
and it could be forced out of its refuge only after centuries of opposition against it on the part of the rabbis.
The last two stanzas follow in a rather free rendition:

> Ye waters, O cease
> Your gurgling and dripping!
> We'll take our sweet ease,
> At eve and at morn,
> Where ample wine flowing
> We quaff from the horn.

> The waters that roar
> Your ears set a-tingling!
> But cease not to pour
> Across your parched lips
> The juice of grapes reddening,
> The wine that smooth slips.

The refrain of this song is as heedlessly irresponsible
as only a student can be:

> Marry, marry, go and sell,
> Sell your house, your field, your beast,
> Bring but gold our thirst to quell,
> Bring but gold to grace the Hanukkah feast.

In spite of this convivial song, the Jewish student
was a teetotaler as compared with the participant in
the drinking bouts usual at the mediaeval universities.
Rarely were complaints lodged against the Bahurim
for unrestrained drinking or indecorous behavior. Of

course, here and there a black sheep was bound to turn up in the flock, and it happened occasionally that a Bahur managed to gain entrance to the wine-cellar of the master and drink his fill.[16] But this was an exceptional occurrence, while the description of the average mediaeval university student by an impartial historian is that "his manners and moral tone generally were in many ways no better than those of the roughest and most uncivilized classes of modern society[17]."

That ill-regulated living was impossible in the Yeshibah, is due not alone to the frugality, sobriety and ascetic habits of the Jews of the Middle Ages, but also to the severe discipline which the rabbis imposed upon those guilty of excesses and frivolity. Once, when a Bahur flung a dish at the head of the beadle with whom he was quarrelling, the Rosh Yeshibah could hardly be restrained from excommunicating the student. The master desisted only at the intercession of all the other students and after the offender had again and again begged pardon of the beadle.[18] The affection in which the teachers held their pupils, so far from making them indulgent toward the faults of the young men, only increased their severity of judgment.

There was but a single occasion throughout the year on which the inexorable rigor of the daily routine gave way to unchecked hilarity. That was at the Purim season. Indeed, the exceptional character of Purim in the life of the Jewish student was so marked that it put its impress on Jewish literature itself. While the Hanukkah conceits have left no trace, the Purim pleasantries of the Bahurim called forth a literary

species in Hebrew which has a double claim to be
called original. Not only did the Neo-Hebrew parody
arise in spite of the lack of a model in classical Hebrew
literature, but it can hold its own, in point of originality, in comparison with the best of similar productions
in general literature.[19] On Purim all was grist that
came to the Bahur's parody mill; he parodied the
Talmud, its venerable commentaries, and the prayer-
book in all its phases.   Not even the most solemn
prayers for the Day of Atonement were spared by the
spirit of parody. There are even hymns and penitential psalms for Purim which are striking testimony to
the sense of humor possessed by the Jew, especially
when one takes into account the merciless cruelty that
held his actual life in its clutches.

It would lead us too far from our present purpose to
give specimens of this rich literature. One typical
example must suffice: The passionate outcry that
forces itself from the lips of the devout Jew at the close
of the *Neilah* prayer: *Le-Shanah ha-ba'ah b'Yerusha-
laim*, "Next year in Jerusalem!", runs in the Purim
parody: *Le-Shanah ha-ba'ah kiflaim*, "Next year for
a double dram." Purim audacity did not shrink back
even before the sacred person of the master. A mock
rabbi occupied the seat of the teacher, and doubtless he
permitted many a joke to escape his lips of which the
rector later took cognizance in all seriousness.[20]

Such innocent play should not deceive us as to the
real character of the relation between teachers and
disciples. Boundless veneration for the teacher and
paternal love toward disciples, these are in very deed

the distinctive marks of Jewish student life in the Middle Ages. When a dangerous illness threatened the life of a famous teacher of the fourteenth century, his pupils and the members of the community determined to fast two days of the week until his recovery was assured.[21] A wish expressed by the master was a command to be fulfilled with alacrity by the disciple. On the other hand, the teacher knew no greater joy than to be of service to his pupils. Touching is the only word that can describe the brief note which tells how R. Isserlein, mentioned above, always divided among the students the fish, or wine, or fruit, sent him for his own delectation.[22] In the house of the famous Rabbi, Jacob Möln ha-Levi, certain parts of the slaughtered animal were not used because there were some among the students whose religious scruples would not permitt them to eat of those parts.[23] If a student took unto himself a wife, the wedding feast was held in the house of the teacher. If a married student celebrated a joyous event in his family, again it was the house of the teacher at which the festivities were arranged.[24]

In sorrow as well as in joy teacher and pupil were lovingly united. When one of his students died, our old acquaintance R. Isserlein was so profoundly affected that he fasted the entire day.[25] In the prayers commemorating the dead, teachers were named along with the next of kin who had departed this life.

It has not been without a definite intention that I have accorded so much space to these trifling details in the life of the student. More than anything else they put us in a position to comprehend the reasons for the success of the rabbi in the Middle Ages. For by no means may the epithet "people of the book" applied to the Jews mislead us into imagining that the teachers of this people were bookish men. The authority exercised by our great teachers radiated from their personality, not merely from their learning. Their individuality was far richer than their word. This is the explanation of their perennial influence. Life can be enkindled only by life; deeds produce deeds. Herein resides the secret of the wondrous power of our old teachers—great in what they did, even greater in what they were. They towered above their writings, for with their word they introduced us into their lives. That personal intercourse with the scholar by far outweighs the effect of his teaching is a principle laid down in the Talmud[26] and accepted at its full value by the later generations of Talmud students. The disciple was admonished to observe the teacher as well as heed his instruction. Our teachers were not in the habit of delivering lectures on psychology to their disciples, abstract disquisitions upon the soul, full of superficial ratiocination and finical introspection. Their whole life itself was laid bare before their disciples—all its motives and emotions, its aims and errors. The pupil observed the master from morn until midnight, and his daily doings were no less potent an influence in shaping the character of the student than his formal instruction and precept. For the Jew of the Middle Ages divine service was not limited to the four walls of the synagogue or the brief hours of public worship.

His whole life in its most material manifestations and in its most trivial activities was a divine service. His workshop, his staff, his table, his household utensils, all were instruments in the fulfilment of his destiny. How such a life was to be lived was a question of fundamental importance, and to fathom its true spirit it was necessary to observe minutely the conduct of the great. The well-nigh superhuman industry with which the master devoted himself to his studies could not fail to exercise an influence upon the pupils. The intellectual enthusiasm of the rabbis communicated itself to all who associated with them. The Bahur completely forgot himself, he pursued learning without thought of a practical purpose, his studies absorbed his being wholly and entirely. The only return he desired from his toil was the happiness which is experienced by the investigator who devotes himself with single-minded interest to the study of a scientific subject.

On the other hand, the rabbi of the Middle Ages was not a monk averse to life with its pleasures and responsibilities. The Talmud, whose study was his life-task, is not a work of abstract speculation; rather is it concerned with the concrete fashioning of practical conduct. The Rosh Yeshibah was not only a scholar, but also a judge who looked upon the administration of justice as the fulfilment of a religious duty. The impartiality of the master, his pitiless severity when the ends of justice were to be realized, taught a lesson which the student could not have derived from the dead letter of the book. A pupil of Rabbi Isserlein

tells us that this rabbi had the sexton make the following announcement before the *Kol Nidre* service, at the
beginning of the Day of Atonement: "R. Isserlein
begs the whole congregation for forgiveness and re-
quests all who think he has done them a wrong to be
good enough to wait until after the Day of Atonement,
when he will satisfy their claims."[27] The narrator goes
on to say that none was ever known to make a complaint against the rabbi in response to this announcement. Can the most erudite lecture on ethics by a
modern professor of philosophy produce so deep an
impression as the simple words of the beadle must
have had?

One of the greatest teachers of the thirteenth
century was R. Meir of Rothenburg, yet his success is
perhaps to be ascribed not so much to his learning and
ability as a teacher as to the attraction which his
character and his conduct exercised upon his pupils.
This was the same R. Meir who for seven years
languished in prison, in which he had been confined by
Emperor Rudolf in the expectation of extorting a
ransom from the Jewish community. Although the
high sum demanded was raised with alacrity for the
redemption of the beloved master, R. Meir refused to
accept the sacrifice, lest it open the road to new
exactions by the powers that be[28]. A character built on
such lines of magnanimity and self-abnegation could
not fail to leave its impress upon the soul of the
youths under his guidance.

We have now reached a point which, though it is
usually ignored, is of fundamental importance in the

history of the Jews of antiquity and mediaeval times. It is the specifically Jewish view expressed in the old saying: "Wisdom cannot become the portion of the evil-hearted."[29] Character and learning according to this view are mutually dependent upon each other. Only he can be an original thinker of creative force whose character rises above the level of the commonplace for, to use the words of a philosopher of modern times, "Great thoughts spring not from the head but from the heart." This view grew to be so essential an element in the make-up of the Jew that for him saint and scholar became almost identical concepts. To mention but one example of modern times, the Gaon, R. Elijah Wilna, perhaps the acutest Jewish critic known to history, is celebrated at once as the *Gaon*, the great scholar, and as the *Hasid*, the great saint[30].

To be creative, mentality must rest upon a complete *Weltanschauung*, upon a view of life that grants the worker a wide outlook upon all human concerns, that calls into requisition all its possessor knows and can do. Information may be useful, but knowledge is power, knowledge which permeates the whole man and which, transmuted into thinking and feeling, has become a live and active force. To impose limitations upon oneself does not necessarily lead to narrowness; on the contrary, the more the domain of knowledge to be cultivated is circumscribed, the more intense becomes the power of him who controls it. Here in part lies the explanation of the remarkable influence which our teachers of mediaeval days exerted. Their knowledge was confined within the boundaries of the Talmud and

the literature growing out of it; but over that field
they ruled absolute. Their knowledge was an integral
part of their ego. They mastered it and it mastered
them, and therefore they were able to exercise mastery
over others. If they were one-sided, it was with a
superb one-sidedness. Knowledge and learning in
them were moral forces because they were not extraneous possessions but constituted their real life.
Their knowledge being a quick force by reason of its
intensity, it was invested with creative, vitalizing
power by virtue of which their views spread abroad
until they became the common property of the people
as a whole. Jewish learning it was that offered full
compensation to a scorned, oppressed and baited
people for all it suffered in the course of tens of centuries; it was Jewish learning that preserved the
clearness and energy of intellects which all else con-
spired to brutalize and deaden. Those who insist that
the Talmud promotes scepticism and therefore have
only words of scorn for it, understand history as little
as they understand the Talmud.

The modern view that the success achieved by a
rabbi is sometimes in inverse ratio to his knowledge, is
correct if success is measured by the amount of salary.
Our whole history, however, is a protest against this
theory; it proves at every point that the rabbi attained
genuine success whenever the congregation recognized
the consummate master in him.

The Bahur who went forth from the Yeshibah to
take charge of a congregation sought to realize the
ideals he had learned to revere in his teacher, the

ideals which possessed the soul of the mediaeval rabbi
and were expressed not in well-sounding periods and
well-turned phrases but in acts and deeds.   Those
ideals may be summed up as an identification of true
knowledge with true faith, a faith not merely metaphysical and abstract but of concrete and effectual
content. The Jew of the Middle Ages was convinced
that his actions were to be estimated only according
to their moral and religious worth, for he was animated
by the belief that God does not view with indifference
the doings of man be they good or evil. If the Jew of
average standing and intelligence held this belief, it
was the distinction of the scholar to verify and apply
it in the walks of everyday life. He recognized but one
judge, his own conscience, and therefore he valued his
independence beyond all things. This feeling went so
far that when changed conditions forced the rabbi to
accept remuneration, his principle remained *noblesse
oblige* and he accepted only the small salary that
exactly sufficed for his needs.[31]

It is an interesting fact which has not received
adequate attention that during the Middle Ages the
smaller towns were the seats of rabbinical learning.
The large city held no attraction for the frugal, modest
scholar. What he demanded of his congregation was
the possibility of gathering numerous pupils about
him, and if that end could be compassed in a small
town, so much the better. Congregations regarded it
as an honor to have a famous scholar fill the post as
their rabbi. They competed with each other for the
distinction, holding out to the rabbi as an inducement

not an abundant salary but the promise to maintain a wide circle of Bahurim. No perquisites were attached to the rabbinical office. Instruction was given free, without any expectation of reward, and ungrudgingly. For, as Ben Sira expresses it and as the Rabbis remark: "Man should in this respect imitate the Holy One, blessed be He. As with God it is a gift of free grace, so should man make it a free gift[32]." As late as the fifteenth century the rabbis refused the fees for divorces which an old ordinance set at a rather high figure in order to stamp divorce as a luxury reserved for the rich. Such fees the rabbis were in the habit of passing over to the sextons and the clerks.[33] The rabbi paid no visits to the rich or prominent members of his congregation; on the contrary, it was regarded as a rare honor by the worthiest Ba'ale Batim to be invited by the rabbi to come to his house. He thus preserved his independence not only of the congregation as a body but to a still greater degree of the individual members composing the congregation. A man so placed could easily forego oratorical tricks. When he delivered an exhortation, he could enjoy the pleasant consciousness that he was bidding others do what he himself had already illustrated in deeds. In point of fact, the preaching of sermons was not the affair of the rabbi. He mounted the pulpit only twice a year, on the Sabbath before Passover and on the Sabbath before the Day of Atonement.[34] On the other hand, his life was itself a protest against all that is base and wicked. He was not in the habit of indulging in brilliant repartee with the ladies of his congregation—for such trifling his time was too precious—and yet to have a son or at least a son-in-law who was a rabbi was the most ardent wish cherished by every Jewish mother.

Nor was the rabbi the teacher of religion to boys and girls; nevertheless his spirit pervaded every household. First and foremost his influence affected the educated and learned members and through them the whole body of the congregation. In the olden time the opinion prevailed that the fathers were to be educated first and then the children, not in the reverse order. Those were the days when the Jew was proud to be a Lamdan, to be one of those who could venture to enter into a discussion with scholars on Jewish learning and literature. The rabbis of those days did not pose as philosophers, political economists, historians and the like, but they never lost sight of the fact that being rabbis they were the ones to pronounce the final, professional and authoritative dictum *in re Judaica*, and therefore due weight attached to their decisions.

The whole life of the rabbi proclaimed the message which a famous Kabbalist summed up in the following sentence: "More difficult is it for the wicked to acquire Gehinnom than for the righteous to acquire Paradise; for Gehinnom is acquired by means of toil and trouble, by strife and passion; but Paradise is acquired by means of patience and gentleness, by charity and rectitude."[35]

IV

THE RELIGION OF THE PHARISEE

A famous doctor of the Synagogue, living in the third century, remarked, "Israel went into exile only after it became divided into twenty-four sects."[1] The pragmatism of this Rabbi is open to serious objection, although modern historians uphold his view that the downfall of the Jewish State was the direct consequence of the internal disunion. That a united Israel would have withstood the power of Rome a little longer than a state torn by dissensions and factions is very likely, but the doom of Jewish Independence was sealed at the moment when Rome entered upon its policy of aggression in the East. However, there can be no doubt that about the time of the downfall of the Jewish State, that is the time of the rise of Christianity, Israel was divided into many sects.

You are, of course, all acquainted with the three main sects of the Pharisees, the Sadducees, and the Essenes, concerning whom we have a good deal of contemporary information, though unfortunately not as adequate as some may believe it. But what do we know about the numerous currents and sub-currents in the wide stream of religious life of the Jews of that period? Take, for instance, the Pharisees; only quite recently scholars have learned to differentiate between the apocalyptic and legalistic wings of Pharisaism, and let me add that even the so-called legalistic Pharisaism was not uniform. In the histories of the Jews we are told that about a generation before the time of Jesus, there lived the two great doctors of the Synagogue, Hillel and Shammai, the founders of the schools later known as the houses of Hillel and Shammai. This statement is, however, far from being quite accurate. A critical study of the old rabbinic sources reveals the very interesting fact that Pharisaism at its very appearance in history, about 170 B. C. E., represented two distinct currents, the conservative and the progressive.[2] Thus Hillel and Shammai far from being the founders of schools, were rather the last representatives of the two wings of Pharisaism. Now I have no intention of discussing the doctrinal differences between the numerous schools, still less those between the different sects. These introductory remarks will give you, however, some notion of the difficulty that lies before us. Our subject is the religion of the Jews in the time of Jesus. But of what Jews? Of the Pharisees, the Sadducees, or the Essenes? And if of the Pharisees, of what branch of the Pharisees, the apocalyptic or the legalistic? And if the latter, of what shade, the progressive or the conservative? And again, what are the sources which we may draw upon for an unbiased and fair presentation of the religion of the Jews at the time of Jesus? Roughly speaking, there are three distinct groups of literary sources to be considered: (1) The literature of the Alexandrian Jews, of which the works of Philo are the most important, (2) the Palestinian Pseudepigrapha, and (3) the vast resources of the so-called rabbinic literature. Now, permit me to describe briefly the point of view from which I shall attempt to approach the subject.

All creative activities of nature consist in producing new forms of existence—new beings and new functions —by means of new combinations of the given elements and the elemental individual. Christianity saw the light in Palestine and the given elements from which it was created must be looked for in the religious thoughts of Palestinian Jewry and not in the Alexandrian Hellenism of the Diaspora Jew. Even granted that Hellenism was not without influence upon Palestinian Judaism—and this influence is to my mind of a very problematic nature—we must not forget that the Jew always had a genius for assimilating foreign matter by impressing upon it his own individuality. Hence it is Judaized Hellenism that might have had its share in the mental make-up of the Palestinian Jew, and not Hellenism pure and simple. The Hellenism of the Diaspora Jew may have been of great importance for the development of Christianity in the second century, but it can be disregarded in the study of the rise of Christianity.

The attractiveness of the new is responsible for the exaggerated claims put up by some scholars for the apocalyptic Pseudepigrapha as the main source for the religious life of the Jew. The most important works of this branch of literature came to light in comparatively recent times, and scholars are human enough to be dazzled by a sudden light. There is, however, no fear in my mind that we shall have to wait too long for a sober judgment concerning the real value of the apocalyptic literature, and this judgment will be that apocalyptic Judaism or apocalyptic Pharisaism was neither the Judaism of the time of Jesus nor the religious atmosphere which the latter and his disciples breathed.

Of apocalyptic Pseudepigrapha it may well be said that the new therein is not Jewish and the Jewish is not new. Only those who misunderstood Pharisaism pure and simple could see in the universalistic and Messianic ideas of apocalyptic Judaism something new and hostile to the former. The true understanding of the religion of the Jews at the time of the rise of Christianity can, therefore, be gained from the Pharisaic sources which express the religious consciousness of the bulk of the nation or Catholic Israel. Taken at bottom the nation was for the most part Pharisaically minded; in other words, the Pharisees were only the more important and religiously inclined men of the Jewish people, who gave the most decided expression to the prevailing belief and strove to establish and enforce it by a definite system of teaching and interpretation of the sacred books.

Our attempt must be, however, to derive the religious thought of the Jew from the spirit of his literature as a whole rather than from formal doctrine alone. Of our subject it is eminently true that the details of a written tradition are intelligible only through the whole. Every member of a living organism depends for its health and function upon the whole more than the whole depends upon its separate organs.

So the true bearing of single features of Pharisaic literature can be learned only from their relation to the whole.

Pharisaism or, to use the more comprehensive term Rabbinism, is inseparable from biblical Judaism, yet not entirely identical with it. Without drawing a sharp distinction between religion and theology, it would be well to remember that the Rabbis were no more theologians than the prophets were philosophers. As the latter did not reason out but experienced the truths to which they gave utterance, so the theology of the former is based not upon cold speculation but upon warm feeling. The most characteristic feature of the rabbinical system of theology is its lack of system. With God as a reality, revelation as a fact, the Torah as a rule of life, and the hope of redemption as a most vivid expectation, one was free to draw his own conclusions from these axioms and postulates in regard to what he believed.

A story is told about Hillel, the great doctor of the Synagogue who flourished about a generation before Jesus, that a heathen approached him with the request to give him the contents of the Torah—the main tenets of Judaism—while standing on one foot. Hillel replied, "What is hateful to thee, do not unto thy fellowman. This is the entire Torah. Go and study the rest, which is merely commentary."[3] Paul, the pupil of Hillel's grandson, Gamaliel, repeated almost literally this idea when he said, "For all the law is fulfilled in one word, even in this,—thou shalt love thy neighbor as thyself."[4]

With all due reverence for such great men as Hillel

and Paul, I am rather distrustful of all attempts at constructing an acrobatic religion. One cannot go on forever standing on one foot. I prefer, therefore, to quote to you the following legend occurring in rabbinic literature in many versions, which will give you a more complete and vivid picture of the religion of the Pharisaic Jew than any learned definition. The legend reads: "When God resolved upon the creation of the world, He took counsel with the Torah—that is Divine Wisdom. She was skeptical about the value of an earthly world on account of the sinfulness of man who would be sure to disregard her precepts. But God dispelled her doubts. He told her that Repentance had been created long before and sinners would have the opportunity to mend their ways. Besides good work would be invested with atoning power and Paradise and Hell were created to dispense reward and punishment. Finally, the Messiah was appointed to bring salvation, which would put an end to all sinfulness."[5]

Divested of its fantastic garb, this legend contains a fair summary of the tenets of the religion of the Pharisaic Jew. God is the creator of the world and in His goodness and wisdom He created man. It is the duty of man to obey Him. He has made known His will by the revelation of the Torah; God rewards those who fulfil His commands and punishes those who disobey. But even the vilest sinner can repent, and if he does he will be forgiven. Wickedness will, however, disappear from among men when the Messiah will arrive and the Kingdom of God will be established on earth.

It would take a dozen lectures to discuss in detail these religious ideas in which Jewish legend saw the essence of Judaism. I will limit myself to a discussion of their bearing on a favorite thesis of a famous theologian of our day concerning the Gospel. Prof. Adolph Harnack grouped the teachings of Jesus under three heads; they are, first, the Kingdom of God and its coming; second, God, the Father, and the infinite value of the human soul; third, the higher righteousness and the commandment of love.[6] I have no intention of discussing the thesis of Prof. Harnack, but whether we accept it or not there can be no doubt that these teachings regarded by him as the message of Jesus do represent fundamental religious ideas. It may, therefore, be profitable in a sketch of the religion of the Jews in the time of Jesus to ascertain what the Kingdom of God, the Fatherhood of God, and the Commandment of Love meant to the Jew of that time.

Any student of the New Testament knows that the expression "Kingdom of God" belongs to the religious language of the Jew; in Matthew's "Kingdom of Heaven" we still have the exact rendering of the Hebrew *Malkut Shamayim*. A feeling of reverence led the Jews at a very early date to avoid as far as possible all mention of the name of God, and Heaven is one of the usual substitutes for it. Hence expressions like "Kingdom of Heaven," "Sake of Heaven," "Fear of Heaven" and many like them are very frequently met with in rabbinic literature. As the term "Kingdom of Heaven" is less expressive of an accomplished fact than of an undefined and undefinable idea, the only

safe way to ascertain its actual meaning is to let the
Rabbis speak in their own language. In what section
of the Torah do we find the receiving of the Kingdom
of Heaven to the exclusion of the worship of idols? ask
the Rabbis. The answer is, In the Shema', the section
containing the words: "Hear—Shema'—O Israel, the
Lord is our God, He is One. And thou shalt love
the Lord thy God with all thy heart, and with all thy
soul and with all thy might."[7] The implicit acceptance
of God's unity as well as the unconditional surrender
of mind and heart to His holy will, which the love of
God expressed in the Shema' implies, this is the
meaning of 'receiving of the Kingdom of God.'

Commenting upon Ps. 81.10, "There shall be no
strange God in thee," the Rabbis remark, "By this is
meant the strange God in the very heart of man, his
evil inclination."[8] The acceptance of the Kingdom of
Heaven meant, therefore, the rejection of selfishness,
which is polytheism in disguise, namely the worship
of God combined with devotion to one's desires and
passions. When Rabbi Akiba, who died the death
of a martyr, was in the hands of his torturers, he
"joyfully received upon himself the yoke of the Kingdom of Heaven," that is, he recited the Shema'.
When asked why he did so, he answered, "All my life
I have recited the words: 'And thou shalt love the
Lord thy God with all thy heart, and with all thy soul,
and with all thy might,' and have longed for the hour
when I could fulfil it. I loved Him with all my heart,
I loved Him with all my fortunes, now I have the
opportunity to love Him with all my soul, giving my

life for His sake. Therefore, I repeat these words in
joyfulness⁹." And thus he died. The idea of the
Kingdom of Heaven was accordingly for the Pharisees
neither eschatological nor political but the rule of God
in the heart of the individual.

To conclude our discussion on this point, I would
add the following remarks on the relation of the
Messianic idea to that of the Kingdom of Heaven. As
in the case of all ideas, the occasion for the rise of the
Messianic idea is to be looked for in the particular
circumstances of the historical factors which deter-
mine the genuine originality of a historical idea. The
material starting point for the Messianic idea is, of
course, to be sought in the particular circumstances
of the national and political life of the Jewish nation.
Israel, in suffering and agony, clung to the hope of
seeing a scion of the glorious house of David as its
anointed king—Messiah—restore its old glories. But
soon the view changes. The Messiah does not merely
mean king; he becomes the symbolic figure of human
suffering from whom alone genuine hope can issue and
who alone can bear within himself the genuine war-
ranty for the restoration and regeneration of the
human race.

Napoleon on one occasion remarked, "From the
sublime to the ridiculous is only a step." The truth
of this saying is best illustrated by the fate that befell
the Messianic idea. This noble product of the religious
genius of the Jew often appears ridiculous in the form
given to it by the phantasmagoria of the apocalyptic

Pseudepigrapha and the fancies of popular imagination. It is, however, time to distinguish more clearly between folklore and theology, and I shall therefore quote to you the following prayer, very likely composed about the beginning of the second century and still recited in the Synagogue, which to my mind represents the Messianic hopes of the Pharisees at the time of the rise of Christianity. The prayer known as the "Kingdom Prayer" reads, "Our God, and the God of our fathers, reign Thou in Thy glory over the whole universe, and be exalted above the earth in Thine honor, and shine forth in the splendor and excellence of Thy might upon all the inhabitants of the world, so that whatsoever has been made may know that Thou hast made it and whatsoever has been created may understand that Thine hand created it, and whatsoever has breath in its nostrils may say, the Lord God of Israel is King and His dominion ruleth over all. O, purify our hearts to serve Thee in truth, for Thou art God in truth."

Here we find expressed not only the universal aspect of the Kingdom of God but also the conception of religion freed from the idea which represents it as serving only the interest of a world beyond and not, primarily and above all things, of the world we live in. Not that the thought of the world beyond was in any way to be curtailed; on the contrary, the Rabbis often speak of the reward awaiting the righteous after their death as consisting not in material pleasure but in enjoying divine glory. Nevertheless, the development of the religious thought of the Jew shows a marked tendency to fix the center of gravity of religion not in the thought of a world beyond but rather to fasten and establish it in the actual life of man on earth. In this respect the Scribes and the Rabbis were the true successors of the Prophets. For the latter morality was the most essential feature of religion, and there is an ethically weak point in even the purest and loftiest ideas concerning the bliss of future life. All these ideas take into account only the individual but in morality society occupies the chief consideration; ethics is, if not entirely, at all events preeminently social. Accordingly the highest ideal of the Pharisees was the Kingdom of God in this world and not in the other world. The position of Rabbinism with regard to mundane morality and supermundane bliss is best expressed in the following saying of a famous Rabbi. After remarking that this world is the vestibule where man prepares for the hall, the world to come, he adds, "Better is one hour of returning to God and good works in this world than all the life of the world to come; yet better is one hour of bliss in the world to come than all the life of this world."[10] No happiness of this life can be compared to heavenly bliss, but the highest that man can achieve is living a religious life in this world.

The realization of morality presupposes, as we have remarked, the existence of society, and this meant for antiquity national society. Even Plato, in his outline of an ideal state, has the Greeks arrayed against the Barbarians, the non-Greeks, in constant warfare. The Messianic ideal, as preached by the Prophets and taught by the Rabbis, is against particularism but not against nationality. It is quite erroneous to assert that the Prophets hated the state as such and desired its destruction because they regarded its very existence as essentially inconsistent with that spiritual life which was their aim. What the Prophets combated was the materialistic view of the national life as they combated the materialistic view of the life of the individual; they were strongly nationalistic but their nationalism was of a spiritual kind. The Messianic hopes of the Pharisees were, as we have seen, universalistic, yet at the same time national. The two ideas of the Kingdom of Heaven over which God reigns and the Kingdom of Israel in which the Messiah, the son of David, holds the sceptre became thus almost identical. This identification gave substance and reality to the idea of the Kingdom of God without diminishing its spiritual value. The combination of the national idea in its spiritualized form with the universal is well expressed in another Kingdom prayer composed at the same time as that mentioned before. It reads:

"Now, therefore, O God, impose Thine awe upon all Thy works that they may fear Thee and that they may all form a single band to do Thy will with a perfect heart. Give then glory, O Lord, unto Thy people, joy to Thy land, gladness to Thy city, a flourishing horn unto David, Thy servant, and a clear shining light unto the Son of Jesse, Thy Messiah. Then shall the just be glad and all wickedness shall be wholly consumed like smoke when Thou makest the dominion of arrogance to pass away from the earth. And Thou, O Lord, shalt reign, Thou alone, over all Thy works on

Mount Zion, the dwelling place of Thy glory, and in Jerusalem, Thy holy city."

We come now to the second head in Prof. Harnack's analysis of the teaching of Jesus,—the Fatherhood of God and the infinite value of the human soul. The term "Father in Heaven" is certainly one of the greatest watchwords of spiritual religion and it is now generally admitted that it was not new at the time of Jesus but a part of the common stock of religious ideas and a natural element in the Jewish religion at that time. I shall not discuss the meaning which Jesus put into this common term of his people, but will limit myself to quoting a few sayings of the Rabbis in which it occurs, that we may be able to ascertain the meaning they gave to it. Rabbi Eliezer ben Hyrkanos, a younger contemporary of the apostles, dwelling on the moral degeneration of his age, exclaimed, "In whom, then, shall we find help if not in our Father in Heaven!"[11] His pupil and later colleague, the famous Rabbi Akiba, remarked: "Blessed are ye, O Israelites! Before whom do you purify yourselves from your sins and who is it that purifies you? Your Father in Heaven."[12] These and many similar sayings show how baseless the view is that the Pharisee thought of God only, or even mainly, as distant and inaccessible or as a taskmaster whose service was hard. The very opening of many Pharisaic prayers, "Our Father" or "Our merciful Father", exhibit the steady faith of those who knew that they were safe in God and certain of being heard by Him.

The words of Rabbi Akiba just quoted contain not

only the declaration of his belief in direct access to God Himself through prayer and repentance, but also the repudiation of any mediator. Every man, says the Talmud, has a patron—a friend, at court. If trouble comes upon him, he does not go directly to the patron but stands at the door and addresses a servant or a member of the household, who tells the patron, "So and so is standing at the door of thy yard." The patron has him admitted or he pays no attention to him. But the Holy One, Blessed be He, is not so. If trouble comes to a man—note that the text speaks of a man generally and not of a Jew in particular—God says, "Let him pray not to Michael and not to Gabriel but to Me and I will answer him at once," as is written, "Everyone that calleth on the name of the Lord shall be delivered."[13]

The methodological error in overestimating the value of the apocalyptic literature as a source for the main current of the religious life of the Jew at the time of the rise of Christianity is fraught with serious consequences for the proper understanding of the problem. In a history of the Jewish religion based upon the study of rabbinic sources, angelology and demonology would hardly play any important part at all,—certainly, not that part which is ascribed to them by those who see in apocalyptic Judaism the religion of Israel in the time of Jesus. The Pharisaic Jew, as we have seen, did not pray to the angels to intercede in his behalf with God that he might be saved from the evil caused by demons, but sought help from God "like a child from his father"—to use the words of a

leading Pharisee of about 80 B. C. E.[14]—that he might
be sustained in his struggle against the evil in himself.
In approaching God, the Pharisaic Jew knew that the
divine rule goes as far as life itself—even to its smallest
manifestation in the order of nature or, in the words of
the Rabbis, "One does not hurt his small finger without it being decreed by Heaven[15]" or, to use a more
familiar phrase, "A bird perishes not without the will
of Heaven."[16]

The man who can come to the Ruler of Heaven and
Earth like a child to his father is thereby raised above
nature and has a value higher than heaven and earth.
The Rabbis often speak of the righteous who by their
noble deeds associate themselves with God in the work
of creation[17]. The thought underlying the figurative
language of the Rabbis is that the universe with its
endless array of life forms and its unchanging laws
reaches perfection only in the presence of the soul of
man who, endowed with free will, rises above nature
by his God-fearing actions and thus becomes an
associate of God in the work of creation.

Man as the quasi-associate of God is mostly spoken
of by the Rabbis in reference to his moral deeds. For
instance, they say, "He who suffers himself to be
insulted without taking offence, thereby associates
himself with God in the work of creation.[18]" This
leads us to the Pharisaic conception of morality and
its relation to the third head under which the whole of
the Gospel is embraced according to Harnack: "The
higher righteousness and the commandment of love."

The following remarks of the Rabbis will indicate to you their view on morality and ethics.

I had occasion above to refer to the saying of Hillel that the commandment of love is the essence of the Torah. More characteristic of the Pharisaic conception of morality is the theory of the Rabbis that the Tetragrammaton, the name expressive of God's being, "I am," stands for love and mercy.[19] In modern phraseology the thought expressed by the Rabbis is: the moral law based on love does not exist by virtue of a divine act or an authoritative fiat; it flows from the essence of God's being, from His absolute and infinite moral nature. The divine Being, knowable to men only in His attribute of love, combined with the endeavor to emulate Him in man's finite way, constitutes at once the rule and the reason of morality. In the words of the Rabbis, "Because I am merciful, thou shalt be merciful,"[20] the reason underlying morality can and should be the same for man as for God. If God can have no reason for morality but the nature of the moral idea, the same holds true of man. The principle of morality is accordingly autonomous, but its archetype is God's. And now let me add one sentence as to the universal character of ethics as taught by the Rabbis. A great leader among them remarked as follows: "The most comprehensive principle of the Torah is expressed in the words: In the day that God created man, in the likeness of God made He him!"[21] In these words of Scripture the Rabbis found expressed not only the unity of mankind as an ethical idea but also the reason thereof—the likeness of man to God.

No description of the religion of the Jews in the time of Jesus can be adequate which would leave out of account one of its main features, namely that it is a Torah religion. It will be noticed that I have used throughout the term "Torah" and not "Law." It must first be stated that the term "Law" or its Greek equivalent "Nomos" is a very misleading rendering of the word "Torah." "To the Jew," Professor Schechter aptly remarked, "'Torah' means a teaching or instruction of any kind. It may be either a general principle or a specific injunction, whether it be found in the Pentateuch or any other parts of the Scripture or even outside of the Canon."[22] "Torah" to the Jew is the sum total of the contents of revelation without special reference to any particular element in it. Eternal truths about God's love and justice, laws and commandments leading the individual as well as society to a noble life, symbolic observances, worship and discipline, diverse as they otherwise might be, are of equally binding power, having all been revealed by the same God. The Jew must embody in his practical life the teachings of Moses and the Prophets concerning God and man. It is not enough to know; the Jew is required to do and to be.[23]

The most distinctive feature of a Torah religion is obedience to the will of God. In the Torah as in nature—the two revelations, for God is the ultimate cause in both—no part may be denied, even though the reason of things and their connection may not be comprehended; as in nature so in the Torah the traces of divine Wisdom must ever be sought for. His ordinances must be accepted in their entirety as undeniable phenomena. They are laws for us, even if we do not comprehend their reason and purpose. They are like the phenomena of nature which we recognize as facts, though their cause and relation to each other are not always understood by us. And as we endeavor to interpret the working of nature by observing carefully its phenomena and their relations to one another, so we shall be able to comprehend the spirit of the Torah by a diligent study of its individual laws and doctrines, teachings and commandments.

Therein lies the great contribution of Pharisaism to the development of Judaism. The Sadducee taught the immobility of the Torah, the Pharisee maintained its immutability, which is not stereotyped oneness but the impossibility of deviating from its own course. To understand the latter, the knowledge of the entire Torah—Law as well as prophecy, commandments as well as doctrines—was an absolute necessity. It was this conception of the Torah that saved it from becoming a sacred relic, a revered mummy without spirit and life.

As true virtuosi of religion, the Rabbis knew that in religion the non-rational elements must not be entirely eliminated if it should not degenerate into a shallow rationalism. But they also knew that religion if not saturated with rational elements must necessarily sink to the level of an anti-cultural mysticism, hostile alike to true religion and to progress. The Torah with its numerous commandments and laws of practice and love, of righteousness and holiness, but also with an

elaborate system of ritual and service offered them
a harmonious blending of the rational with the non-
rational elements of religion. Their guide in life was:
It is good that thou shouldst take hold of the one, yea,
also from the other withdraw not thy hand. Obey the
will of God as expressed in His revealed Torah, try to
penetrate into the spirit of the word of God, but
whether you are able to discern the reason of a divine
commandment or not, your first duty is to fulfil it, and
its fulfilment will be unto you a source of inspiration
and joy.

Conformity to the will of God and communion with
God are the two outstanding features of a spiritual
religion. The Pentateuch and the Psalms, the *Halakah*
and the *Haggadah* are not contrasts but necessary
complements to one another. Of course no one will
deny that a Torah religion, that is one that lays great
stress upon conformity to the will of God, might
become for some a set of rules and forms without
inwardness or spirituality. But no less undeniable is
the fact that a religion which overemphasized communion with God might degenerate into antinomianism. The one as well as the other has frequently
happened and is happening daily. To characterize,
however, rabbinic Judaism as legalism is as justified
as to identify Christianity with antinomianism. The
Rabbis, who after all ought not to be entirely ignored
in judging or rather in sentencing Judaism, are at least
as severe in their censure of legalism as the Church
Fathers in their denunciation of antinomianism.

The precepts of the Lord are according to the words

of the Psalmist not only right, but also "rejoicing the heart." It may therefore not be out of place to correct another prevailing error with regard to rabbinic Judaism. We hear quite often of the yoke of the law under which the Pharisees groaned, but little is said of the joy they experienced in the fulfilment of the divine commandments; שמחה של מצוה is the expression used by the Rabbis. In a passage of the daily prayer of the Jew, which was composed very likely in pre-Christian times, we read as follows: "With everlasting love Thou hast loved the House of Israel, Thy people; Torah, commandments, statutes and judgments Thou hast taught us. Yea, we will rejoice in the words of Thy Torah and Thy commandments forever. And mayest Thou never take away Thy love from us. Blessed art Thou, O Lord, who lovest Thy people, Israel."[24] Can there still be any doubt that those who lived and died for the Torah considered it as a blessing, the affluence of God's mercy and love?

With respect to the work of art which we term religion, says a modern philosopher,[25] idealization is as necessary as elsewhere, and is the primary condition of a right understanding for all its adherents, but no less so for the foreign student. In my attempt to sketch the religion of the Jews at the time of Jesus, I was guided by this thought, that without idealization even the historical ascertainment of facts would be impossible, at least insofar as such an attempt aims at presenting a unitary and spiritual view of its matter. Of course I have not lost sight of the absolute necessity of an exact study of the available sources. For without this latter it would not be possible for the process of idealization itself to come into operation; a mere phantom would ensue. But I am thoroughly convinced that statistics may become as dangerous to theology as theology is to statistics. We shall never do justice to the religion of a group by following the method of statistics and attempting to ascertain the average, because there is no such thing as the average in religion. As each man's emotions, needs and longings must differ, so must each man's religion differ. Each man lives his religion in his own way. To gain insight into the life of a foreign religion, we must never forget that where there is no sympathy there is no understanding. Where there is sympathy, however, it is sure to find its reward.

V

JEWISH THOUGHT AS REFLECTED IN
THE HALAKAH

It was not without hesitation that I accepted the kind
invitation extended to me to deliver the Zunz Lecture
of this year. Greatly as I appreciated the honor conferred upon me, I did not find it an easy task to free
myself from a deep-rooted conviction that, to speak in
the words of the great Frenchman, Pascal, most of the
mischief of this world would never happen if men were
contented to sit still in their parlors and refrain from
talking. As a compromise with this strong conviction,
I have chosen as my subject, "Jewish Thought as Reflected in the Halakah." On a subject of this sort one
would talk only when one has something to say, or at
least thinks so,—otherwise one would be prompted to
keep silence.

To be candid, keeping silence strongly commends
itself to one who has spent the greater part of his life
in the study of the Halakah and, believing himself to
have a good deal to say about it, is at a loss how to do
so within the limited space of a single paper. It would
be impossible within the compass of anything less than
a substantial volume to present an analysis of the ideas
comprised or implied in the term Halakah, or even to
set forth the various senses in which the term has been
employed. It has often been observed that the more

109

claim an idea has to be considered living, the more various will be its aspects; and the more social and political is its nature, the more complicated and subtle will be its issues and the longer and more eventful its course. The attempt to express the "leading idea" of the Halakah I must perforce leave to those whose forte is omniscience and whose foible is knowledge. What I propose to do is something less ambitious than to sketch the nature and scope of the Halakah. It is more closely connected with the problem of the nature of Jewish history.

The Talmud remarks: "He who studies the Halakah daily may rest assured that he shall be a son of the world to come."[1] The study of the Halakah may not commend itself to everyone as a means of salvation. Some may desire an easier road thereto; but we may well say that he who studies the Halakah may be assured that he is a son of the world—the Jewish world —that has been. Not that the Halakah is a matter of the past; but the understanding of the Jewish past, of Jewish life and thought, is impossible without a knowledge of the Halakah. One might as well hope to comprehend the history of Rome without taking notice of its wars and conquests or that of Hellas without giving attention to its philosophy and art. To state such a truism would be superfluous were it not for the fact that the most fundamental laws of nature are often disregarded in dealing with the Jews, and their history has undergone strange treatment at the hands of friend and foe alike.

If we further remember that Jewish historiography

in modern times dates from the days when the Hegelian conception of history reigned supreme, the "peculiar" treatment of the history of the "peculiar people" is not in the least surprising. Historians who believed with Hegel that "history is the science of man in his political character," and consequently were of the opinion that there could be no history of a people without a state, could not but ignore the Halakah, a way of life that was rarely sustained by the power of the state but was frequently antagonized by it. What was the result of this conception of history applied to the Jews? The three main subjects dealt with in works on Jewish history in post-biblical times are: religion, literature, martyrology, to which a little philosophy with a sprinkling of cultural history is added; but of actual history in the modern sense of the word we find very little indeed. History as now generally understood is the science establishing the causal nexus in the development of man as a social being. The Jew may well say: *homo sum, nihil humani a me alienum puto*. State or no state, even the Jew of the diaspora lived for almost two thousand years a life of his own and has developed accordingly a character of his own.

Modern students of man teach us that three elements contribute to the formation of his character— heritage, environment, and training. What is true of individual character holds good also of national character. We hear a good deal of the importance of heritage or race, to use the favored phrase of the day, in appraising the character of the Jew and in the interpretation of his history. Dealers in generalities especially are prone to call in the racial features and characteristics to save the trouble of a more careful analysis which would show that these racial qualities themselves are largely due to historical causes, though causes often too far back in the past to admit of full investigation. The explanation of history from the narrow point of view of race is tantamount to affirming, as Hegel did, that the whole wealth of historic development is potential in the beginnings of mind, a view which it would be impossible to justify historically. The lessons of history indicate rather that at certain times men of genius initiate new movements which though related to the past are not explained by it, and that there are various possibilities contained in a given historic situation. Which of the possibilities is to become real would depend solely upon the training of the people confronted with the historic situation. Nothing is easier and nothing more dangerous than definitions. I shall not define what Halakah is; yet one is safe in asserting that its chief feature is education of oneself or training. Accordingly, the Halakah is a true mirror reflecting the work of the Jew in shaping his character.

No man who is badly informed can avoid reasoning badly. We can hardly expect to understand the causal nexus of our history if we disregard the most valuable source of information we seek. Here is a plain example in arithmetic to prove it. The literary output of the eighteen centuries from the beginning of the common era to the year 1795, the date of the emancipation of the Jews in France and Holland when the modern history of the Jew begins, contains seventy-eight per cent of halakic material.   We may easily convince ourselves of the exactness of this statement by looking at the classification of the Hebrew books in the British Museum, the largest collection of its kind in the world, prepared by such an eminent and careful bibliographer as Zedner. Yet it is not the quantity of the halakic Literature that makes it so valuable a source of Jewish history; by far more important is its quality.

Historians divide historical sources into two main groups: (a) historical remains and (b) tradition. By the first group we understand all that remains of an historical event. For instance, we find in certain parts of Germany ruins of Roman castles, places with Roman names, burial-grounds containing the bodies of Romans, their armor, pottery and so on. Let us suppose for a moment that the writings of Cæsar, Tacitus and other Roman historians treating of the relations between Rome and Germania had disappeared; these remains of the actual life of the Romans in Germany would suffice to establish beyond any doubt the fact that at a certain time in history the Romans lived in Germany and were its masters. The second group of historical sources, tradition, is much less reliable, since it is only a subjective reflection in the human mind of historical events and can therefore be made use of only after a critical analysis has separated the subjective element of reflection from the objective facts reflected. We often hear of the lamentable dearth of sources of Jewish history. As far as historical tradition is concerned, the correctness of this statement is

beyond dispute; but of historical remains we have in
the Halakah a veritable treasure of material. The
Halakah, as its meaning "conduct" indicates, comprises life in all its manifestations,—religion, worship,
law, economics, politics, ethics and so forth. It gives
us a picture of life in its totality and not of some
of its fragments.

You will ask how it could happen that all the historians and scholars who devoted their lives and great
abilities to the study of Jewish history ignored its most
important source, the Halakah? The answer to this
question is not a difficult one. The importance of the
Halakah as an historical source is equalled by the difficulty of its utilization. Its faults lie not in its substance
but in the form which the conditions of its growth have
given to it. It is a system extremely hard to expound
and hard to master. So vast is it and so complicated,
so much are its leading principles obscured by the way
in which they have been stated, scattered here and
there through the vast expanse of the "sea of the Talmud," in an order peculiar to the latter, which is the
perfection of disorder, that it presents itself to the
learner as a most arduous study, a study indeed which
only a few carry so far as to make themselves masters
of the whole. Hence the favorite phrase that a general
impression of the Halakah suffices without the study
of its details. Of course this is a cover for incapacity.
To understand the whole, the knowledge of the parts
is as indispensable in the study of the Halakah as in
any other branch of human thought.

I do not wish to be misunderstood. Not everything

that happens is history, and, consequently, the first
requirement of the historian is to distinguish between
essentials and non-essentials, between historical and
non-historical happenings.   The individual performs
countless acts daily which the most conscientious and
careful Boswell would pass over in silence as irrelevant.
So also in the lives of nations and peoples, many things
happen daily that are of no historical value. Not all
the minutiae of the Halakah are historical material,
but to quote the saying of an old Jewish sage: "If there
be no knowledge, how could there be discernment?"[2]
To distinguish the essential from the non-essential in
the Halakah one must master it entirely if one is not
to become a prey to his subjective likes and dislikes,
—and we all know how Jewish history is marred by
bias and prejudice.

The problem of subjectivity in the presentation of
Jewish history leads me to remark on another aspect
of the Halakah,—its authoritative character. Writers
on the phase of Judaism that comprises Jewish theology and ethics in post-biblical times, have based their
studies exclusively on the Haggadah, which means
that they erected their structures upon shifting sand.
Whatever else the Haggadah may be, it certainly is
either individual, consisting of opinions and views
uttered by Jewish sages for the most part on the spur
of the moment, or creations of popular fancy. The
haggadic sayings of the rabbis belong to the first division; the apocryphal-apocalyptic writings belong to
the second.

All work, it is true, is done by individuals. We have

nothing beyond the dicta of definite—known or unknown—persons. Yet the great men of a people give
the impulses only, and all depends upon what the mass
of the people make thereof. It is doubtless as important for the history of Judaism to know what Hillel
said, what R. Akiba thought and what R. Meir taught
as it is important for Christianity to study the writing
of Augustine, Luther and Calvin. But not all Christians are Augustines or Luthers, nor all Jews Hillels
and Akibas. The great moulders of Christian thought
did indeed succeed in making the masses of Christianity
accept their doctrines at solemn councils and representative covenants, but that was not true of the
spiritual leaders of the Jews. Even if we admit that
whatever is alive in the nation finds expression in the
works and words of individuals and that many individual contributions are products of the national spirit,
there still remains a vast array of intellectual products
that are temporary, accidental and individual, in which
the national soul has but a small share. The devil,
according to Shakespeare, quotes Scripture. But if he
is really as clever as he is reputed to be, he ought to
quote the Talmud, as there is hardly any view of life
for and against which one could not quote the Talmud.

No less uncritical is the attempt made by many
theologians to give us a system of the religious thought
of the Jew based upon the apocalyptic literature, the
fantastic fabric of popular imagination. As the author
of a large work on Jewish legends, I believe myself to
be above suspicion of lacking sympathy for the creations of popular fancy. Theology, however, is a rational

system of religious values and cannot be built up of material furnished by fancy and imagination. As often as I read books on Jewish theology, and I may say with Faust: *Ich habe leider auch Theologie studiert*, the diametrically opposing views expressed in them remind me of the following story so popular in my native country, Lithuania. A rabbi, trying a case— for the rabbi of olden times was more of a judge than a theologian—after listening to the plaintiff, exclaimed: "You are right, my son;" and then made the same remark to the defendant, after the latter had pleaded in his own behalf. The rabbi's wife, who was present at the trial, could not refrain from remarking to her husband: "How can both litigants be right?" To which the rabbi in genuine meekness, as becoming a husband and a rabbi, replied: "You, too, are right, my dear." I frequently feel like saying to the diametrically opposed theologians: What you say is so profoundly true and so utterly false! You are profoundly right in what you tell us about the beliefs and doctrines of this rabbi or that apocalyptic author, but you are utterly wrong in your attempts to stamp as an expression of the Jewish soul what is only an individual opinion or a transitory fancy.

It is only in the Halakah that we find the mind and character of the Jewish people exactly and adequately expressed. Laws which govern the daily life of man must be such as suit and express his wishes, being in harmony with his feelings and fitted to satisfy his religious ideals and ethical aspirations. A few illustrations will often explain better than long abstract statements, and I shall therefore present a few concrete examples of the Halakah applied to the study of Jewish thought.

At the risk of causing Homeric laughter I shall begin *ab ovo*, not as the poet did, with the egg of Leda, but rather with that no less famous one that, to speak with Heine, was unfortunate enough to be laid on a holiday. He who does not appreciate Heine lacks the ability to appreciate something genuinely Jewish, and I, for one, greatly enjoy his merry remarks on that unfortunate egg. But grave historians, or rather theologians, the majority of whom are not usually distinguished by a sense of humor, do not show deep historical insight in ridiculing the great schools headed by Shammai and Hillel for discussing the question whether an egg laid on a holiday is permitted for use or not.[3] We hear a great deal of Judaism being a view of life for which religion is law. I am at present not interested in showing the fallacy of this dictum nor in inquiring why we hear so little about the second part of this equation, to wit: for the Jew law is religion. But if it be true that religion is law for the Jews, the conception underlying Jewish law must necessarily be expressive of Jewish religious thought. The discussion of the old schools about the egg is tantamount to the question of the extent to which the principle of intent is to be applied. *Actus non est reus nisi mens sit rea*, say the Roman jurists, and similarly the Rabbis: Actions must be judged by their intent. Since, according to biblical law, food for the holy days must be prepared the day before, the progressive school of Hillel maintained that

an egg laid on a holy day must not be used because,
though prepared by nature, it was without the intent
of man and hence can not be considered prepared in
the legal sense. As strong men exult in their agility,
so tendencies that are strong and full of life will sometimes be betrayed into extravagancies. It may be
extravagant to prohibit an egg laid on a holy day on
account of not having been intentionally prepared for
food. But of what paramount importance must intention have been to the religious conscience of the Jew
if it could assume such an exaggerated form as in the
case before us! And could there be a better criterion
of the development of a religion than the importance
it attaches to intent, the outcome of thought and
emotion, in opposition to merely physical action?

Now let us examine another Halakah that might
throw light on the question as to the relation of thought
and emotion to acts and deeds in Jewish theology.
Sin, we are told by leading theologians, consists, according to the Jewish conception, in acting wrongly,
and hence forgiveness, or, to use the more technical
term, atonement, is of a purely mechanical nature.
Originally there were different kinds of sacrifices, the
sin offerings, the guilt offerings, and so forth, by means
of which the sinner could right himself with God.
Later the Rabbis substituted prayer, fasting and alms-
giving for the sacrifices which, after the destruction of
the Temple, could no longer be brought. So far our
theologians. And now let us hear what the Halakah
has to say about it. In a large collection of laws treating of marriage with conditions attached, which is to

be found in the Talmud, we read: If one says to a woman, I marry thee under the condition that I am an entirely righteous man, the marriage is valid, even if it is found that he was a very wicked man, because we apprehend that at the time of the contraction of marriage he repented in his heart. If one says to a woman, I marry thee under the condition that I am a completely wicked man—sin is homely but also attractive!—the marriage is valid.[4] For even if it is found that he was very pious, we apprehend that at the time of the contract he had thoughts of idolatry. Sin as well as forgiveness are thus understood by Jewish law to be entirely independent of acts and deeds; the evil thought in the heart turns the perfectly just into the completely wicked, and vice versa, the change of heart changes the completely wicked into the perfectly just.

The ethical principles and ideals that shaped and formed the Halakah have been made a subject of study by many; however, as we are still in need of a thorough investigation of Jewish ethics, a few remarks on the Halakah as a source of Jewish ethics may prove to be profitable. I shall, however, content myself with touching upon those parts of the Halakah that treat either of ceremonial law or of the forms of civil law; my purpose in doing so being to show to what use the knowledge of these minutiae may be put.

Whether Jewish ethics are of a positive or a negative nature is a question often propounded, and of course answered according to the nature of the quotations one is able to gather from Jewish writings.[5] A favorite argument for the negative character of Jewish ethics is drawn from the number of the commandments, which is said to consist of two hundred and forty-eight positive and three hundred and sixty-five negative. I doubt whether the good Rabbi who first computed these numbers was aware of the consequence of his statistics.[6] There can, however, be no doubt in my mind that modern theologians are not aware of the fact that statistics are as fatal to theology as theology to statistics. A prompt and decisive answer to the question concerning Jewish ethics is given by the Halakah in its ruling: that in all conflicts of laws the positive takes precedence of the negative.[7] This legal maxim applies of course to conflicts of ceremonial laws, but it is the outcome of the legal mind or, to use the more adequate term of the Germans, *das Rechtsbewusstsein*, of a people which conceived ethics as something very positive.

Many of us are undoubtedly acquainted with the favorite diversion of many popular writers who deny to the Jew any claim to creative genius; his religion and his ethics are said by them to be merely different manifestations of his commercial spirit; *do ut des* being the guiding power of his life. Hence the insistence upon the dogma of reward and punishment in his religion and the utilitarian character of his ethics. We have had enough of theology for the present and I shall not enter upon a discussion of the dogma of reward and punishment. Yet I cannot help quoting to you the very wise words of one of the finest minds among contemporary thinkers. The world, says Mr.

Balfour, suffers not because it has too much of it—the belief in reward and punishment—but because it has too little; not because it displaces higher motives, but because it is habitually displaced by lower ones. To those who maintain the utilitarian character of Jewish ethics my advice is: study the part of civil law in Jewish jurisprudence which treats of gifts. While the ancient Roman law, as has been pointed out by the great jurist and legal philosopher Ihering,[8] does not recognize gratuitous transfer of ownership, but only for value, the promise of a gift attained an independence of form in the very earliest stages of the Halakah. For the Roman law gift is a sort of exchange; one makes a gift in order to receive a gift in return, or, in the words of the Roman jurists: *ad remunerandum sibi aliquem naturaliter obligaverunt, velut genus quoddam hoc esse permutationis*.[9] The Halakah, on the other hand, had overcome the egoism of man, and beneficence and love dictated by altruism had come to their full right in legislation as well as in life.[10] The importance of this phenomenon only he can fail to recognize who sees in the forms of the laws mere forms and not the expression of ideas.

The only point where liberality comes to the surface in the Roman law is in regard to wills, and it is highly interesting for the appraisal of the Jewish character to notice that Jewish law is rather inclined to limit the power of the testator to the extent that it prohibits the disinheritance of an ungrateful and wicked son in favor of a good and dutiful son.[11] It has been noticed by others that bequests have psychologically not the value of a gift—the gift of the cold hand is compatible with an icy cold heart; it is not a gift of one's own, but from the purse of the legal heir. In the long course of the development of the Jewish people the underlying bond was the family; the ties of blood were of absolute and undisputed strength. Consequently, the Halakah is not in favor of any measure that might disrupt this bond of union. In this connection I may call attention to the fact that the Halakah failed to develop the law of adoption, notwithstanding the fact that the Bible offers some precedents in certain forms of adoption.[12] The idea of blood relationship forming the basis of the family was too strong with the Jew to permit the development of a law that would undermine it.

This leads us to the burning Jewish question of the day: Are the Jews a nation or merely a religious community? Of course I am not going to discuss it from the point of view of the Jew of today, but justice to my subject requires that we discuss this question from the point of view of the Halakah. And the answer to this question is given unmistakably in the following two laws of inheritance. A Jew, converted to paganism, inherits his father's estate; a pagan, who is converted to Judaism, does not inherit his father's estate, whether the father also becomes a convert or not.[13] The idea underlying these Halakot is that the ties of blood binding the Jew to the Jewish people can never be loosened, and that, on the other hand, by becoming a Jew, a pagan severs his national connections with those to whom he previously belonged. There is a logical contradiction in these two laws of inheritance as formulated by the Halakah. But what is life but a conglomerate of logical contradictions? The Halakah would not be a true mirror of Jewish life, if it were free from all logical inconsistencies. The Jew is bound forever to his people, and yet anybody who enters Judaism becomes a true son of Israel.

A little reflection will, however, convince anyone who comes to the question with an open mind that both these theories concerning Judaism, the purely nationalistic as well as the purely religious, are alike incomplete and, being incomplete, are misleading. They err, as all theories are apt to err, not by pointing to a wholly false cause but by extending the efficiency of a true cause far beyond its real scope. Considered from an historical point of view there is no such thing as nationalism in general. History knows only a particular form of nationalism. It is not the military or economic organization of a state which makes it a national body but the spiritual idea represented by its people. When we speak of the Greek nation we primarily think of the form in which the genius of this nation expressed itself. And is not Jewish nationalism an empty phrase if we do not connect with it Jewish religion and Jewish ethics, Jewish culture and the Jewish mode of life which gave it its individuality?

VI

THE GAON, RABBI ELIJAH WILNA

We are assembled here to-night to commemorate the two hundredth anniversary of the birth of the Gaon, R. Elijah Wilna. We wish to do honor to the memory of the scholar with whom a new epoch began in the study of rabbinic literature, to pay our tribute of admiration to the last great theologian of classical Rabbinism and to draw inspiration from the contemplation of the life of a saint, a life of most rare spiritual depth.

R. Elijah Wilna, called the Gaon par excellence, came of a family celebrated for the learning and piety of its members. Students of heredity might find it highly interesting to study the stock from which the Gaon sprang and to ascertain what it contributed to the extraordinary qualities of his soul and intellect. I shall refer to but one of his ancestors, Rabbi Moses ben David Ashkenazi, around whom arose a large cycle of legends which are current among Lithuanian Jews to this very day and were told to the young Elijah as he in turn told them to his children.[1]

Rabbi Moses was a small shopkeeper, and when appointed Chief Rabbi of Wilna about 1670, he refused to accept any remuneration from the community, being satisfied to eke out a living from his shop, and hence he became known as Rabbi Moses Kraemer, that is, Rabbi Moses, the shopkeeper. The members of the

community thought that the least they could do for
their beloved Rabbi was to patronize his shop. However, when he noticed an unexpected increase in business, he insisted that his wife, who of course was
managing the shop, should keep a careful record of the
profits and as soon as she had enough for her weekly
expenses, should close the shop for the rest of the week.
"It would be," he said, "unfair competition on my part
to take advantage of my being a Rabbi."[2] That such
a poor business man should have been called "Kraemer"
(merchant), is not without a touch of humor.

Rabbi Moses Kraemer was, according to the testimony of his contemporaries, one of the greatest Talmudists of his time. Nothing, however, is known of
his literary activity. Characteristic of the man is the
witty remark made by him in reply to those who criti-
cized him because he attempted to change an old
established custom. He said: The words of Scripture
al tifnu el ha-obot are usually translated, "Seek not
after the wizards," but they might also be rendered,
"Seek not after the ancestors"—a play on the words
abot "ancestors" and *obot* "wizards." Scripture thus
teaches us that one must use his own judgment as to
what is right or wrong and not exclusively depend upon
custom established by ancestors.[3] This remark reminds
one of his great descendant, the Gaon, whose principle
was, use your own eyes and not the spectacles of others.
R. Moses Kraemer's son, R. Elijah, was one of the
leaders of the Wilna community distinguished for his
learning and piety. He was known as R. Elijah "the
Saint" at a time when the Jews were still very chary

of epithets of this kind.⁴ His grandson was R. Solomon, described in a contemporary document as one whose profession is the study of the Torah, and— one is almost inclined to say therefore—living in straitened circumstances.⁵ R. Solomon and his wife, Treine, lived in Seltz, a small town near Brest, Lithuania.

On the first day of Passover of the year 5480, that is April 23, 1720, there was born to them a boy, their first child, whom they called Elijah after his great-grandfather, R. Elijah the Saint.⁶ The child had an unusually beautiful face, "as beautiful as an angel" are the words of his biographers, and to see him was to worship him.⁷ When the child grew older, people marvelled no less at the lad's beautiful soul and his mental gifts than they had done at the infant's angelic beauty. Even if we discount heavily the stories told about the Gaon's youth, there can be no doubt that he was a real prodigy. At the age of six he was advanced enough in his studies of the Bible and the Talmud to dispense with the assistance of a teacher. When six and a half years old he delivered in the great Synagogue of Wilna a learned discourse taught him by his father. Put to the test by the Chief Rabbi of Wilna, the lad showed that he possessed sufficient knowledge and acumen to enable him to deliver such a discourse without the assistance of others.⁸

Lively feeling and clear thinking accompany each other much oftener than is commonly supposed. The combination of mysticism and criticism, of which the Gaon is the best example, was inherent in his nature

and discernible no less in the young child than in the
ripe man. The tussle of the dialectic athletes—*Fech-*
terschule der dialektischen Athleten Heine calls the
Halakah—attracted the phenomenal mentality of the
young child, and his imagination was nourished with
the delicious fruits of the Haggadah—"A garden," to
quote Heine again, "most fantastic, comparable to that
planted by the great Semiramis, the eighth wonder of
the world." The Haggadah of the Talmud led him to
the mystic literature, and we have the Gaon's own
words to the effect that he had studied and mastered
this branch of literature before he was thirteen.[9] Notwithstanding these occasional flights, he remained on
solid ground. His main studies centered about the
Talmud, and his mathematical genius led him early
to recognize the deep truth that to understand a literature dealing with life, one must consider facts and
facts only. He studied at a very tender age mathematics, astronomy and anatomy. He even contem-
plated taking up the study of medicine, but was prevented from doing so by his father, who apprehended
that as a physician his son would not be able to give
all his time to the study of the Torah, since it is the
physician's duty to assist suffering humanity. The
study of botany he was forced to abandon because he
could not stand the uncouth life of the Lithuanian
farmers, from whom he attempted to acquire the
knowledge of plants. It was a principle of his that to
understand the Torah one must be well versed in secular knowledge, and he tried to live up to it.[10] One may
state with certainty that he was in possession of all

the knowledge he could derive from Hebrew sources. However, not satisfied with these materials, he encouraged the translation of Euclid into the Hebrew language,[11] and what is still more characteristic of his wide vision, he wished to see the works of Josephus made accessible to Hebrew readers that they might be helped by them in their study of the Talmud.[12]

The sphere of the scholar is circumscribed by the walls of his study, while the realm of the saint is limited to his soul. The outer life of the scholar and saint is briefly told. He married early,[13] in accordance with the rule laid down in the Mishnah, "At eighteen the age is reached for marriage." His wife was Hannah, the daughter of a certain R. Judah from the town of Kaidan, and it is said that for a time the Gaon lived in this town,[14] returning to Wilna at the age of twenty-five. A document of the year 1750 informs us that R. Elijah the Saint was granted a small weekly allowance from the legacy left by his ancestor, R. Moses Rivke's, for the maintenance of those of his descendants who would devote themselves to the study of the Torah.[15]

Though living in complete retirement, his fame spread rapidly. When comparatively a young man, thirty-five years old, he was approached by the greatest Talmudist of the day, R. Jonathan Eybeschuetz, to state his position with regard to the controversy that was then raging among the Jews of Germany and Poland. I have no intention of entering even into a brief account of the controversy between Eybeschuetz and his cantankerous opponent, Emden. The interest of the student of history ought to be in the flower which

history puts forth and not in the muck in which it
grew. For our purpose it will suffice to quote a part of
the Gaon's reply to Eybeschuetz. He writes: "Oh,
that I had wings like a dove, then would I fly to restore peace and quench that strange fire, the fire of
contention. But who am I that people should listen
to me? If the words of the Rabbis, the heads of the
holy congregations, are not listened to, who would care
about the opinions of a young man hidden in his
study?"[16]

A few years later, at the age of forty, the Gaon seems
to have partly given up his seclusion, and though re-
fusing up to the end of his life to accept the position
of Rabbi, for all practical purposes he became the
spiritual head not only of the community of Wilna but
also of the entire Lithuanian and Russian Jewry.[17] He
changed his mode of life in compliance with the injunction of the old sages that the first forty years of one's
life should be devoted exclusively to acquiring knowledge and the years following to imparting it.[18] The
first step in his changed attitude towards the public
was the establishment of a model synagogue. The
changes introduced by him as, for instance, the abolition of a goodly part of the Piyyut and the introduction of congregational singing, were certainly intended
to give decorum to the service and intensify the devotion of the worshippers.[19] The synagogue served at
the same time as a house of study where a select number of prominent scholars sat at the feet of the Gaon,
and though they were a handful only, they succeeded
in causing the influence of the master to spread far and

near.[20] Especially the community of Wilna, the metropolis of Lithuania, felt such reverence for the Gaon
that a word of his sufficed to annul the most solemn
resolutions of a powerful board of Parnasim. When,
for instance, the Board of Jewish Charities in Wilna in
a fit of efficiency decreed that no one should be permitted to solicit contributions, all of which should go
directly to a central body, the Gaon maintained that
philanthropy must never lose all sense of humanity,
which would be the case if all the needy were required
to apply in person to the administration of charities.
He therefore not only annulled the decision of the
Board, but made them put at his disposal a certain
sum of money to be distributed by him to those who
in his opinion deserved to be spared the humiliation of
appearing before the officers of the community.[21]

The incident which more than anything else brought
the name of the Gaon before the great masses of
Jewry, not only of Lithuania and Russia but also of
Poland and other countries, was his bitter fight against
Hasidism. That the rush of the flood of this movement stopped at the gates of Wilna and that even in
countries like Galicia and Poland the large communities, the seats of Jewish intelligence, were not swept
away by this flood, is mainly due to the Gaon. The
Gaon issued his decree of excommunication against the
Hasidim on the night following the Day of Atonement
of the year 1796. On the eve of the next Day of Atonement he became very ill and died a few days later, on
the third day of the Feast of Tabernacles, October 17,
1797, at the age of 77 years and six months. The Feast

of Joy was turned into days of mourning for the community of Wilna, for they felt that their greatest intellectual and spiritual light had been put out.[22]

R. Abraham Danzig in his funeral oration over the Gaon speaks of seventy books composed by the latter,[23] and the same statement is made by R. Israel of Minsk, a disciple of the Gaon.[24] One who has had the opportunity to examine the exhibition of the works of the Gaon, arranged by the Jewish Theological Seminary, will not consider this statement exaggerated, especially if he considers that many a work of the Gaon is still awaiting publication and that not a few have been lost.[25] Yet it may well be said of the Gaon that he was too fond of reading books to care to write them. He was, to use a happy phrase of Doctor Schechter, *Der ewige Student* (the perpetual student) who read and studied in order that he might become a better and a wiser man. It is quite certain that all the works of the Gaon were written before he was forty, in his so-called student years, when for his own use and benefit he annotated and commented on nearly all the books he read.[26] Some of the works ascribed to the Gaon were really composed by his disciples, who put into writing the lectures and remarks of the master, and are therefore to be used with great care. No teacher would like to be held responsible for the lecture notes of his students—even of the cleverest of them.[27]

To one concerned with the study of Jewish mentality the works of the Gaon will furnish very interesting material. They consist of commentaries on nearly all the books of the Bible; treatises on biblical geography, chronology and archaeology; commentaries on the Mishnah and Talmud of Jerusalem, critical notes and annotations to the Tannaitic Midrashim, the Mekilta, Sifra and Sifre, as well as to the Babylonian Talmud; commentaries and notes on the classical works of the mystic literature like the Sefer Yezirah and the Zohar; treatises on astronomy, trigonometry, algebra; a grammar of the Hebrew language; and, last but not least, his most important work, the commentary on the Shulhan Aruk.[28]

To give an adequate estimate of the Gaon's phenomenal mentality and his lasting contribution to the different branches of Jewish learning would require more than a dozen lectures. Here I shall merely attempt to make clear his claim to originality.

Most of the biographers of the Gaon maintain that his importance consisted in having abolished or, to be accurate, in attempting to abolish the dialectical method of studying the Talmud, i. e., the Pilpul. However, one must not overlook the fact that the Talmud in its main contents is a structure of dialectics. One might as well study calculus without applying the mathematical laws of equation as the Talmud without using dialectics. It is true the Gaon had only words of scorn for those who build the roof before laying the foundations,[29] but the study of the Talmud was not for him any more than it was for his predecessors a matter of a purely archaeological-historical nature, having no bearing upon life. The development of talmudic law in all of its departments but especially in the domain of civil law would have been an impossibility without the application of dialectics, and the Gaon was the last one to decry its importance and justification.[30]

Of course, there are dialectics and dialectics, there is legitimate use and there is pernicious abuse thereof. Many a great Talmudist before the Gaon saw the evil of unbridled dialectics, but none of them recognized its cause, and hence they were unable to remedy it. The originality of the Gaon consists in the fact that he not only diagnosed the disease but also established its cause and found its remedy.

Book infallibility without authoritative interpretation is no better than a mighty sword without a mighty hand to wield it. It hangs on the wall as a glorious memory; it cannot do its work. In the long run the rule-of-thumb infallibility will not serve. If the dogma of book infallibility is to play an efficient and enduring part in history, there must be an authoritative body to translate the book into law. The infallibility of the Bible necessitated during the second commonwealth the authority of the Sanhedrin, whose legitimate heirs were the Patriachate in Palestine and the Academies in Babylonia. The conception of the Talmud as infallible arose in a time when the Babylonian Geonim possessed a practical monopoly of spiritual prestige. With the extinction of the Gaonate about the middle of the eleventh century, the last authoritative body disappeared from among the Jews. The great danger confronting the spiritual life of the Jews in the Middle Ages lay in the difficulty of continuing Jewish tradition. In other words their problem was how to maintain the authority of the Talmud in the absence of any authoritative interpretation, and the result was the endless multiplicity of authorities. For the views of every competent scholar, especially if they were written down, came to be considered authoritative. Multiplicity of authority, however, is identical with no authority, and hence the rise of the Pilpul, by means of which the differences among the authorities were as far as possible explained away.

Now dialectics is a system whereby the interpreter can first put into a text any given set of ideas and then with a grand air of authority take it out of the text. Under a bold dialectical method the text of the Talmud lay helpless. Like a wax nose, the interpreter could shape and twist it as he pleased. The attempt to maintain the authority of the Talmud by upholding the authority of all its interpreters by means of dialectics could not but lead to exegetical abuse of the worst kind, and in the long run it endangered the very authority which the Pilpul wished to safeguard, the authority of the Talmud. The tacit proviso was that dialectics must be kept within the bounds marked out by authority. But the leopard does not change his spots when he is put into a cage. It is true, behind the commentators and the codifiers stood the Talmud, but it stood behind them and could not be reached save through them.

After these preliminary remarks we may be in a better position to understand the originality of the Gaon, the father of the criticism of the Talmud. The first condition of criticism is the emancipation from

tradition, and the Gaon was bold enough to declare
that the interpretation of the Talmud must be based
on reason and not on authority. Yet the Gaon did not
belong to those whose motto was, to quote a witty
Frenchman, *Les grands pères ont toujours tort*, or in
homely English, "Whatever was good enough for our
fathers is not good enough for us." His admiration
and reverence for the post-talmudic scholars was boundless, but to use his own words, "No personal regard
where truth is involved."[31] Criticism involved, according to him, two elements, religious conscience and
reason. If the Talmud is the great treasure of the
Synagogue, then it is an act of conscience to bring it
forth from behind tradition into direct touch with
everybody. Again, if conscience insists upon a first
hand knowledge of the Talmud for the man who needs
it for his guidance in life, reason insists upon the same
thing for the sake of the object to be known. For the
scientific mind guarantees to every object, great and
small, the right to be seen as it is.

With the shaking off of the yoke of authoritative
interpretations, the critical principle was conceived.
But it might have taken centuries before it came clearly
to the light. Criticism was a lost art for the last centuries of antiquity and the entire Middle Ages, and
was rediscovered in comparatively modern times. The
genius of the Gaon, however, was so great that he not
only conceived the critical principle but also showed
the way it should be applied. Living as he did in an
isolated world without being in the least influenced
by the spirit of the eighteenth century, he nevertheless

evolved the essential canons of criticism which it took
the best minds of several centuries to attain.

The contribution of the Gaon to external and internal criticism of the Talmud—for obvious reasons I
prefer these terms to those commonly used, "lower
and higher"—are numerous and of lasting value. He
was the first Jewish scholar to see clearly that ancient
documents, copied and re-copied as they have been
for centuries with very little care and exposed at every
fresh transcription to new risk of alteration, were bound
to reach us full of inaccuracies.[32] He, therefore, before
using a written source, set about to find out whether
the text was sound, that is in as close agreement as
possible with the original manuscript of the author,
and if the text was found to be corrupt, he undertook
to emend it. Many a law, many a view of the later
authorities was thus shown by the Gaon to have been
based on passages of the Talmud corrupted in trans-
mission, and they collapsed as soon as the true readings
were discovered or restored. It would be easy to fill
pages with lists of happy emendations by the Gaon.
One may say without exaggeration that a great part
of the tannaitic literature would have remained words
of a "writing that is sealed" if not for the ingenious
emendations of the Gaon. No one down to our day
has equalled him in the art of conjectural emendation.

External criticism, however, is only a means to an
end, leading to internal criticism which deals with interpretation and examines the accuracy of authors,
thus enabling us to gain a profound insight into past
ages. The Gaon was no less the founder of internal

criticism of the Talmud than of external. Plato, comparing the power of a book with that of a living teacher, declared that the book is helpless at the mercy of the reader. The truth of the statement is best seen in the lot that befell the books of Plato himself. Students have misread them, carrying into them their own wisdom and ignorance, making Plato speak a language widely different from his own. The same may be said of the Talmud. So long as the talmudic scholars studied the Talmud only, they could not help misunderstanding it. The Talmud or, to be accurate, the Babylonian Talmud, is only a part of a very vast literature, and a knowledge of the whole is indispensable for the understanding of the part. The Gaon did not limit his studies to the Babylonian Talmud but extended them over the entire field of cognate literature, to the tannaitic sources that form the basis of this Talmud as well as to the Yerushalmi, its twin brother. Accordingly, the Gaon had historical-critical problems to solve. So long as the old form of Talmud studies reigned, there could be no critical problems connected with the Talmud because the real facts in the case could not force themselves into notice. For the Gaon, however, it became necessary to ask for an explanation of the striking likeness between the Mishnah and the Tosefta or between the Babli and the Yerushalmi and their almost equally striking diversity. Following his healthy instinct for facing facts boldly, he could not but come to the conclusion that as the interpretation of the Talmud must be independent of post-talmudic authorities, so must the interpretation of the pre-talmudic literature be independent of the authority of the Talmud.[33]

The Gaon was described above as the last great theologian of classical Rabbinism. Leibnitz somewhere said of Kepler that he was not aware of his own great riches. We may apply the same characteristics to the Gaon. He did not give us a systematic presentation of his theology. He was very likely not aware of having a system of theology, and yet it would not be a very difficult task to cull from his works the material necessary for a rabbinic theology. And he was the last great theologian of classical Rabbinism. The classical ages of religion are either the periods of great beginnings when with all the power of originality they attract all forces and all interests to themselves, or the great organizing periods when all existing culture is bent into obedience to the highest religious ideas. In these classical ages great unity or at any rate great harmony prevails in the spiritual world. Judaism enjoyed such a golden age during biblical times and again later during the Middle Ages when religion was the all in all in the spiritual sphere. The Jewish Middle Ages, as Zunz so aptly remarked, lasted to the beginning of the eighteenth century, and hence the Gaon may well be described as the last theologian of classical Rabbinism. Though living many centuries after the great exponents of the religious philosophy of the Jews, Saadya Gaon, Gabirol, Maimonides, Gersonides, and many others, he is nevertheless a better representative of Rabbinism than they. He among all the theologians of classical Rabbinism is the least influenced by foreign thought, by Greek-Arabic philosophy, and his theology has therefore a claim to be considered rabbinic and nothing else.

The central thought of his theology is that self-perfection or, to use his own words, the perfection of character is the essence of religion, and that the Torah is the only medium through which this purpose can be achieved.[34] "The Torah," I give his words literally, "is to the soul of man what rain is to the soil; rain makes any seed put into the soil grow, producing nourishing as well as poisonous plants. The Torah also helps him who is striving for self-perfection, while it increases the impurity of heart of those that remain uncultivated."[35] Self-perfection cannot be achieved without hard training, and hence there is a strong current of asceticism in the Gaon's theology.[36] But it ought to be pointed out that his asceticism is essentially of a different nature from that taught by the predominating religion of the Middle Ages. He does not see in the material world the seat of evil; he does not even teach us to despise the enjoyment of this world. What he maintained is that asceticism is a necessary means to self-perfection. Men's desires must be purified and idealized but not done away with.[37] In the severe struggle between the ideal and the material world it is the Torah and its commandments that give man the weapons which if used properly assure him of victory.[38] I have quoted these few theological remarks of the Gaon because they throw light upon the fundamental principles of rabbinic Judaism. It may be said of the Gaon's theology that the old became new, appropriated and applied by a great original mind.

Torah, of course, means for the Gaon as for any Jewish theologian the written word and the unwritten tradition. The Gaon, however, more than any Jewish theologian before him, strained the claim for the binding power of the Talmud, the depository of the unwritten Torah, to the utmost.[39] So-called historians point to this as a proof of the reactionary tendency of the Gaon's theology. They fail to see that he set up the authority, almost the infallibility of the Talmud as a bulwark against the authority claimed for many of the post-talmudic codifiers and interpreters. The Gaon's directions to his disciples were, "Do not regard the views of the Shulhan Aruk binding if you think that they are not in agreement with those of the Talmud."[40] In this statement the novel feature is the denial of the authority of the Shulhan Aruk and not the emphasis laid upon the authority of the Talmud, which was never questioned by rabbinic Jews.

The earliest documents in which the Gaon is mentioned, one dating from a time when he was thirty,[41] the other from a time when he was thirty-five,[42] call him Rabbi Elijah the Saint, and to this day his synagogue in Wilna is known as the synagogue of the Saint, the "chosid's klaus." It is true the Gaon strongly protested against the epithet "Saint" being conferred upon him, maintaining that he merely attempted to fulfil the duty incumbent upon every Jew, to live in accordance with the Torah, and that he only should be called "Saint" who does more than is ordinarily expected of man.[43] However, the greatness of the Gaon rests on the wonderful concentration with which he gathered up all the most significant elements in rabbinic Judaism, the inwardness and depth with which he realized the thought of preceding ages, and on the magnetism of his personality which streamed forth from him to others. The last great representative of classical Rabbinism is the most classic type of the man in whom deep inner experiences, energetic thought and absolute faith in authority united in a close and characteristic union. The ideals of rabbinic Judaism thus became realized in him.

There was a certain kind of spiritual chasteness in him which made it impossible for him to draw out his innermost treasures even for his own inspection, still less for the inspection of others. For under inspection the stamp of inwardness is apt to tarnish. We must be silent on our own internal life or it may cease to be internal. Accordingly the Gaon was extremely reticent about his inner experiences, and it is therefore very difficult to get a clear conception of them. Their main feature is that in the study of the Torah and the fulfilment of its commandments he experienced the prophetic fervor, the joy and the inspiration of personal communion with God as well as the high privilege of serving Him. The service of God was everything to him, and he used to say, "Elijah can serve God without any rewards," the joy of serving Him being sufficient reward in itself. Notwithstanding his austerity and asceticism, he never experienced a depressed or sad state of mind. He always was, as we are informed by his biographers,[44] in a joyful mood and in high spirits, though his trials were not few. For several years he and his family had to suffer actual hunger and other privations by reason of the dishonesty of a petty official of the community who kept for himself the weekly allowances granted to the Gaon from a legacy administered by the community. The Gaon preferred to suffer rather than to inform the authorities of the dishonesty of the official, being of the opinion that according to the Torah it was his duty to suffer silently.[45] He argued that putting a man to shame is declared in the Talmud to be equal to bloodshed, and one must not cause bloodshed even to save one's life. He was not at all conscious of the heroic element in his suffering, but believed that he only did his duty and he enjoyed his suffering as a service to God. He often sold all his furniture to assist the poor or gave away his last meal.[46] He did it joyfully, holding that a man's duty is always proportionate to his capacity, and he quoted the Talmud to show that in ethics there must always be progressive taxation.[47]

In these days when the harrowing catastrophe that came over the Jewry of Eastern Europe makes one almost despair of the future, it is a source of consolation to contemplate the life and works, the intellect and character of the Gaon. Lithuanian Jewry especially may on this day of the bi-centenary of its greatest son draw new hopes and aspirations. A dried up tree cannot bring forth delicious fruit; and if the fruit be good, then the tree must be good too. The vitality of rabbinic Judaism is clearly proved by the production of such a giant of intellect and soul, and in this sense the words of Scripture become true, "The memory of the righteous shall be for a blessing."

RABBI ISRAEL SALANTER

I

The following anecdote is told about Rabbi Joshua ben Korha, who flourished about the middle of the second century. A man once left a will which caused the Probate Court no little embarrassment. The will read as follows: "My son shall not receive his inheritance until he becomes foolish." The judges, after long deliberation, betook themselves to Rabbi Joshua to get his advice in the difficult case. As they approached his house, they saw him crawling on all fours with a cord in his mouth, held by his little son, who was playing horse with his father. When the judges finally were ushered into the presence of the Rabbi, they placed before him the difficult question that was the cause of their visit. Laughingly the Rabbi said: "I have given you a concrete illustration of your case; for everyone becomes foolish as soon as he has children." The testament was therefore interpreted as meaning that it was the wish of the deceased to have his son married and the father of children before he received his patrimony.[1]

We shall not tarry to consider the legal side of this narrative. This was attended to by the parties interested in the contest over the will. It will pay us better to consider the psychological aspect of the story a little more closely.

In the mechanical world as well as in the world of feeling, it is a truth that every primary force is one-sided in its action. It persists in one direction so long as no other force appears to counteract or thwart it.[2] Thus it happens that our feelings under strong excitement carry us along with such force that we are impelled to acts which, under other circumstances, we should regard as foolish. Rabbi Joshua sank the dignity of the scholar in the pride and affection of the father that dominated him for the moment. The Rabbis teach us this truth in their peculiar way. The pity is that writers of history, and especially of Jewish history, have often ignored it in judging the heroes who have influenced the course of events.

The law is the same in the intellectual as in the mechanical and emotional world. There is no great thought that has become an impelling power in history which has not been espoused at its origin by men willing to put all their physical and spiritual powers entirely at its service. Men who produce spiritual movements are themselves primary forces, their inner natures are filled with a single thought, and with this peculiar thought they identify their personality to the exclusion of all else, indeed to the point of isolation from all else. Our culture is therefore the resultant of a number of one-sided forces, whose originators would hear nothing of compromise, but which end in a harmonious union, because no force is strong enough to hold the field alone. The history of facts embraces only the feebler part of reality. To comprehend and properly appreciate historical events, we must go back to those primary ideas which, though never completely realized, are still the only creative forces to be considered. Therefore, we must take as the starting point of history the records of those men who, regardless of actual conditions, in their enthusiasm for one particular thought viewed life through the prism of this thought and saw nothing else.

The essential thing in this world is not to serve this or that ideal indifferently, but, with all one's soul, to serve the ideal which one has chosen. If we look at history from this point of view, we shall have to admit that the average and commonplace persons do not represent the nation so well as its heroes. On the contrary, as has been well said, "The true mind of a people at any time is best ascertained by examining that of its greatest men." What is true of the general history of a people is eminently so in the history of its religion. For in the history of religion the experience which furnishes us with the needful touchstone is that of the religious life, and for this we must have recourse to those who have best lived that life, that is to say, the saints.

Furthermore it is the saint who displays in a special degree the excellencies which characterize the religious ideals of the nation. In order, then, to understand the religion of the Jew and the history of the Synagogue, we must make diligent use of the lives of the saints.

The dearth of biographical material so conspicuous in the sources of Jewish history is one of the main reasons why it is inadequately understood and judged. The most unusual movements of Judaism have generally the fewest documents and their most remarkable leaders are the least known. The great in Israel's later history whom we know best, belong to a set of men whom it is easier to describe collectively than separately, whose minds were formed by one system of discipline. Only rarely can we gratify our desire to study Jewish ideals not written upon paper but upon living souls. In modern times such religious geniuses were Rabbi Israel Baal Shem Tob, the founder of Hasidism, and his younger contemporary, the Gaon, Rabbi Elijah Wilna, the one the complete embodiment of emotion and feeling, the other the personification of religious thought.

In the words of the first father of the Synagogue, Simeon the Just, these two men realized in their lives two of the three ideals which make the essence of Judaism: *Torah* and *Abodah* or, in modern parlance, religious thought and religious emotion. The founder of Hasidism was entirely absorbed in religious emotion, the Gaon's life was devoted to the searching and explaining of the Torah.

A life wholly consecrated to the third fundamental principle of Judaism, *Gemilut Hasadim*, ethics and morality, was that of Rabbi Israel Lipkin Salanter.

The history of the short-lived but very interesting moralist movement in Lithuania is practically the biography of this man.[3] Rabbi Israel was born on the 3d of November, 1810, in the Russian border province of Samogitia, in Lithuania. His teacher in Talmud and Rabbinics was his father, Rabbi Wolf Lipkin, who was both rabbi and scholar. While still a youth, he married and settled in Salant, the birthplace of his wife. It is from this place that the name by which he is best known is derived. Influences are subtle things, even in one's own case, yet we can clearly discern the influence of two great men of this place who, however diverse they were in capacity and character and mode of life, left their ineradicable marks upon their young and impressionable disciple. The one was the rabbi of the place, Rabbi Hirsch Braude, who was one of the keenest dialecticians among the Talmudists of his generation at a time when dialectics reigned supreme in the domain of the Talmud. Salanter, as a Talmudist, was never able to deny the influence of this master, and he endeavored to transfer this system of dialectics to another sphere of thought, that of ethics.

Quite different was the influence that proceeded from his other master, Rabbi Zundel, whom one would be inclined to describe as a lay saint were it not for the fact that the Jews have no monks, and to them the contrast between the laiety and the clergy does not mean the same as to other peoples.

Rabbi Zundel,[4] though a great scholar, never accepted the position of rabbi but was satisfied to eke out a living from a small shop he kept, or from any odd job that came his way. He even refused to be recognized by any external signs as belonging to the intellectual class and would therefore dress like a common man, disregarding the custom of the country, where even the poor scholar could be distinguished by his garb. This plainness of dress and simplicity of manner were often the causes of great discomfort and unpleasantness to him. Once while travelling among a rather rough lot of people, he was taken to be one of their own class, and as he was unwilling to participate in their vulgar actions and still more vulgar conversation but spent all his time in praying and in studying the Talmud by heart, they decided to punish him for giving himself airs. Surprising him while he was asleep, they attempted to mark him by singeing his beard on one side of his face, and thus disgrace him, as no good Jew would ever dare to shave his beard. Just as they were on the point of carrying out their intention, they heard him exclaiming in great ecstasy, "Only one moment more!" Observing that he was awake, they desisted, though they did not quite understand the meaning of his words by which he expressed his great joy on being able to suffer insults without resisting. His great ideal in life was to make the whole of it a continuous divine service, and the means of realizing this ideal consisted for him in the study of the Torah with its strenuous and solitary discipline of thought and action. From his master, Rabbi Hayyim of Volozhin, he not only learned boundless reverence for the Gaon, Rabbi Elijah Wilna, the master of his master, but he also attempted to live his life in accordance with the ideals set up by this austere and ascetic saint.

The simplicity, humility and saintliness of Rabbi Zundel attracted the young Salanter, who never neglected an opportunity to be near the master that he might be able to see a saintly life with his own eyes instead of studying it from books. It is told that once when Rabbi Zundel noticed the young man following him, he turned suddenly around and said to him: "If you want to lead a pious life, study *Musar*." These simple words were the decisive factor in the life of Salanter. From now on the driving power in his very active life was the conviction that the study of the Torah and the fulfilment of its commandments, important and absolutely necessary as they are for the salvation of the Jew, do not lead to the desired goal as long as one does not work seriously and steadily at the education of self. This, however, can only be gained by a thorough study of the Musar literature, i. e., the ethico-religious books. How it is to be studied we shall see later; for the present we would remark only that in the importance attached by him to the study of Musar we can see the indirect influence of the Gaon, who declared it to be the religious duty and inviolable obligation of every person to fix a certain time of the day for reflection and meditation.[5] This teaching of the Gaon was made living to the young Salanter by Rabbi Zundel, whose powerful impression on him was so enduring that even in later life the disciple remembered the master with the greatest admiration, and he described him as "a ladder set upon the earth, with its top reaching to heaven."

"To keep aloof from men and to live in retirement from the world" was the highest ideal after which Rabbi Zundel strove, in imitation of that great hermit,

the Gaon. Without doubt they also thought of the
salvation of their brethren who were in and of the
world; but they tried to further it by example only
and at most, in cases of pressing necessity, by rare and
short apparition. It is therefore not surprising that
for a time Salanter was in great perplexity, swaying
between the relative merits and advantages of the
active and the contemplative life. We thus find in
him not merely noble actions, but life in the true
meaning of the word, that is, development and
struggle. The outcome of this struggle could not
be doubtful. Preëminently religious, however, as the
motive power of his inner life was, it was essentially
of an ethical bent, and hence he could not but come to
the conclusion "that true salvation can be gained only
by the service rendered by the individual to the
community." He became convinced that there is no
virtue, strictly speaking, for man as a solitary individual in the world; that virtue begins with socia-
bility. The idea of solidarity, טובת הכלל, is at the root
of all our aspirations toward the good. But not only
morality, religion also in its higher form, he maintained, can be achieved in social life only, and it is a
false show of self-sacrifice when religious duties are
performed in partial or complete isolation, as in the
cloister or the Bet ha-Midrash. Salanter, therefore,
came to the conclusion that it was his duty instead of
avoiding the multitude to seek them out in order to
enlighten, console and improve them.

While still in the very small town of Salant, Rabbi
Israel, at the age of about twenty-five years, became

the leader of a small group of students and business
men whom he introduced into the study of *Musar*.
His fame as a great Talmudist spread very rapidly,
and he was scarcely thirty years old when he was
appointed head of the Meilishen Academy in Wilna.
It is perhaps not without interest to note the fact
that his salary amounted to four rubles a week. One
is almost inclined to believe that then as now salaries
were often in inverse ratio to merits. One takes it for
granted that the greater the scholar, the smaller his
demands upon life.

In Wilna Salanter found for the first time in his life
a large field to display his energies and talents. He
had arrived in that "little Jerusalem of Lithuania" at a
very critical moment in the history of Lithuanian and
Russian Jewry. The Haskalah movement which for
about half a century was struggling in vain to gain a
foothold in Lithuania, received about 1842 a strong
impetus through the activity of Max Lilienthal,[7] the
"emissary of Haskalah" and the agent of the Russian
government in its endeavor to dejudaize the Jews as a
preliminary step toward their conversion to Christianity. It is true that the plain uneducated Lithuanian
Jew showed more discernment in judging the "friendly"
policy of a most tyrannical government than did the
learned German doctor, and Lilienthal had soon to
give up the hope of ever realizing his reforms. The
agitation, however, caused among the different classes
of Lithuanian Jewry by the Lilienthal episode, did not
abate even when the educational plans of the government came to a sudden stop, and Lilienthal, their

prime mover, finally recognizing whose dupe he was, emigrated to America. Large numbers among the educated classes who hitherto had known only of one form of intellectual activity, the study of Talmud and Rabbinics, began more and more to devote themselves to secular studies, preferably to *belles lettres* in Hebrew and other languages, which they found more attractive and enjoyable, as they satisfied not only the intellect but also the emotions. And, as it is natural for the lower classes to copy the example set by the higher, Jewish studies and consequently Jewish ideals lost their attraction in the eyes of the common people.

To the credit of Salanter it must be said that not only was he the only one among the representatives of strict Talmudism who saw the danger confronting it, but he was also the only one who attempted to protect it against the threatening peril. He cannot be said to have been very successful in his main activities; some will declare that he failed completely, yet surely nobody will deny the religious fervor and sincerity, the high and saintly moral standards of the man who single-handed attempted to fight a world in arms.

Salanter, who lived only two generations after the rise of the great Hasidic movement that threatened to divide the Jewry of eastern Europe into two hostile camps, had learned from the upheaval caused by a small band of religious enthusiasts two practical things. The one was that the preponderance of intellectualism in religion estranges the great masses, and the other, that those who are to lead them must possess other qualities besides those of scholarship and saintliness. A favorite saying of his was that the Hasidim as well as their opponents, the *Mitnagdim*, err—the former in believing that they have leaders, the latter in maintaining that they have no need of them. His activity was accordingly directed toward the achievement of two objects, the attraction of the masses of the people by emphasizing the emotional element of religion, and the training of men who would in the true sense of the word be spiritual leaders of the people.

Shortly after his arrival in Wilna, he established a *Hebrah Musar*, an institute that had for its object the study of ethical literature—for example, the works of Bahya, Gabirol, and Rabbi Moses Hayyim Luzzatto. Members of the organization were recruited from all classes of society—professional scholars, business men, artisans and laborers. At his instance new editions of a number of ethical works were published in 1844 and 1845 for the use of the members of the institute as well as for others who might take up the study of these works if made accessible to them. Salanter was, however, not satisfied with the establishment of a center for those desirous to devote part of their time to the study of ethics, but he served those seekers after truth as guide and leader, frequently delivering lectures before them on the subjects of their studies. In order that his work might spread all over Lithuania, and likewise continue after his death, he selected a few chosen individuals, distinguished by learning, piety and high moral standards, to be trained as the spiritual leaders of the people.

In spite of the wide sphere of activity he had created

for himself in the metropolis of Lithuania and although
he enjoyed the greatest respect of the entire community,
his stay in Wilna was not of very long duration. There
were many reasons why he left that city. It suffices
here to state that he wanted to avoid an office which
it was sought to impose upon him. In 1848, the
Russian Government opened the Rabbinical Seminary
in Wilna, and pressure was brought to bear upon him
to accept the professorship of Talmud. That it was his
clearsightedness and not fanaticism that forbade the
acceptance of this office is shown by the result or
rather lack of result obtained by this class of institutions in Russia. His sound judgment warned him
against becoming the instrument of a government
whose politics were directed to the end of extorting
money from the Jews to be spent for institutions
established for the sole purpose of destroying Judaism.
The opposition of Salanter and many of his party
to the Haskalah and its schemes was not the result
of hostility to secular knowledge, the war-cry of
the *Maskilim*, but was mainly rooted in the firm
conviction that a government furthering the spread of
secular knowledge among the Jews and at the same
time curtailing their civil and political rights, can have
but one aim in its mind—the destruction of Judaism.
There can now be no doubt that this was a just
estimate of the policy of the Russian government at
that time. With equally fair certainty it may be
stated that Salanter was in principle not at all opposed
to secular knowledge. Later in life he counted among
his very close and intimate friends the leaders of the

German orthodoxy, men of the highest type of modern education. It is therefore not at all surprising to find Maskilim cite the authority of Salanter against those who opposed secular knowledge absolutely.

In the year 1848 he left Wilna and settled in Kovno, the second largest Jewish community in Lithuania. The close commercial relations which existed between this city and Germany were not without far-reaching effects upon the life of its Jewish inhabitants. At the time of the arrival of Salanter in Kovno, it was the most modern community in Lithuania, a real hotbed of the Haskalah. When he left it two decades later, it had become the stronghold of orthodoxy and remained such for half a century longer. This change may be said to have been exclusively the work of Salanter who put his stamp upon the spiritual life of this large community.

It was in Kovno that the development of the Musar movement reached its pinnacle. Here arose the first *Musar-Stuebel* (moralist conventicle). The central figure was Salanter and around him gathered a large number of capable young Talmudists as well as many merchants and artisans who were attracted by the high enthusiasm and kindling eloquence of the master. The energy and devotion of Salanter are the more to be admired as his achievements were gained in the face of violent opposition. The opponents were not only the Maskilim but also many among the representatives of the strictest Talmudism. Chief among the latter was the Rabbi of Kovno, Rabbi Lceb Shapiro, a critical mind of the first rank and a man of very

independent character[8]. He was frequently in the
habit of giving a slight twist to verse 19 of Psalm
135 and applying it maliciously to the Musar-Stuebel:

O House of Israel, Bless ye the Lord!
O House of Aaron, Bless ye the Lord!
O House of Levi, Bless ye the Lord!
O ye that fear the Lord, Bless ye the Lord!

There is a house for Israel, he said, a house for Aaron,
a house for Levi, but there is no mention of a separate
house for those who fear the Lord, hence there is no
need of establishing conventicles for them[9]. This *bon
mot* shows at the same time the course of the opposition which the Musar movement provoked. It is the
deep seated opposition of the talmudic Jew to every
separatist movement. Against the study of the Musar
literature neither Shapiro nor his friends had anything
to say; what they condemned was the forming of a
society which tended to set its members apart from the
rest of the community as "the moralists." The opposition to the Musar movement and its leader was
carried on with great bitterness and was not entirely
free from personal animosity against Salanter and his
disciples. As to the latter it must be stated that their
admiration for the master whom they tried to imitate
and emulate was sincere and profound, but genius is
not to be copied. A good deal of the criticism levelled
against the Musar movement had its origin in the
extravagancies of those whom the Talmud describes as
"disciples who did not wait upon their masters sufficiently," they are those who attempted rather to ape
the great than to mirror them.

After living in Kovno for about twelve years,
Salanter was forced by a severe illness—a nervous
disorder—to change his abode and settle in Germany,
where he hoped to regain his health through the
famous skill of its physicians. He spent the rest of his
life in Memel and Koenigsberg. In these communities
new problems awaited him, and, notwithstanding the
weakened state of his health, he continued his various
activities.   These two cities, on account of their
proximity to Lithuania, contained large numbers of
Jews of that country, some of whom had settled there
permanently and others, especially those engaged in
importing Russian merchandise into Germany, were
forced by their business to spend there many a month
of each year. Salanter saw the danger lurking in these
large masses of Jews living unorganized in a foreign
country, with the Jews of which they neither could nor
would form a union. He set himself therefore the task
of organizing communities of Lithuanian Jews in these
two cities and thanks to his untiring energy and
devotion to his people, he succeeded within a short
time. He was, however, not interested in organization
for its own sake. What he desired was to transplant
the cultural and religious life of the Lithuanian Jews
to these communities, and his endeavors were not
entirely in vain. The Jewish community in Memel
continued up to the great war to be the only one of its
kind. Its life resembled that of Kovno and Wilna
much more closely than that of Berlin or Frankfort.

A plan that engaged the fertile mind of Salanter
for many years was the popularization of the Talmud,

that is, first to make the Talmud accessible to the
great masses of the Jews and further to introduce its
study into the non-Jewish colleges and universities.
Being firmly convinced that the knowledge of the
Talmud is absolutely necessary for the culture and
religious welfare of the Jew, he could not but look with
alarm upon the gradual disappearance of talmudic
learning from among the great masses of Jewry, even
those of Lithuania, the classic land of talmudic study.
To stem the tide of ignorance *in re talmudica*, he
advised the following means: The publication of a
dictionary of the Talmud in Yiddish to help the average business man or artisan among the Lithuanian or
Polish Jews in his studies of the Talmud, and the
replacement of Rashi's commentary on the Talmud
by a more modern one that could be put into the hands
of beginners. As usual, Salanter was not satisfied with
formulating plans, but immediately set about to carry
them out. His plan of a Yiddish dictionary of the
Talmud, it is true, did not proceed far, for there were
not enough Talmudists who could and would engage
in such a work, but the plan of a modern commentary
advanced so far that he received a promise of collabo-
ration from a goodly number of prominent Talmudists.

The spread of the knowledge of the Talmud among
the educated classes of the Gentiles, Salanter believed
would benefit them as well as the Jews. He was of the
opinion that the dialectics of the Talmud are the best
means for developing the mind of the youth at colleges
and universities, who might greatly profit by supple-
menting their studies in classics and mathematics by

courses in Talmud. A better acquaintance with the Talmud by the educated Gentile world would at the same time remove many prejudices against the Jew and his post-biblical literature, which are mostly to be ascribed to the false notion the world has of the Talmud.

Salanter's plan was to petition the authorities of institutions for higher learning in Germany to introduce the Talmud into their regular courses of study. As he did not master the German language, he looked for a man whom he could entrust with the preparation of such a petition that would necessarily have to contain a clear and precise description of the Talmud and its educational potentialities. It seems that Salanter met with some opposition among the Rabbis, who looked with disfavor upon any attempt at secularizing the Talmud[10].

During his long stay in Germany, he became acquainted not only with the spiritual leaders of the Orthodox but also with the many lay members of this party whom he tried to interest in his educational schemes for the Lithuanian Jews. He finally, in 1878, succeeded in finding a wealthy man in Berlin[11] who set aside a considerable sum of money for the purpose of establishing in Kovno a great Yeshibah for the training of Rabbis, known as the Central Body of the *Perushim*, כולל הפרושים. Perushim were young married men who had left home and family—*Perushim* means those who separated themselves—to devote themselves to study. This idea was quite an original cre-

ation of Salanter as all the other Yeshibot up to that
time were mainly frequented by young unmarried men.

As the bachelor Rabbi is entirely unknown in
Eastern Europe, and maturity is almost a prerequisite
of the spiritual leader, it often happened that men who
spent their entire youth and a part of their manhood
in preparation for the ministry were forced to look for
other vocations to enable them to support their wives
and children. It could not but result in the increase of
an intellectual proletariat—the training of a rabbi
does not tend to produce a successful business man—
and the gradual elimination of the poorer classes from
the Rabbinate, as only the sons or sons-in-law of the
wealthy could afford the long preparation. To remedy
these evils Salanter established the new educational
institute which enabled the poor Talmudist to continue his studies after graduating from the Yeshibah
by providing him and his family with the necessary
means.

The sum donated by the Berlin Maecenas for the
maintenance of the Institute, though very considerable, was not sufficient to assure its permanency, and
Salanter, though burdened by old age and many ail-
ments, took upon himself the heavy task of gaining the
support of larger classes for his scheme. He addressed
a stirring appeal to the Jewish communities of Russia,
which was not in vain[12]. The *Kolel* (Central Institute)
thus firmly established by him, not only continued to
exist for a long time after his death up to the recent
war, but even gained in importance very considerably.
For a number of years it was the most important

center of the higher Jewish learning in Lithuania. The Kolel bore through all the years of its existence the stamp of Salanter by being the only institution of its kind where the study of Musar formed a part of the curriculum.

At the same time while working feverishly at this scheme, Salanter found time and strength to go to Paris to organize there a Russian-Polish community. The conditions in the French metropolis were not dissimilar to those in Koenigsberg and Memel. The lack of organization among the Jews of Eastern Europe who had settled in Paris was greater and in some ways more deplorable than that which Salanter found among his countrymen living in the two cities of Eastern Prussia. The religious life of the French Jews had already at that time reached such a low state that not much good would have been achieved by amalgamating the newcomers with the native Jews even if it had been possible.

After spending almost two years in Paris he succeeded in bringing some order into the chaotic condition of the Eastern Jews. He returned in 1882 to Germany and there took up his residence in Koenigsberg to continue the work that he had interrupted for several years. This however was not granted to him. He died there on the second of February 1883 at the age of seventy-three and a half.

II

In order properly to estimate the essence of the moralist movement inaugurated by Salanter, it is necessary not only to understand his character and personality but also to become acquainted with the cultural and religious life of the Lithuanian Jews, among whom this movement first arose and developed. The Jewish people, as one of the oldest of the cultural races of the world, place a very high estimate upon intellectualism—indeed sometimes too high an estimate. The older and the more deeply rooted the culture of a nation, the more strongly it is impressed with the truth that "knowledge is power," not only material but also spiritual power. This intellectualism so highly praised by the Jewish people naturally varies with age and country. For Maimonides and his followers in Spain and Provence Judaism consisted essentially of philosophical intellectualism culminating in love of God and love of man. However radically different the Polish-Lithuanian Jew of the eighteenth and nineteenth centuries may be in his entire *Weltanschauung* from the Spanish Jew of the thirteenth century schooled in a scholastic Aristotelianism, both have this belief in common—that it is knowledge that makes a man a man, and a Jew a Jew. The only difference is that the Polish-Lithuanian Jew puts talmudic dialectic, in which he is unsurpassed, in place of Aristotelian philosophy. The rise of the Kabbalah in Provence in the thirteenth century was a reaction against Jewish Aristotelianism of the Middle Ages and similarly the rise of Hasidism in the middle of the eighteenth century was an attempt to aid the emotions in regaining their legitimate place in the spiritual life of the Jew. In Lithuania, the classical land of talmudic learning, the emotional doctrine of Hasidism never secured a firm foothold. The form that Hasidism took in certain parts of Lithuania, the so-called *Habad*, is more intellectual than emotional. To attribute the failure of the Hasidic movement in that country to the violent opposition of the Gaon Rabbi Elijah, the greatest intellectual-religious genius among the Lithuanian Jews, is to take a part for the whole. His opposition did but express the attitude, the natural bent, and the acquired traits of the Lithuanian Jew who seeks first of all to satisfy his intellect. Reaction against the too great preponderance of intellectualism could, however, not fail to make its appearance even in Lithuania. About one hundred years after the rise of Hasidism in the Carpathian Mountains among uncultured and ignorant villagers, we find a parallel phenomenon among the sharp-witted Talmudists of Lithuania. Rabbi Israel Baal Shem Tob, the founder of Hasidism, was a person of "emotion and feeling" and rejected intellectualism instinctively without having intimate knowledge thereof. On the other hand, R. Israel Salanter, the father of the moralist movement, was himself one of the greatest Talmudists of his time and, therefore, although his great heart was not able to be satisfied with a one-sidedness of logic and reason, he nevertheless could not fall into the other extreme of regarding religion as a matter of feeling exclusively.

The keystone of Salanter's teaching is best given in his own words: man is created to labor and to carry on the war of the Lord—the development of the divine in man—and accordingly it is his duty to take great pains in the service of God. It is not sufficient to follow one's good impulses and to do only that which according to one's nature is not very difficult. Such a one does not serve God, he might even be described as one who "casts off the yoke of God," since he permits nature to take its course and does not work in the service of the Lord. The essence of this service consists in man's moral-religious effort to do things which his natural inclinations oppose, and to refrain from others to which he is prompted by them. The development of the moral-religious personality is therefore only possible by the education of self or, to use the favorite phrase of Salanter and other Jewish moralists, by Musar, i. e. self-discipline. One might as well, says Salanter, attempt to see without eyes or hear without ears as to expect moral development without self-education; moral intelligence is the result of education and is not acquired at will.

Man does no wrong wilfully, says Socrates, and similar is the saying of the Rabbis: man does not commit sin unless the spirit of folly has entered into him[13]. The aim of education in general as of self-education in particular is therefore, according to Salanter, to give the reason full power over one's actions, for he who does not act as he thinks, thinks incompletely. To think rightly and completely means of course for Salanter and those to whom he addressed himself to square one's actions with one's belief in God and His revealed will, the Torah. How then, he asked himself, does it happen that people of great intellectual power who are past masters in human wisdom and in the knowledge of Torah do not understand and are, from a moral-religious point of view, idiots or weak-minded? What should the self-education of a man be that would give him the necessary intelligence which makes "the truly wise man," who "sees the consequence of his action?" Salanter's answer to these perplexing questions is that only thought transmuted into emotion has effect on our life or, in his own words: our impulses are swiftly running currents which drown our intelligence if the latter is not carried over them in the boat of emotion and enthusiasm. The purely intellectual idea has no motive power, which can be acquired only by the addition of an emotional and passionate element. Though rational life is moral, life as a whole is non-moral because the emotions are not working. It is therefore not enough for us to form correct opinions; we must pass from mere comprehension to profound conviction; and this requires feeling; we must be carried away. We remain cold even in intense intellectual work. "A passion yields only to a passion," and hence in order that our correct ideas may culminate in correct action, in other words that we may not be carried away by impulses but act in accordance with reason, the mental representation of our action must kindle a desire.

We shall now be able to understand the great importance which the dogma of Reward and Punishment plays in the teaching of Salanter. The precise and detailed definition of this dogma, he remarks, is of no great consequence, what matters is that we firmly

believe that there exists after this world a condition of
happiness or unhappiness for every individual. The
bliss of the righteous surpasses any pleasure conceivable to human imagination. On the other hand, the
suffering of the wicked is such that compared with it
the greatest earthly pain might be described as
pleasure. Faith in the existence of God, Salanter
maintains, is of small value in true religion as long as
it is not supplemented by the belief in a just God who
rewards good deeds and punishes evil ones. It is faith
in this sense to which the Rabbis refer in their often-
quoted saying[14]: The 613 commandments of the
Torah were reduced by the prophet Habakkuk to one,
viz.: "The righteous liveth by his faith."

We would do great injustice to Salanter if we maintained that self-interest was for him the only motive
power of religion and morality. If there be any need to
disprove such a faulty conception, it suffices to quote
his words in the last essay published by him; he writes,
"The road that leads to eternal bliss is to follow the
path of the Torah and fulfil all its commandments for
the sake of the Lord. The true service of God is that
which is free from the motive of receiving rewards;
a person who behaves in this way may be truly described as "serving God," while he who does what is
pleasing to God with the view of receiving reward, may
really be described as "serving himself[15]." As a practical moralist, however, Salanter could not dispense
with the dogma of Reward and Punishment. He was
firmly convinced that there is but one way to correct
a vice, namely to recognize the dangers it entails,

and there is but one way of acquiring a virtue, and
that is, to see clearly the advantages it brings.
Hence he taught that the first step in self-education is
the acquisition of the fear of the Lord or, as the Rabbis
say, "the fear of sin." By frequent pondering and long
meditation upon the consequences of our actions for
which we shall be held accountable by a just God, the
idea of Reward and Punishment becomes vividly
impressed upon our mind.   Only when the idea is
transmuted into feeling does it become a motive power
for our actions. These meditations must therefore be
of a nature to stir our hearts and act on our emotions.
Salanter accordingly attributed great importance to
the mode of studying Musar which, to be effective,
must be different from merely intellectual studies. In
the Musar Stuebel, by oneself or together with others,
preferably at twilight when the falling darkness creates
a melancholy atmosphere, one can surrender oneself
entirely to one's emotions, one can weep and recite in a
loud voice those soul-stirring words of the Prophets,
Psalmists and later moralists on the vanity of human
life, or give oneself over to reflect in silence upon death,
which will bring one before the Heavenly Judge to give
an account of one's life.

The sharpening of one's sense of responsibility by
the means described is, however, only the first step
leading to Musar, self-discipline. When a person is
thoroughly permeated with the thought of responsibility in the hereafter for his actions in this world,
he has acquired the means necessary for the *Kebishat*

Yezer ha-Ra, the suppression of the evil inclination. There are, says Salanter, three stages of the worship of the Holy One, blessed be He. The first is to arouse one's sense of imperfection, the fear that one may not be perfect in the sight of his heavenly Father. By frequent meditation and soulful study of the sayings of our wise men and the dicta of our moralists, this sense is created and then one is in a position to conquer his *Yezer*, which finally leads to "the changing of the Yezer." The Yezer ha-Ra and its opposite, the *Yezer Tob*, are defined by him as follows: The evil Yezer is of a two-fold nature—it is (1) the sensual desire in man that often makes him mistake momentary pleasure for the true happiness which he craves, so that he does not act in accordance with the moral-religious principles which he has established in his mind, but succumbs to the pressure of his impulses of passion. The frequent yielding to his sensual desires finally produces in man (2) an impure spirit or, to use modern parlance, the decay of his spiritual energy, with the result that he becomes a slave to his evil habits, committing at the slightest incentive the most depraved actions. Similarly the good Yezer is of a two-fold nature—it is (1) moral-religious clearsightedness unimpaired by passion and evil habits which commands man to struggle against the temptation of passion and sensual desires and to be guided in his actions not by the immediate pleasures which they produce but by their remote consequences. By continually increasing his fund of moral views and strengthening his power of true reason the (2) spirit of purity or, as we might say, automatism of morality is given to him, so that without struggle and combat he always wills the good and the right.

The suppression of the Yezer consists first in the incessant discipline of one's will-power, in order to strengthen and steel it so that it gains perfect control over his passions and no evil temptations have sway over him. Meditation and continuous practice in self-control are the only means of achieving victory. More difficult, and to some extent more important, is introspection and self-analysis. The suppression of the Yezer is not possible without improving "the qualities of our souls" and, as no two men are alike either in temperament or in character, every one must study himself very carefully. Every one, Salanter says, is a world in himself, the knowledge of which is the very first prerequisite for his dealings with the "outer world."

The recognition of one's errors and deficiencies is thus the beginning of salvation, as without it no moral improvement is possible. One must learn to recognize with absolute sincerity the secret springs of his acts. Sincerity is especially important in self-criticism because our judgment of good and evil is not an act of pure reason but is greatly influenced by emotion and sentiment. Accordingly without deep sincerity we should find little to criticise in ourselves; our self-love would blind our judgment. We often, remarked Salanter, meet with people who are extremely conceited and vain, though we fail to detect the slightest reason for their good opinion of themselves. The true reason is that self-love often excites in man so strong a feeling of self-importance that he is unaware of his shortcomings and deficiencies, while those of his neighbor are seen clearly by him. Salanter even goes a step further and maintains that absolute truth can be attained only in the field of material facts directly provable or in the domain of science demonstrable by the methods of logic, while in our moral judgment there is always an element of feeling. In self-criticism our main effort must be directed toward eliminating or at least reducing to a minimum this element of self-love and turning our scrutiny upon ourselves in the same way that we would exercise our criticism upon others.

Our critical abilities should be directed toward our own actions not toward the actions of our fellow-men. We all have an amazingly critical keenness when it is a case of picking to pieces, not our own conduct, but that of our neighbor. We should search again and again the depths of ourselves in the midst of our restless life; we must criticise and correct our actions without pity. We must not allow ourselves to rest on the laurels that we award to ourselves or that others too easily bestow upon us, but should utilize the time rather in self-criticism.

As we devote ourselves to the cultivation of our intellectual powers, so we must pay heed to the development of our moral potentialities. Salanter established the rule among his disciples that each should associate himself intimately with one of his fellows for the purpose of observing and being observed and exchanging friendly cautions and admonitions.

In this way all would attain to the self-knowledge that corrects conduct.

The discovery of our faults will not discourage us if we look to the future instead of to the past. Repentance was indeed a doctrine upon which he laid great stress, yet for him as for nearly all Jewish theologians and moralists, repentance is not remorse for the past but a serious attempt to profit in the future by the lessons of the past. When he spoke to the people he was in the habit of making them recite with religious fervor the verse from Lamentations, "Turn Thou us unto Thee, O Lord, and we shall be turned." "Return to God" is the Jewish conception of repentance, and while Salanter was hammering into the minds of the people the great need of self-criticism, that they might be able to change their lives and return to God, he was no less indefatigable in preaching courage. No ailment of the soul, he says, is worse than discouragement; man must again and again renew the idea of courage in his mind. He must not become discouraged if he fails to observe any improvement in his moral qualities after long labor of self-discipline. He should know that his work was not in vain but has left its beneficial effects which, though invisible at the moment, will become visible in time. Drops of water continually falling upon a rock will finally wear it away though the first drops seem to produce no effect at all. It is the same with self-discipline; its effects cannot fail to penetrate our hearts if we practise it continually.

Another form of discouragement against which Salanter warns us is that which has its source in the exaggerated importance attached to the influence of heredity; he writes: "One should not say what the Lord made cannot be changed; He planted in me an evil nature, how can I hope ever to unmake it?" It is not so; man is not only master over the qualities of the soul with which he is born but he is also able to change them.

We all know how great the power of man over animals has been; he has succeeded in imposing his will upon them so that not only originally wild and ferocious animals have lost their ferocity but many species have also been tamed and their natures changed. The same applies to man; he not only can suppress his passions and impulses but he can also change his nature from evil to good by constant study and practice. One must remember further that in the worst of men there is something good and the best are not without a touch of depravity. Hence self-education is the main factor in our development.

Salanter in almost every address was in the habit of quoting the verse from Proverbs: "If thou seekest (wisdom) as silver and searchest for her as for hidden treasures...." The burden of all his exhortations was that the moral life of man is like the flight of a bird in the air; he is sustained only by effort and when he ceases to exert himself he falls.

Moral effort or, to use his own term, the suppression of the evil Yezer, important as it may be, is, however, only the prelude to *Tikkun ha-Middot*, the improvement of character, by which he meant the reduction of virtue to a second nature. Moral effort is the negative part of

self-education, which must finally lead to the positive,
viz. the entire change of our impulses and inclinations,
our passions and desires. We draw nearer to the ideal
by always thinking of it, by examining everything in
its light. The continuous effort, however, is fatiguing,
and therefore when swept by great passions, we are
unable to withstand them though we thought we had
gained control over our will. Accordingly our only
safeguard lies in moral knowledge which must be
sufficiently clear to lay hold on us and carry us away;
this knowledge must become a passion with us so that
we act automatically under its imperious injunction.
Impressions upon our emotions such as may be produced by the realization of retribution after death,
though they may tend to weaken certain passions
and impulses, are not able to change them. Their
change can be accomplished only by means of knowledge. We must make ourselves the object of contemplation and, dissecting the stirrings of our hearts, seek
to comprehend their complicated machinery. Then
and then only will virtue become instinctive in us, so
that even our unconscious actions will be directed by
it. We must not forget that it is our less conscious
thoughts and our less conscious actions which mainly
mould our lives.

There are two forms, says Salanter, of intellectual
knowledge. The child, for instance, who has just
learned his alphabet has great difficulty in combining
the letters though he knows well their individual
sounds. After exercising for some time he is able to
read fluently without being in the least conscious of

the single letters and their functions. The same holds good in moral knowledge. For a time we must practise increasing the power of our will over our passions until we become so accustomed to virtue that we perform it unconsciously without being aware of any effort. This will happen when our moral ideals become sentiments by reason of being impressed upon our understanding. The truth of this view Salanter attempted to prove in quite a homely way. He writes: "In our country—Lithuania—the average Jew has trained himself in the observance of the dietary laws to such an extent that without any effort he not only abstains from the use of prohibited food but even abhors it. On the other hand, dishonesty in commercial relations is a frequent occurrence. Many do not trouble themselves to find out whether their dealings with their fellow men are always honest, and not a few will even attempt to cover their dishonest actions when they are found out. Now when we ask, how does it happen that the ceremonial law is automatically observed at great sacrifice of comfort and money, while the ethical is often disregarded—a sin which according to the Rabbis neither the Day of Atonement nor death can atone[16]—we can give only this answer: The long training of the Jew, theoretically and practically, in the observance of the dietary laws has had the result that in following his own nature he feels an abhorrence for everything ritually unclean, while the ethical teachings of the Torah theoretically never formed such an important part of the body of Jewish studies as the dietary laws, and practically did not offer themselves

as an exercise in virtue but as something convenient
and useful. This, however, is greatly to be regretted;
the ethical teachings of the Torah are a most important part thereof, and in practical life we must train
ourselves so that we may no longer obey the dicta of
morality reluctantly as a severe rule, but that we may
follow them with the natural bent of our desires."

Great care, however, must be taken that the automatism of virtue is not turned to that obnoxious form of
stoicism which makes man indifferent to the desires
and needs of his fellow man. Equanimity and calm-
ness of temper and mind, says Salanter, is a great
virtue; we must never allow ourselves to be ruffled
even when the greatest misfortunes befall us. "Trust
in God," the religious term for this virtue, is, however,
an abominable sin if applied to shift from us our
obligations towards our fellow men; one must not
trust in God at the expense of those who seek our help.
Humility is not only a virtue but a demand of common
sense, as it is absurd to be proud of a superiority that
we owe to the chance of birth or the munificence of
Providence; and as to vanity, Salanter could only see
in it the most grotesque trait of character. Yet he
admonishes us to be very careful of the susceptibilities
of others and never fail to pay them our respects in the
forms established by society. Withdrawing ourselves
from social life is very commendable if it affects only
ourselves, but it is the foremost duty of man "to go
among the people" and associate closely with them
for the benefit and the good of our fellow men. Consequently the positive part of self-education consists not

only in acquiring virtue as an instinct, but also in studying to comprehend and understand the desires and impulses of men, so that we may be able to feel their sufferings and wants. The task of combining these two opposites is hard but not impossible.

In spite of Salanter's originality, he has not given us a new system of ethics. He lacked philosophic training and systematic ability. His importance consists mainly in this that he emphasized and sought to put into their proper light certain aspects of Judaism which previously had been heeded but little or not at all.

The keynote of his teaching is that the aim and task of the Jew is to strive to secure the ethically ideal condition of man and of the world, no matter how far off and perhaps unreachable it may be. Judaism is for him no theoretical system, teaching speculative truths or scientific knowledge concerning a certain province of thought, but it is a doctrine intended to lead man to his moral ennoblement by prescribed ways and means. So far as the moral life is concerned the concrete plays a preponderating and decisive part. On the other hand it cannot dispense with speculative or, let us rather say, religious truths. In fact, it requires some religious truths as a support and a guarantee for the binding force of the moral law. Other religious truths, again, strengthen the will, or are of spiritual value in moral development, because they fuse together practice and theory into a harmonious unity. If morality is to be not merely a theory but a real factor in the life of man, he must so train his thoughts and feelings that his moral consciousness becomes too strong to allow him to act otherwise than morally. The religious truths which are indispensable to the ethical education of man and without which he cannot develop morally, are: Belief in God, Revelation, and Reward and Punishment.

We have seen above what important rôle the doctrine of Reward and Punishment plays in his teachings, and we may add here that Revelation or, to use the rabbinical term, the Torah is of still greater consequence. In his public addresses, Salanter hardly ever touched on any other subject than ethics and the study of the Torah. The latter is to be considered from two different angles. First, as the revealed will of God, it is the only safe guide for our religious and moral life. Hence the duty incumbent upon every one, not only on the professional scholar, to occupy himself with the study of the Torah that his conduct may always be in accordance with the divine Will. The study of the Jewish civil code however, to take one instance, is a religious work not only because it enables the student to know what is right and what is wrong in a given case, but also because it refines and deepens one's conscience. Consequently, strange as it may sound, it is from the point of view of religion more important for the business man than for the Rabbi— the judge—to be thoroughly acquainted with the civil code. The former is often tempted to dishonesty, and by continuous study of the commercial law of the Torah he will be in a better position to withstand his temptations, of which the Rabbi is innocent. Besides the practical parts of the Torah, the study of any portion thereof is a remedy against the Yezer. "The spirit emanating from the Torah makes spiritual him who occupies himself with it."

It would be underrating the importance of Salanter to measure him only by the standard of his theories on ethics. Of him, as in general of all Jewish moralists, it may be said that the practical produced the theoretical, and not vice versa. The ethical system of the Greeks developed at a time when rapidly growing skepticism threatened to destroy the basis of morality and in part did actually destroy it. The ethical systems framed in those days were the dikes erected by speculative minds to hold in check the devastating flood of immorality. Compare this phenomenon with the long and eventful history of the Jews, and it will become evident that with them there was nothing certain and absolute except God, the source of moral truth. When all things round about tottered and reeled, there always remained one fixed immovable point, that God is good, holy and just, and that it is the duty of man to walk in His ways, the ways of holiness, justice and love. The Jewish moralists, therefore, considered it their chief task not to elaborate new doctrines and speculative truths, but to impress the old lessons with ever greater emphasis upon the consciousness of the people. Their aim was to find means of augmenting the effectiveness of the old truths. And as they always proceeded from the principle that the most successful pedagogic method is teaching by example, they tried to illustrate in their

own conduct the truths they wished to inculcate. The
Jewish moralists, so far from setting up ideal teachings
for the sake of setting them up, demonstrated con-
cretely how the ideal can be made real in the daily
walks of life.

III

It has been well said that a man of rare moral
depth, warmth or delicacy may be a more important
element in the advance of civilization than the newest
and truest idea derived from the fundamental principles of the science of morals. The leading of souls to
do what is right and humane is always more urgent
than mere instruction of the intelligence as to the exact
meaning of right and humanity. If therefore the saint
has his place in history, Salanter is one of the outstanding figures in Jewish history of recent times. What
most appeals to our imagination and sympathy in history is heroism, and saintliness is only another word
for heroism in the domain of ethics and religion. The
heroism of the saint is well described by the famous
French critic, Sainte Beuve, as an inner state which
above all is one of love and humility, of infinite confidence in God, and of strictness toward one's self
accompanied with tenderness for others. Saintliness is
however at the same time preeminently subjective,
mainly on account of the great diversity of the means
which help to produce the state common to all saints.
The glimpses we gain of the life of a saint are therefore
of incalculable value to us for the understanding of the
religious milieu that produced him. Salanter, for

instance, was the product of rigorous Talmudism, and
hence to become better acquainted with his heroic life
is tantamount to coming nearer to a true understanding of talmudic Judaism.   Purity, asceticism and
charity are the characteristic practical consequences of
the inner conditions of all saintly souls; the forms,
however, in which these virtues express themselves
vary essentially, and the variation is a safe indication
of the culture amidst which the saint arose.

Boundless reverence for the weak and the suffering,
the helpless and the needy, best describe the particular
form that Salanter's love for his fellow man took. The
Lord "dwells with him that is of a contrite and humble
spirit," hence Salanter felt himself in the presence of
the divine whenever he saw suffering and pain that
produce a meek and contrite spirit.   His religious
enthusiasm, that is his love of God, instead of quench-
ing his love of man, ennobled and transformed it. Too
numerous are the stories told about Salanter's kindness and goodness to be given here; a very few characteristics of the saint, may however, be mentioned.

During his sojourn in Kovno it happened on the eve
of Yom Kippur, when the Synagogue was filled with
devout worshippers awaiting in solemn awe and
silence the Kol Nidre service, that suddenly ominous
murmurs and whispers arose on all sides. Salanter,
wonderful to relate, had not yet arrived. The assembly waited half-an-hour and an hour, and still no
trace of the Rabbi. Messengers were sent hither and
thither to search for him. All returned from their
errand unsuccessful. After long waiting and watching,

it was resolved to begin the prayers without Salanter,
a course calculated to increase the excitement. All
sorts of probable and improbable rumors were circu-
lated about the sudden disappearance of the beloved
leader. When the congregation was on the point of
dispersing, Salanter appeared in the Synagogue. The
joy was great, and equally great was the amazement of
the good people when they learned the reason of his
absence. On his way to the Synagogue, Salanter told
them, he heard a little child cry bitterly. He drew
near to investigate why it was whimpering and found
that the baby's mother, in order to be at the Synagogue
in good time on this holiest of occasions, had put it to
bed earlier than her wont. The child had soon awakened from sleep at an unaccustomed hour and was
crying for its mother. As none of the women in the
neighborhood signified her willingness to forego at-
tendance at divine services upon the Holy Kol Nidre
night, he resolved to stay beside the baby's cradle
until its mother returned. To appreciate this act of
Salanter, it must be remembered what the service at
the Synagogue on the eve of the Day of Atonement
meant to a man like him who was in the habit of
withdrawing from the world for forty days preceeding
Yom Kippur, and spending his time in prayer and
devotion.

His great compassion and pity for the poor and
helpless often was the cause of clashes between him
and the official heads of the communities where he
lived as a private man. He had settled in Kovno
shortly after the cholera had wrought great havoc

among the Jewish population of that city, especially among the poor classes. The hospitals were overfilled with sufferers, so that quite a number were not properly cared for. Salanter insisted that the great Synagogue of the community be temporarily used as a hospital and poor-house. Needless to say that his plan found ill favor in the eyes of many who looked upon it as an attempt at desecrating the house of God. Possibly they were right, as there was hardly any need of such an extreme step to be taken. Salanter, however, in face of suffering and distress could not see their point of view. Courteous and gentle as he otherwise was, he lost his temper on this occasion. Interrupting the address he was delivering in the Synagogue, he pointed his finger in righteous anger at the president of the Congregation, a man distinguished for learning and piety alike, and cried out: "You will have to answer to the Lord for the suffering of the poor. God much rather prefers His House to be used as a sleeping place by "Motel the carpenter"—a very disreputable person but a homeless beggar—than as a place of worship by you." Not long after this incident, Salanter betook himself to the home of the man he had offended, to ask his forgiveness, but he never changed his mind with regard to the justification of his plan to turn the Synagogue into a poor-house[17].

A year before this he had gotten himself into the bad graces of the spiritual leaders of Wilna. In the year of the frightful cholera epidemic Salanter, after having taken counsel with a number of physicians, became convinced that in the interest of the health of the community it would be necessary to dispense with fasting on the Day of Atonement. Many a Rabbi in this large community was inclined to agree with his view, but none of them could gather courage enough to announce the dispensation publicly. During the several years of his stay in Wilna he lived strictly the life of a private man, and in his humility would not decide a question of ritual, not even if it occurred in his own house, but would refer it to one of the local Rabbis. When he saw, however, that none of them would act in this case, he thought self-assertion to be his highest duty. He affixed announcements in all Synagogues, advising the people not to fast on the coming Day of Atonement. Knowing, however, how reluctant they would be to follow his written advice he, on the morning of the Day of Atonement at one of the most solemn moments of the service, ascended the reader's desk. After addressing a few sentences to the Congregation in which he commanded them to follow his example, he produced some cake and wine, pronounced the blessing over them, ate and drank. One can hardly imagine what moral courage and religious enthusiasm this action of his required from a man like Salanter to whom obedience to the Torah was the highest duty. He found strength for his heroic action only in the thought that what he did was for the benefit of others. Many years later he used to dwell on this episode and thank with great joy his Creator for having found him worthy to be the instrument of saving many lives. He was convinced that many a person weakened by fasting would have

fallen a victim to the frightful disease, and that
therefore in making people eat on the great Fast he
saved many lives. Others, however, did not share his
conviction of the necessity of dispensing with the fast
and he was severely censured by them, not only for
what he did, but also for having assumed the authority
belonging to the official leaders of the community. It
is not unlikely that the unpleasantness created by this
incident was one of the reasons for Salanter's leaving
Wilna for good.[18]

Poor as he was all his life, he had little of worldly
goods or, to be accurate, nothing to give others, but he
did give them more than this—he gave himself, heart
and soul, to those whom he knew to be suffering. The
poor and the needy could always count upon his
readiness to assist them. No time of the day, no
season of the year, no cold winter night, and no
scorching summer day could prevent him from walking
for hours from house to house to solicit help for those
in need. Once a poor scholar confided to him that if he
were able to preach he might succeed in maintaining
himself and his family by taking up the profession of
an itinerant preacher, but as the theory as well as the
practice of preaching were quite unknown to him, he
must forever give up the hope of gaining a livelihood
in this way. Salanter, however, did not despair; he
composed a number of sermons, and after spending
several weeks in teaching the poor scholar how to
deliver them, he dismissed him well prepared for his
new calling.

As in the environment of a saint there are often

found many who are the very reverse of saints,
Salanter's kindness and sympathy were not rarely
misused. Sometimes undeserving people would succeed in obtaining from him letters of recommendation,
but he would never revoke them, even if informed by
reliable persons of the deception practised on him. He
used to say that a letter of this sort becomes the
rightful property of the person to whom it is given
and it would be plain robbery to revoke it.

The fear of being the cause, even in the remotest
manner, of injury to the poor, was always present before his eyes. Once when, in obedience to the rabbinical ordinance, he was washing his hands before sitting
down to a meal, his disciples noticed that he was
exercising great care not to use a drop of water more
than the minimum required by the law. In amazement
they exclaimed: "Rabbi, does not the Talmud say
that he who lets water flow abundantly over his
hands will be rewarded with wealth in equal abun-
dance?"[19] "True, but I do not want to enrich myself
at the expense of the labor of the water carrier,"
replied Salanter. He did not for a moment question
the binding character of the rabbinical ordinance
concerning the washing of hands before meals, but
that did not prevent him from remembering and acting in accordance with his great moral principle.

At another time while walking in the outskirts of the
city, he noticed the cow of a Jewish farmer straying
away and trying to enter a neighboring garden belonging to a Gentile. Knowing the ill-feeling of the Gentile
farmers towards their Jewish neighbors in that part of

the country, he had no doubt that if the animal should be caught it would be killed or at best kept for a high ransom. He therefore attempted to lead the cow back to the Jewish farmer, but inexperienced as he was in work of this kind, he miserably failed in driving the animal back. Yet he did not give up the fight, and for several hours he held on to the cow, and in this way prevented her from entering the dangerous zone until he was released from his task by people coming along the road. To have permitted the cow to run its own way, he thought, would have been negligence in his duty towards the poor farmer.

No less cautious was he in avoiding offense to the sensibilities of the poor. He was passionately fond of snuff, but he denied himself the pleasure of taking it at sessions of the Charity Board, when the poor appeared to present their cases. He shrank from taking out his silver snuff box in their presence, lest its splendor cause them to feel their poverty more keenly[20].

The ascetic impulse is a general phenomenon in saintliness, and the Jewish saint does not form an exception to the general rule. Yet there can be no doubt as to the correctness of the view that Judaism is not an ascetic religion. That the highest development of a non-ascetic religion should culminate in ascetic saintliness will appear to many as an inexplicable riddle. If, however, we examine more carefully the form of Jewish asceticism, we shall find the answer to this puzzling question. A religion that sanctifies even the so-called animal appetites and desires of man,

elevating them into worship and religious exalta-
tion, and instead of despairing of the flesh, highly
recommends the satisfaction and joy of the body,—
such a religion could never produce the excesses of
asceticism found among other religions to whom the
body and the material world are the seat of evil. With
very few exceptions, which were of a pathological
nature, we hardly ever find among the Jewish saints
ascetic mortification or immolation, and even asceticism as sacrifice to God is very rare among them.
Jewish asceticism takes almost always the form which
a famous psychologist describes as the fruit of the love
of purity that is shocked by whatever savors of the
sensual.

The life of Salanter offers many instances of this
special kind of asceticism. Of fasting and vigils he did
not have a high opinion; indeed, he often used to
admonish his disciples to eat and sleep as much as
they needed. There was little need to preach temper-
ance and sobriety to the Lithuanian Jew, distinguished
for extraordinary frugality. Far more stringent was
the watch he kept over the things which proceeded
from the mouth. He would at times refrain for days
and weeks from talking. Idle talk, indulgence in what
is ordinarily called conversation, was abhorrent to
him, and he employed it only as a means to brighten
up people in depressed spirits. The silence he cultivated had its motive neither in the desire for self-
mortification nor in that of expiation, but was the
direct outcome of his highly developed sense of the
purity of life. To his soul whatever was unspiritual

was repugnant, and any inconsistency or discord between the ideal and the real was exceedingly painful to him. The average conversation, even of the educated, with its plenitude of insincerity and multitude of pretentions, shocked his spiritual sensibility to such an extent that he preferred silence to speech.

There was also always present with him the fear of being admired by others for qualities of heart and soul above what he merited. This fear was so strong with him that he was once found weeping after delivering a brilliant discussion on a talmudic subject; he was afraid that the display of his brilliancy would make people exaggerate his intellect; and what could there be worse than deception? His scrupulousness as to veracity and sincerity knew no bounds. The first essay published by him contains the note that it was put into literary form by somebody other than the author himself, who is rather a poor stylist. He was once asked, how is one to explain the great success of "the liberals" in their fights with "the true believers," since according to a saying of the Sages, "Truth lasts, untruth perishes." The answer he gave was: "Sincerity makes an untruth seem to be a truth, while insincerity makes a truth seem to be an untruth; the liberals succeed because they are sincere; their opponents fail because they are not always sincere."

Salanter lived all his life in dire poverty, as a matter of choice, as there were many who would have considered it a privilege to provide him with comfort. He never accepted the position of Rabbi and only for a short time did he occupy a public office, that of the head of a talmudic school. He was firmly convinced that he could do his work best by being entirely independent of the public, and after a great inner struggle he decided to accept the offer of one of his disciples to support him entirely. This disciple was the only one from whom he accepted assistance, but only as much as was absolutely necessary to keep body and soul together. When Salanter's wife died he found a small sum of money among her effects which she had saved from the weekly allowance granted to her and her family by their benefactor. The money was distributed by Salanter among the poor. He argued, "The money granted to me by my disciple was for my needs, but not to enrich myself; hence I have no right to it nor have my children, the heirs of my wife, and as the original owner refuses to accept it, the poor have the next claim to it."

Though an indefatigable student all his life and in great need of books, he never possessed a single volume. When he died, his room contained, beside a threadbare suit of clothes, nothing else than his *Tallit* and *Tefillin*. It would be a great mistake, however, to believe that Salanter, like the ascetics of other religions, idealized poverty as the loftiest individual state and sang its praises. One of his disciples, trying to persuade him to accept from a rich admirer a new Tallit, said to him, "You are certainly in need of one and the decorum of the services requires that the Tallit be not threadbare. I too hope to buy one as soon as I have the money." And the master's answer was, "I also will buy one as soon as I shall have the money."

Judaism teaches that wealth is a blessing, as it gives time for ideal ends and affords exercise to ideal energies. Jewish saints, therefore, never denounced the possession of earthly goods, provided man does not turn the blessing into a curse by his greed and passion for money. The saint, however, knew also the high moral value of poverty: liberation from material possessions, freedom of soul, and manly indifference. Salanter's craving for moral consistency and purity was developed to such a degree that he could neither occupy a public office in the community nor accept comfort and luxuries from the hand of others. He for a time thought of becoming an artisan that he might be able to support himself by "the labor of his hands," but when he saw the impossibility of such a plan, he gladly submitted to a life of want and hardship.

"Love your enemies" is not a Jewish precept, and one may doubt whether there are any examples of compliance with it. The nearest approach to it is that magnanimity which "repays evil with good," and the life of Salanter is full of acts of this kind. "Imitation of God," he used to say, "is explicitly commanded in the Torah, and accordingly it is our duty not only to confer an act of kindness upon those who have done harm to us, but to do it at the very moment we are wronged. God is kind to the sinner at the time of his sin and rebellion, since without the kindness of God that gives him life and strength he would not be able to sin, and we are to imitate Him so as to be like Him. We must be kind to those who sin against us, at the time of their wrongdoing." He took scrupulous care all his life to act in accordance with this rule. No sooner did he hear of an injury done to him than he hastened to find out whether he could not confer some kindness upon the person who injured him. The continuous practice of this kind of magnanimity, he taught further, develops tolerance and indulgence towards all men.

In one of his letters to his disciples, Salanter expresses the hope that the spark coming from his soul might kindle a holy fire in their hearts. His hope was not in vain. His was one of those conductive natures who, as was well said by a famous author, are effective because the effluence of their power and feeling stirs the hearer or onlooker to a sympathetic thrill. A Jewish saying, "Words that come from the heart enter into the heart," expresses the same thought. Few people who came in personal contact with him could withstand his charm and his power. His influence over the masses as a preacher was unique in the annals of Eastern Jewry. The inner fire of his spirit shot out its lightning flashes, dazzling the inward eye with the clearness of the truth he revealed to the consciences of his hearers. He brought the people no new doctrines to arrest their thought; he was a flame enkindling the smouldering faith of his hearers; for a while he would lift them up into the clear atmosphere of heaven where their souls stood revealed to themselves and their hearts were aglow with unwonted desire of the higher life. He saw truth so clearly that he was able to make others see it.

Salanter's power was, however, in himself not in his words, and we would do injustice to the man if we judged him by his few literary remains. Yet even they reveal not only an intellect of originality but also a soul of rare purity and great nobility, a worthy link in the long chain of Saints in Israel.

VIII

ZECHARIAH FRANKEL

The opening of a new century has given occasion to numerous attempts to designate some decisive characteristic as descriptive of the period just closed. Thus the nineteenth century has been variously styled the era of the steam engine, of electricity, the age of individualism, of criticism, of democracy; but seeing the diversity of standpoints from which the development of mankind can be considered, any uniform opinion as to what has been the nineteenth century's distinctive characteristic is hardly to be expected. A railroad magnate and a professor of philosophy, for instance, would hardly agree; the latter would look upon this city's elevated railroad as an ingenious device to spoil the pleasure and comfort of one's daily walk, while the former would consider all the time and work expended upon the clearing up of obscure passages in the Dialogues of Plato as bootless waste of energy. When, however, we come to the consideration of the question from a Jewish standpoint, the task becomes somewhat easier. If we ask ourselves what was the most striking gift of the nineteenth century to Jews and Judaism, there is only one answer that can be given: "the science (*Wissenschaft*) of Judaism," or, to use the popular though less accurate term, "Jewish science."

Emancipation, Reform and Zionism are phenomena which strike deep into Jewish life both spiritual and material, but they are all phenomena which rest upon the same Jewish science. The claims of the latter to be the most important Jewish event of the past century are supported by the fact that it is a genuinely Jewish creation. And, indeed, although Jewish science received strong impulses from without, its origin lay entirely within the fold.

It is an error to maintain, as is frequently asserted, that Jewish science began with Zunz, and that the German "critical school" was an indispensable forerunner of it. More than a generation before the birth of Zunz, whose great merit in the field of Jewish learning I would be the last to deny, there lived in Lithuania a certain Elijah of Wilna,[1] commonly called the Gaon, who indeed deserves in full the title of "founder of Jewish science." His son Abraham,[2] Manasseh ben Porat,[3] Wolf Einhorn,[4] David Luria[5] and others, represent this Lithuanian school of the Gaon which was indubitably free from all extraneous influence, while his point of view, persisting in Krochmal and Rapoport, assumed modern forms. It is only when thinking of these last named, who consciously adopted modern methods, that we may call Jewish science a creation of the nineteenth century.

Undoubtedly this fact that Jewish science is thoroughly Jewish in its origin must be the reason why the Jewish public knows, or cares to know, so little about it. The genealogy of a baptized Jew may count upon numerous readers in a Jewish paper as soon as he has attained prominence and fame in some department of human activity. Nay, even the Jewish pulpit will sing

the praise of a Jewish thinker whose hatred for his
people is exceeded only by his contempt for Judaism.
The esteem in which such a one is held in the Christian
world suffices to stamp him almost as a Jewish saint;
while really Jewish thinkers or men who have devoted
the whole of their lives to Judaism, men whose gifts
and abilities would have brought them eminence and
admiration in any other branch of human knowledge,
are passed over by this same good Jewish public as
worthy of no attention whatever.

I therefore esteem it a privilege to be allowed to
sketch before you the life and activity of a Jewish
spiritual hero, a man who was a Jew not alone by
descent and faith, but who lived and labored for his
people and religion. To-day is the one-hundredth anniversary of the birthday of Zachariah Frankel, and I
propose to devote a few moments to the memory of
this great scholar, this deeply religious thinker, the
zealous and tireless worker for the cause of Judaism
and the Jew. It is not, of course, to be expected that
I should occupy your time with a detailed biography.[6]
Nor is it possible to comprise in one address a complete
resumé of the many-sided importance of such a man.
I shall content myself with speaking of Frankel as a
theologian, as the father of the "positive historical
school," and as the historian of the Talmud or, to be
accurate, of the Halakah.

Frankel, the scion of a Prague family distinguished
for learning, wealth and standing, was born on *Simhat
Torah*, in the Jewish year 5562, that is, September
30, 1801.

He received his secular and rabbinical training in his native city, and for a short time studied classical philology and mathematics at the University of Pesth, where in 1831 he was graduated as doctor of philosophy. A year later he was appointed by the Government as District Rabbi of the District of Leitmeritz, and at the same time he was elected Rabbi of Teplitz, the leading congregation of the district. At his instigation, or at least with his approval, the congregation of Teplitz introduced a number of innovations in the service of the Synagogue which, though far from being radical, were looked upon by many as deviations from strict orthodoxy. He distinguished himself by being the first rabbi in Bohemia to introduce German sermons into the Synagogue. In 1836 he became Chief Rabbi of Saxony and of its capital, Dresden, where he remained eighteen years.

While we cannot speak here of Frankel's activity as Rabbi, we cannot omit to mention the considerable share he took in the emancipation of the Jews of Saxony. Not alone did he obtain for them the privilege of public observance of their religion, the erection of a synagogue and school, which had been hitherto forbidden, but he distinguished himself by his zealous activity in securing the abolition of the humiliating Jew-oath, to which his treatise, *Die Eidesleistung der Juden*, 1840, contributed not a little. Prince John of Saxony entered the parliament with the work in his hand, and the result of the legislative debate was the abolition of this outrage.

Frankel's success as rabbi was the more remarkable, as by nature he was not a fiery orator, possessed no imposing personality, but appeared as a genuine type of the close student—the bookworm, endowed rather with the qualifications necessary to make him a scholar among scholars than a leader of the masses. This knowledge of his own weakness proved also his strength in that he refused the call to Berlin as Chief Rabbi in 1843, while in 1854 he accepted with gratification the presidency of the Rabbinical Seminary in Breslau, then just established. He occupied the chair of Talmud and Codes at the Seminary and yet found time not only to edit the *Monatsschrift* which he had founded in 1852, but also to contribute largely to it. Increasing years induced him, in 1869, to transfer the editorship of his magazine to Professor Graetz; but he remained actively at the head of the Seminary until his death, on February 13, 1875.

Let us now pass to a consideration of Frankel's theological standpoint. Although in his communication to the *Hamburg Tempel Verein* he assumed a standpoint which must undoubtedly be styled new, inasmuch as it ran counter to both strict orthodoxy and reform, his actual leadership of a new and living school in Judaism must be considered to have begun upon his departure from the celebrated Frankfort Rabbinical Conference. We are yet too close to that period to give an unbiased judgment concerning that Conference; I, for my part, care not to be designated as a heretic by the one side or as a fanatic by the other. Let us merely examine how far Frankel was justified in warning the reformers of his day that they lacked all scientific principle, lacked all the necessary earnestness, and were wanting in spirituality and perception of the true demands of the times. That these accusations were totally groundless, no one will assert to-day. As for Frankel's first reproach, that of lack of all guiding principle, it must be remembered that when in the course of the debate he insisted again and again upon some consistent statement of principles which reform was to follow, he was interrupted by cries that in principles his fellow delegates were unanimous. How ill-founded such a statement was will become evident to us when we remember that in that conference the abolition of Sabbath and Holy Days found champions while, at the same time, discussion waxed warm as to the propriety of supplying the ritual bath with "drawn water."

The truth is that even the two most prominent spiritual leaders of the conference, Geiger and Holdheim, were not agreed upon principles. The latter, in his conception of Judaism, was a Polish Pilpulist in modern garb; the former was a historian from the critical school of the German universities. Holdheim desired the reform of biblical Judaism, which naturally would lead to almost complete negation, seeing that one portion thereof is now no longer specifically Jewish and another not Jewish at all. Geiger, on the other hand, wished to reform rabbinical Judaism; as a historian he recognized that Rabbinism is itself reform. He desired to retain the spirit while changing the external form. *"Ex lege discere quod nesciebat lex,"* was the formula used eighteen centuries earlier by a great reformer to state his doctrine of a Torahless Judaism.

These facts about the Frankfort Conference may serve not alone to justify Frankel's charge of a lack of principle in Reform, but also to explain how it came about that he took part in this convention, whose spiritual leaders were Geiger and Holdheim. The very want of unanimity and clarity of purpose in the camp of Reform must have confirmed Frankel in his expectation that if Reformers would only come together for an illuminating public discussion of principles, the conservative elements would attain supremacy, even if only because the majority of the Reformers at that date had neither the courage nor the steadfastness of conviction to break definitely with Rabbinism and traditional Judaism. Some such intention in Frankel was evidently divined by the leaders of radical Reform, who opposed with all their might the discussion of any question of principle in the conference, and inasmuch as the guidance of the deliberations rested in their hands, they were successful in their opposition.

But Frankel held a trump card in his hand which he very cleverly played, and instead of simply staying away from the conference, which thus determinedly excluded questions of principle, he awaited a fitting and striking opportunity clearly to present his divergent standpoint before the conference, and so bring it to the attention of that large Jewish audience in Germany which was following the deliberations of the Frankfort Conference with the closest attention. His success was attested by the many enthusiastic addresses he received afterward both from extreme Orthodoxy as represented by Rabbi Solomon Trier, and from the party of moderate progress.

These congratulations were evidence of the gradual growth of a new party of which he was the acknowledged leader, showing that he could have selected no better moment for his public utterance than that in which all eyes were riveted upon Frankfort. It was here that he first gave expression to the designation "positive-historic" Judaism as his religious standpoint, an expression which, for half a century, remained the shibboleth of the party founded by him.

As to what is to be understood by this term or, in other words, what was Frankel's conception of Judaism, it is remarkable to note how little clearness there exists concerning it. His opponents on both sides sought to represent him as a man of compromise, as one who would theoretically permit no barriers against critical investigation but in practice would make the authority of tradition paramount. But this conception explains nothing and raises the question, how Frankel came to assume such an unnatural as well as unscientific position. Psychologically, of course, the case is possible that one in whom religious sentiment and critical acumen struggled for the mastery might see himself forced arbitrarily to draw the line between theory and practice and in this way maintain a certain inward equilibrium. But such a psychological explanation would hardly apply to the case of Frankel, who was a fairly consistent personality. Nor can a creative mind produce a "creatio ex nihilo," and only when the conditions are present can a great mind fashion the material at hand.

This "positive-historic" school has demonstrated its strength and viability in the last fifty years especially by its building up "Jewish science," and no one would care to seek the origin of all it has produced in the psychology of one man. The best and only correct answer to the question, "What is positive-historic Judaism?" was given by Frankel himself—"Judaism is the religion of the Jews." The best illustration of his conception of Judaism is precisely the instance which induced Frankel to leave the Frankfort Conference, on which occasion he, for the first time, made use of the expression "positive-historic" Judaism. The matter in hand was a discussion of the question whether and to what extent the Hebrew language should be retained in the Synagogue; and whent he majority decided that Hebrew must be kept there only out of consideration for the feelings of the old generation, Frankel took his departure. It may at first seem somewhat strange that he calmly sat through all the radical discussions concerning Sabbath and marriage laws, while he perceived danger to the Jewish religion in such a matter as the abolition of the Hebrew language. Indeed, the very lively debate which followed Frankel's address concerning the great importance of the Hebrew language for synagogue worship serves to show how few of those present understood him. Of his opponents only Geiger hit the nail on the head with his remark that language was a national thing, and as such only should it be allowed

importance. The underlying principle at stake is this:
does the essence of Judaism lie exclusively in the
Jewish religion, that is, in ethical monotheism, or is
Judaism the historical product of the Jewish mind and
spirit? The Hebrew language is of course not a
religious factor, and even from the strictest standpoint
of the *Shulhan Aruk*, it would be difficult to adduce
any fundamental objection to the use of any other
language in prayer. Still it is true that in the long
development of the synagogue service the Hebrew
tongue became that which the sensuous cult of classic
nations or of Catholic Christianity was to those
religions, or church music to Protestantism, an instrument conducive to lofty impressiveness and edifi-
cation. The recollection that it was the Hebrew
language in which the Revelation was given, in which
the Prophets expressed their high ideals, in which
generations of our fathers breathed forth their sufferings and joys, makes this language a holy one for us,
the tones of which re-echo in our hearts and awaken
lofty sentiments. In a word, Hebrew is the language
of the Jewish spirit, and in so far an essential component of our devotional sentiment. It is true that
pictorial representations working upon the eye, or
musical sounds, may move our sentiment and attune
us devotionally; but this is true of mankind in general
and not only specifically of the Jews. The *Jewish*
divine service must therefore specifically influence
Jewish minds, hence Frankel considered the Hebrew
language as the sole instrument which can give it this
Jewish tinge. In this sense Geiger was consistent in

opposing its use as the expression of Jewish nationalism and in opposing Frankel.

The same conception of Judaism underlay Frankel's attitude toward the Law, and it is not correct, as is sometimes said, that he allowed his critical spirit free rein until he came to some point of importance for theology and then refused to allow criticism to carry him further. I do not propose now to examine Frankel's position regarding biblical criticism, and am willing to grant the statement (repeatedly made) that he considered the Bible as a *"noli me tangere"* to be correct. It must, however, be remarked that Frankel never deduced the authority of the Law from the plenary inspiration of the Bible as the word of God, and the foremost representative of the positive-historic school next to Frankel was a man who, upon this point, may fairly be styled almost radical. Neither for Frankel nor for Graetz was Law identical with Bible; but in the course of time, whether for weal or for woe, in the development of Jewish history, the former became the specifically Jewish expression of religiousness. The dietary laws are not incumbent upon us because they conduce to moderation, nor the family laws because they further chastity and purity of morals. The law as a whole is not the means to an end, but the end in itself; the Law is active religiousness, and in active religion must lie what is specifically Jewish. All men need tangible expression to grasp the highest ideas and to keep them clearly before them, to say nothing of the ordinary masses for whom abstract ideas are merely empty words. Our need of sensuous expressions and practical ceremonies brings with it the necessity for the material incorporation of religious conceptions, and various peoples have given them varying forms. The Law is the form in which the Jewish spirit satisfies this need. In the precepts, which are the dramatic representations of the inward feelings, Judaism found a material expression of its religious ideas; through them its abstractions became realities and in them the essential needs themselves, reverence and recognition of the divine will, were expressed. Every form became thus spiritualized and living, bearing within itself a lofty conception.

We may now understand the apparent contradiction between the theory and practice of the positive-historic school. One may, for instance, conceive of the origin and idea of Sabbath rest as the professor of Protestant theology at a German university would conceive it, and yet minutely observe the smallest detail of the Sabbath observances known to strict Orthodoxy. For an adherent of this school the sanctity of the Sabbath reposes not upon the fact that it was proclaimed on Sinai, but on the fact that the Sabbath idea found for thousands of years its expression in Jewish souls. It is the task of the historian to examine into the beginnings and developments of the numerous customs and observances of the Jews; practical Judaism on the other hand is not concerned with origins, but regards the institutions as they have come to be. If we are convinced that Judaism is a religion of deed, expressing itself in observances which are designed to achieve the moral elevation of man and give reality to his religious spirit, we have a principle in obedience to which reforms in Judaism are possible. From this point of view the evaluation of a law is independent of its origin, and thus the line of demarkation between biblical and rabbinical law almost disappears. Characteristic of Frankel's attitude toward this problem is the statement given by him in his *Darke ha-Mishnah* concerning *Sinaitic Traditions*, which caused a great deal of controversy.

In the first section of the Darke ha-Mishnah Frankel makes the assertion that the frequently recurring talmudic expression, *Halakah le-Mosheh mi-Sinai*, "a tradition of Moses from Sinai," properly designates those ordinances whose reason and origin were unknown and which, being of remotest antiquity, were looked upon as if they had actually originated on Sinai. Strict Orthodoxy, of course, perceived in this statement a declaration of war against traditional Judaism inasmuch as it denied Sinaitic authority for the "Oral Law." Men like Samson R. Hirsch and Benjamin Auerbach in Germany, Wolf Klein in France, Gottlieb Fischer in Hungary—to mention only a few—attacked Frankel vigorously, accusing him of undermining traditional Judaism.[7] But there were not lacking, on the other side, defenders like Raphael Kirchheim, Saul Kaempf, and to some extent also Solomon L. Rapoport[8]. Curiously enough Frankel took no further notice of these attacks other than to publish an explanation (*Erklärung*) in the *Monatsschrift*, in which, however, the same unclearness of thought and indefiniteness of expression concerning

the term "Sinaitic Tradition" prevail as in the Darke
ha-Mishnah. This was the very cornerstone of offense,
and both sides desired a clear statement on the
point. To give our opinion today upon this controversy, we can only say that both Frankel and his
orthodox opponents were equally right, each from his
own particular standpoint. The Mishnah as well as the
Talmud do employ the expression quoted to designate
the laws whose origin is acknowledged to be of later
date; but it is no less true that they hold that many
Halakot were imparted orally upon Sinai in addition
to the Written Law. Even if we knew nothing of such
Halakot, the expression "Sinaitic Tradition" used in
old sources to describe laws whose origin was no longer
known, would imply that there were traditions which
were revealed to Moses on Sinai, otherwise this term
would never have been used. Strict orthodoxy, therefore, was correct when its champions insisted upon the
recognition of this theory.   But it is clear also that
Frankel, for whom, as we have seen, the authority of
the Bible depended essentially upon the fact that its
doctrine had penetrated into the mind and sentiment
of the Jewish people, could not make the authority of
tradition dependent upon the adoption of such a theory of "Sinaitic Halakot."   What distinguishes these
Halakot from others is their origin in high antiquity,
during the formative period of Jewish history.   Just as
the character of an individual man is in its essence
formed before he attains manhood, though the circumstances of his life modify it, giving prominence to some
points and leaving others undeveloped, so in those

early centuries were formed that set of ideas and type of mind which took shape in these provisions.

"The Law" is essential to the Jewish religion, but not the laws; though, of course, seeing that the former presumes the latter, if Reform is to be a forward development of Judaism a norm must be maintained, lest Judaism suffer like the bundle of arrows in the fable, and each individual arrow being broken, the whole bundle will be shattered. This norm, according to Frankel, was the talmudic position that whatever observance is spread through the whole community must not be abrogated by any authority. Frankel, according to his conception of Judaism, could not well arrive at any other conclusion. That which the whole community has adopted and recognized may not be repealed; to do so would be to dissolve Judaism, which is nothing else than the sum of the sentiments and views which dominate Jewish consciousness. In reply to the question as to who must be taken as the representatives of Jewish consciousness, Frankel could only make the reply that only those who saw in Judaism a very definite form of expressing religious thought and feeling, only those who recognized the Law as specifically Jewish, could have the right to decide what portions of it had incorporated themselves into the national consciousness.

Theoretically Frankel's definition of Judaism gives up a large field to Reform; practically, however, Frankel did not follow up the consequences of his doctrine. This must be partially ascribed to the fact that in the proceedings of the radical Reformers he recognized only a species of religious indifferentism totally repugnant to him, and was therefore inclined to side with Orthodoxy, though he differed from it in very essential doctrines. Take, for instance, his belief in the Messiah, which was far from Orthodox as can be seen by his letter to the *Hamburg Tempel Verein*. In view of the present Zionistic movement, it will be of interest to recall the following utterance. "The desire that in a certain corner of the globe—naturally, of course, in the land of our ancestors, so full of the holiest recollections—our nationality should again appear and that we should enjoy the respect which sad experience teaches us falls to the lot only of those who possess worldly might, contains in itself nothing wrong; we evidence thereby only that in spite of centuries of suffering and misfortune, we do not despair of ourselves and cherish the idea of a self-dependent and a self-reliant reanimation." The warmth with which Frankel in this letter posits the firm belief in the restoration of the Jewish nation, and his sharp and bitter criticism of the attenuation and the spiritless superficiality which avoided any expression of national character, shows clearly that Frankel realized that Judaism possessed a far broader basis than that of a mere religious community. These words contain a germ of the purely national conception of Judaism which finds expression in many a Zionist tendency of to-day. For Frankel, it is true, nationalism does not belong to the essence of Judaism, but it is nevertheless necessary for its existence. Breath is not a part of man, it comes to man from without, yet no one can live without breathing. So nationalism is the very air in which Judaism breathes.

The view that only that is Jewish which lives in the consciousness of the Jewish people inclined Frankel, it is true, towards conservatism; but it likewise stimulated him most powerfully to creative thought. His indisputable scientific importance lies undoubtedly in the fact that he is the historian of the Halakah; his efforts in this department constitute a scientific analysis of the national consciousness as expressed in the Halakah, the national mode of life. His researches demonstrated how the individual details of the Halakah came into being and how from small beginnings they poured themselves into that stormy ocean, the "sea of the Talmud." To the landsman the ocean seems one huge immeasurable flood, obeying a single law of ebb and flow and offering a uniform force. Yet in truth we know that the movement of the ocean is the result of many forces; the seeming uniformity covers the energy of a hundred currents and counter-currents. The sea is not one mass but many masses moving along definite lines of their own. It is the same with the "sea of the Talmud." The uniform character of the Talmud exists only for those who merely survey its surface, but not for those who understand how to penetrate its depths. Frankel therefore endeavored to discriminate between those tendencies of the Halakah which were always current, and those which were dictated by the newly-arising needs of the day. The difficulties of his task and the measure of success he attained can only be given in outline; details would require many lectures. The only source of Halakah, that is, of religious practice and its theoretical foundations as it developed in the period between the return from the Babylonian exile and the sixth century of the Christian era, is the talmudical literature. But the Talmud is like the Jew whose spirit it represents. Just as it is extremely difficult to-day to indicate in any individual Jew what about him is strictly Jewish, what he owes to foreign influence, and what is the result of a combination of both these elements, so is it also with the Talmud. The larger portion of this work in its present shape is the product of the fifth century; a small but most important portion of it dates from about the beginning of the third century—the Mishnah and other tannaite collections. Its various component parts, however, have been welded together and can be resolved into their origins only by the exercise of a sharply discriminating analysis.

An important problem is the relation of the Babylonian Talmud to the Palestinian; in spite of their common origin, they are widely divergent. In short, the history of the development of the Halakah must occupy itself with such problems as the following: The oldest traditions of the Halakah must be discovered in the literature as we have it; the codified Halakah of the Tannaim must be examined in its progressive stages; the treatment and tradition of this tannaite Halakah at the hands of the Amoraim must be examined.

Frankel was not only one of the first to point the

way that the critics of the Halakah must go, but himself traversed a goodly portion of the route, especially in the following works: *Ueber den Einfluss der Palaestinensischen Exegese auf die Alexandrinische Hermeneutik* (1851), and *Ueber Palaestinensische und Alexandrinische Schriftforschung* (1854), in both of which he endeavors to trace the old Halakah in the Greek translation of the Bible. Important as both these works are for the understanding and proper valuation of the Septuagint, their chief importance for Frankel and, indeed, for Jewish science, lies in the detection of the oldest components of the Halakah contained therein. He shows how the translators of the Bible into Greek as early as the third century before the common era were influenced in their understanding of the Bible by the traditions of the Halakah. The elucidation of the second of the above mentioned problems is the aim of Frankel's chief work, the *Darke ha-Mishnah* (1859).

This is Frankel's most important work; in five sections it treats of (1) the origin and development of the Oral Law in the time of the Scribes, from the return from Babylon to the Maccabees; (2) an account of all the Tannaim mentioned in the Mishnah and of their chief legal and ethical doctrines; (3) the relation of Rabbi Judah's Mishnah to the preceding halakic collections that formed its basis; (4) a concise but quite new presentation of the methodology of the Mishnah; (5) a short conspectus of all other tannaitic works, such as the Tosefta, the Mekilta, etc., as well as of the old commentaries of the Mishnah. Of these sections of unequal length and of unequal importance, the second is undoubtedly the most valuable even to-day, and in research concerning the mishnaic doctors, one invariably falls back upon Frankel's clear, comprehensive and judicious work, a testimony of his erudition and his fairness alike.

Frankel's other great work was the *Mebo ha-Yerushalmi* (1870). This work consists like the preceding one of five sections of unequal length and unequal importance. It treats of (1) the politico-economic conditions of the Palestinian Jews at the time of the Amoraim, the authors of the Palestinian Talmud; (2) the linguistic peculiarities of Palestinian Aramaic and the style of the Palestinian Talmud; (3) the method of the Yerushalmi and its relation to the Babli; (4) an alphabetical index of all the Amoraim mentioned in this Talmud with short bi-ographic-chronological notes; and (5) the commentators and editions of the Yerushalmi. The remaining essential of a history of the Halakah, as stated before, concerns the treatment of tannaite doctrine by the Amoraim, or the relation of the Palestinian Talmud to the Babylonian. In the *Mebo* Frankel discusses this brilliantly. He attempts to show that the Mishnah existed in Palestine even in late days in varying versions, some of which received general recognition, and a selection from them was made in Tiberias. This Mishnah of Tiberias with a few changes and emendations became the standard text in the Babylonian Academies. He showed also that the other tannaitic collections commonly designated as *Baraitas* existed in different editions in Palestine and Babylon. Such facts naturally entailed different treatment in the two Talmuds, the characteristics of which Frankel clearly and exhaustively describes.

To indicate Frankel's position among the fathers of Jewish science, we might say that he is the historian of the halakic literature. Judaism was for him a historic process and not merely a theological doctrine. His scholastic interest centered in the Halakah, which reflects the process. His strength however was not in following up the individual phases and the inward development of the Halakah but in the fact that, with extraordinary acumen and a very happy gift of combination, he recognized the result of the various tendencies of the Halakah just as soon as they evidenced themselves in literary form.

A correct objective estimate of Frankel's importance for the history of the Halakah may best be attained by comparing him with Geiger. The latter, a historian pure and simple of Jewish theology, evidences a finer understanding as a critic of the Halakah than Frankel as far as the principles of its development are concerned, but is extremely unfortunate as a historian of the halakic literature and as interpreter of halakic texts. Frankel's true superiority over Geiger—and indeed one might say over almost every other Jewish scholar of modern times in Western Europe—consists in the fact that he united in himself old-Jewish learning and modern critical schooling, so that it is difficult to say whether he was more an old time Lamdan or a modern scholar.

The other founders of Jewish science were either
Talmudists who had acquired modern education of
themselves—Krochmal, Rapoport and others—or modern savants who chose Jewish science as their special
study like Zunz, Jost and Geiger. Frankel was the
exception; from his earliest youth he harmonized
within himself the *Yeshibah bahur* and the university
student, and to this rare combination he owes his
proud position among the founders of Jewish science.
The historian of a certain period or of a tendency of
thought must bring himself into deep and close connection with his material; he must, on the one side,
be so much at home in his sources as to feel their
continued connections with history and, on the other
side, if his opinions are to be objective, he must
consider the problems before him historically—that is,
as separate and apart. The modern scholar who
attempts to examine Judaism and its literature usually
lacks either this intimate acquaintance with the
historical material or a full consciousness of the
thoughts to be presented; while the Talmudist pure
and simple is still too much preoccupied and influenced
by that on which he is to give an opinion. Frankel's
merit was that he did not skim the surface of the "sea
of the Talmud," but plunged into its depths and
never permitted himself to be swayed hither and
thither by its deep currents. The whole future of
Jewish science depends upon whether we shall number
among ourselves many more men who, like Frankel,
shall combine harmoniously the old and the new.

IX

ISAAC HIRSCH WEISS

Highly significant of the vagueness and confusion of ideas that prevail in certain circles is the fact that the apostles of "universal Judaism" are at the same time the spokesmen and exponents of the doctrine of "provincial Judaism." Old Judaism is too narrow and limited, its chains must be snapped! This is proclaimed to all who will hearken, and in the very next sentence the Jews are exhorted to Americanize, to Germanize Judaism, so that nothing Jewish remains. Hence Judaism embraces all mankind but the Jew.

As is the case with most shibboleths, an element of truth underlies the expression "provincial Judaism." Judaism in ancient times and during a large part of the Middle Ages had spiritual centers, which kept the spiritual unity of Judaism intact, despite the fact that the Jews for more than two thousand years lived scattered in all parts of the globe. These centers changed from time to time. The first was the temple, then came the patriarchate, then the academies in Palestine and Babylonia. Consequently neither Hellenism nor later the Roman civilization caused any essential differentiations in Judaism. Here and there, it is true, we hear a good deal about the contrast between "Hellenistic Jews" and "Palestinian Jews," but this is because we know very little about the former, and as a result one can ascribe everything to them. It may be stated, however, in this connection, that the most important creation of Jewish Hellenism, the translation of the Bible into Greek, points toward the endeavor rather to Judaize Hellenism than to Hellenize Judaism. We have a Greek Bible, but have we a Hebrew Plato? It was not until the end of the tenth century when, on the one hand, the academies of Babylonia had begun to lose their importance and, on the other hand, freshly pulsating life stirred in the Jews of Italy, Spain, France and South-western Germany, that the hitherto unimpaired spiritual unity of Judaism vanished forever. Not that it was the endeavor of Judaism from now on to lose itself in the civilization surging about it. On the contrary, Judaism has always come out of its contact with a different civilization strengthened, spiritually enriched, deepened and developed. From this point of view the term "geographical Judaism" is a justified expression for an influence which since the tenth century has been, and to this day continues to be, an important factor in the history of the Jew. Rashi and Maimonides, who are among the greatest men of mediaeval Judaism, are typical products each of the country in which he lived. The systematizing genius of Maimonides could have developed as little in Champagne as could the naturalness and depth of Rashi, unclouded by philosophic speculation, have been fostered under the high culture of the Arabs. Each, however, found complete satisfaction in Judaism, not in an Arabic or a French Judaism, but in Judaism *par excellence*.

The dispersion of the Jews to all quarters of the globe was beneficial, then, in this respect, that Judaism in its totality could not be too strongly influenced by any one civilization. The philosophic tendency of Spanish Judaism stood at the opposite pole from the tendency of Franco-German Judaism, and they met in Provence, with the result that neither of the two attained predominance. In recent times a similar phenomenon is to be observed. The three great masters of the science of Judaism—Krochmal, Zunz and Rapoport—may not be considered apart from their environment. No one but the foster-child of a German university could do what Zunz did—bring order into the chaos in which he found the history of Jewish literature. And it was Krochmal, the Hasid, who from his early youth had made himself familiar with the metaphysical speculations of the Kabbalah in its hasidistic form, who explained the deep philosophy of Judaism on the basis of its historic development. Moreover, the Polish Pilpul in the unsurpassed acuteness of its dialectics was the most favorable soil for producing a critic like Rapoport, whom modern science had only one thing to teach—how to make use of the weapons he had at hand.

A man who could avail himself of the critical skill of a Rapoport, the philosophy of a Krochmal and the clearness of a Zunz could arise only in a country in which talmudic learning and modern culture existed alongside of each other. This was nowhere possible except in that part of Austria in which Germanism had made fair progress without at the same time destroying old rabbinical Judaism. These conditions existed in Bohemia and Moravia in the first half of the nineteenth century, as similar conditions had existed in Provence in the thirteenth century. Although inhabited for the most part by Slavs, Bohemia and Moravia were the field for the Germanizing experiments of Emperor Joseph II. The persons used by the Emperor for this purpose were in the main such poor specimens of humanity that Germanism as a contrast to Judaism won few respecters or admirers, but in its practical aspect it was more successful. The acquisition of the German language laid the foundation for modern culture.

The life of Isaac Hirsch Weiss reflects the Jewish history of his native land, Moravia. Only Moravia could produce the historian of Jewish Tradition. Germany had no men who possessed the requisite talmudic-rabbinic knowledge, and the Poles, as a result of their one-sided talmudic education, lacked system and clearness. The life history of this great scholar assumes even greater importance if one recalls that it is the history of a man who has lived ninety years. He is not only the greatest Jew of Moravia, but the last representative of "geographical Judaism." The conflict between German and Slav in his province, it is true, was never so strong as it is now. Nevertheless, that which is specifically Moravian-Jewish disappeared, and at best nowadays one finds only here and there someone who knows how to tell Jewish stories and pass them off upon the credulous as history.

Isaac Hirsch Weiss[1] was born at Gross-Meseritsch, Moravia, on Shebat 29, 5575, that is, February 9, 1815. According to the custom of the land, he received his early education in the Heder. But at that time the Heder in Moravia had already been somewhat modernized, for instruction was not confined to the Talmud but was given in Hebrew grammar as well, which is still regarded as a forbidden branch of learning in various parts of Russia and Poland. The text-book used was Ben-Zeëb's *Talmud Leshon 'Ibri*. For a century this Hebrew grammar was the one that was liked best, while its author was in certain circles among the most hated of men. The judgment that Weiss pronounced upon the Heder is worthy of mention here. Naturally, he was not blind to certain of its defects, but he admitted that piety, firm belief, love of Judaism and the teachings of Judaism are to be found more frequently among the old *Melamdim* than among modern religious instructors, and that the Melamdim are better entitled to be called "religious instructors," since their life, in furnishing the best example of true religion, exercised a much greater influence upon their pupils than religious instruction imparted according to all the rules of pedagogy, but lacking religious seriousness.

Weiss did not remain in the Heder a long time. His parents sent him, when scarcely thirteen years old, to the Yeshibah in Trebitsch, the leader of which was then Rabbi Hayyim Joseph Pollak. Pollak was a prominent Talmudist who, at the same time, was very well versed in the mediaeval philosophic literature of the Jews, which circumstance made him an almost unique personality in his day.[2] To his philosophic and modern culture was due the fact that he went his own way in interpreting the Talmud. Instead of the hair-splitting dialectics cultivated in the Yeshibot under the name Pilpul, Pollak in his lectures upon the Talmud adopted the philologico-critical method later carried to brilliant perfection by his pupil Weiss.

But Weiss early in life seems to have been seized by a love of change. After he had devoted himself to study for two years under the guidance of Pollak, he went to Eisenstadt in Hungary, where he entered the large Yeshibah conducted by Rabbi Moses Perls. There was great similarity in more than one respect between the two teachers of Weiss. Like Pollak, Perls was an opponent of the Pilpul, and his interpretation of the Talmud was logical and critical. Although he had no modern learning at all, he was no enemy or scorner of it, as were most of the Hungarian rabbis of his time. On the contrary, he regarded scientific knowledge as extremely useful to a Jewish scholar. It was a favorite saying of his that secular knowledge bears the same relation to the Torah as zero bears to one. Knowledge without the Torah is zero, and the Torah without knowledge is one; the two together are as one placed before zero, or ten.

The Yeshibah in Eisenstadt, however, was fundamentally different from that in Trebitsch; in fact, religious conditions on the whole were essentially different in Hungary and Moravia. The Teutonizing policy of the Emperor Joseph II had attained its end

in Moravia, at least so far as the Jews were concerned.
As early as the beginning of the second third of the
nineteenth century the larger number of Moravian
Jews spoke and wrote German. But a knowledge of
German was identical with the possession of modern
culture; for in his zeal for knowledge a Bahur of the
Yeshibah was not satisfied with the mere ability to
read German; he strove also to acquaint himself with
German literature and philosophy. Conditions in
Hungary were different. The reform movement in
various German lands provoked a reaction which made
itself felt most keenly in Hungary. The radical reformers, striving to "de-Judaize" Judaism, brought it
about that in many orthodox circles every innovation
however innocent, every concession to modern conditions however insignificant, was absolutely and un-
qualifiedly rejected. In earlier times it had not
occurred to anyone to identify secular culture with
irreligion. Even at the end of the eighteenth century a
man like the Gaon, R. Elijah Wilna, maintained that
"the Jewish scholar must be master of all the seven
branches of knowledge."[3] Now there were people who
damned a man simply if he did not devote all his time
and ability to the Talmud.

Accordingly, when Weiss came to Eisenstadt he was
not a little surprised to find that among the Hungarian
Bahurim there was not even one who possessed any
Jewish knowledge beyond a knowledge of the Talmud,
and who certainly, then, had no secular culture. But
what was worse than their ignorance was their in-

tolerance. If a colleague dared to think differently from them, they sought to persecute him.

As a consequence Weiss did not remain long in Hungary. At the end of two years he went to Nikolsburg, Moravia, where R. Nahum Trebitsch had founded a large Yeshibah. Although he was back on native soil, Weiss was not wholly satisfied with the change, because the methods of his new teacher did not altogether suit him. On the other hand, he was very much pleased that he was now in a position to devote himself to secular knowledge along with his rabbinical studies. Since he was one of the best Bahurim, it was very easy for him to exchange lessons with a Bahur who did not do well in his talmudic studies, but had a modern education. Weiss taught the Bahur Talmud and rabbinics, for which the latter instructed Weiss two hours every evening in non-Jewish branches of learning. The progress made by Weiss in his secular studies was rapid, so that he returned to Eisenstadt in 1834 in order to undergo the entrance examination to the university. However, he gave up this idea and returned to his father's house in order to continue his rabbinical studies.

Although the scion of a family of rabbis and educated as such, Weiss appears never to have seriously entertained the idea of becoming a rabbi. After his marriage with the daughter of Baer Oppenheim, rabbi at Eibenschitz, he lived for several years in his native city, Gross-Meseritsch, and devoted himself entirely to the study of the talmudic-rabbinic literature. For a couple of years he was also the leader there of a small but not unimportant Yeshibah. At the same time he was active in a literary way, although after the old style, writing *novellae* to the Talmud and to the Shulhan Aruk. These studies brought him into relations with the leaders of Talmudism, with whom he carried on a correspondence, and Responsa to Weiss occur in the Responsa collections of Rabbi Joseph Saul Nathanson, rabbi at Lemberg, and of Rabbi Hirsch Chajes, rabbi of Kalisz.[4]

To this period of his life belong his first attempts in the field of Hebrew Literature. Though they in no way bear marks or give signs of the future investigator of Jewish Tradition, yet they are highly significant of the beginnings of the science of Judaism. Enthusiasm for the Hebrew language, which originated in the newly-awakened esthetic feelings, was a necessary preliminary condition to the existence of a historico-critical perception. Rapoport and Krochmal were the disciples of the *Measfim*, and like the Measfim their first achievements were in the field of Hebrew poetry and language. Similarly, the first literary attempt of Weiss was a Hebrew poem, which appeared in 1846 under the title "Poetry by Ignatz Weiss in Gross-Meseritsch," in the Hebrew journal *Kokebe Yizhak*. His first scientific essay appeared the following year in the same journal in the form of a biography of Abba Arika, which followed the plan and method of the similar master creations of Rapoport, but fell far below the level of its models. Nevertheless, it gave proof of the thorough talmudic learning and critical skill of its author.

These were the years of stress and storm, during which the former Bahur developed into a great critic and historian. An epigram of Weiss published in 1852 in the above-mentioned journal shows that he not only had internal conflicts to encounter, but external reverses to endure as well. The heading of the epigram is taken from Ecclesiastes 9, 11: "Bread is not to the wise," and the epigram itself reads: "On the ladder of thought thou seekest to climb to heaven; and below, on earth, no one concerns himself about thee. Rather remain on earth, obey the foolish demands of life; then thou wilt find many friends, and thou wilt not want for bread."

Through some friends to whom Weiss had entrusted his entire fortune he lost it completely, and was wholly without means. This was the occasion that led Weiss in 1859 to go to Vienna, where he hoped to find some suitable work more easily than in a smaller city. And he did not have to wait long. In the second year of his stay he was appointed Hebrew proof-reader in the printing establishment of Zamarski & Dittmarsch. His connection with a publishing house caused the appearance of his compendium of legal decisions, rules and customs of the entire Jewish ritual, which was printed in 1861 in Vienna under the title *Orah la-Zaddik*, together with the prayer-book of Rabbi Jacob Lissa. The book was very successful. But later, when its author emerged from the chrysalis state and appeared in his character as a critic of the Talmud, it occurred to a certain fanatic to buy the plates of the book and destroy them.

A year later the first important scientific work of Weiss appeared, his edition of the *Sifra* or *Torat Kohanim*, the tannaitic Midrash on Leviticus, with the commentary of Abraham ben David, the great critic of Maimonides. The historic-linguistic introduction as well as the exegetic-critical notes written by Weiss to this edition of the Sifra give proof of his talmudic learning and his critical training. He who read between the lines needed no special explanation to tell him that Weiss' point of view was no longer the traditional but the critical. However, it was not the hypercritical attitude of a Geiger, who often in his presentation of the Halakah concerned himself little with what the old sources had to say, and considered only whether the statements of the sources accorded with his pragmatic conception. If not, he said that the statements had been altered in later times for a special purpose, and were therefore historically unreliable. Geiger, in his notice of Weiss' book,[5] said of its author, "Naturally he adopted the ordinary talmudic standpoint, and there is no question of historical criticism." But while one has to admit that to admire by tradition is a poor thing, it is still better than to criticise by caprice, and "the ordinary talmudic standpoint" so disdainfully spoken of by Geiger, is often nearer the truth than the criticism of Geiger. The representatives of the old school showed that they had much keener insight into the nature of Weiss' work. They recognized the new in it, and accordingly denounced it as heretical.

Many years ago when, in the house of my teacher, a distinguished Talmudist of Lithuania, I was studying the Sifra in the Weiss edition under his guidance, I was astonished to see that the introduction was lacking in all copies of the book to be found in our Yeshibah. My teacher gave me no explanation of the curious fact. It was not until a number of years later in Germany, when a complete copy of the Sifra as edited by Weiss fell into my hands, that everything became clear to me. The introduction contained so much that seemed heretical in the eyes of orthodox Talmudists that they determined to destroy it in order to be in a position to use the text.

Yet it was not until 1864 that Weiss came out quite openly and with courage and skill sought to advocate his conception of rabbinical Judaism. The occasion for this was presented by the Kompert trial, which made as great a sensation in the middle of the "sixties" as the Dreyfus affair did in recent times. The story of the lawsuit is briefly as follows:

In the *Jahrbuch für Israeliten* published by Wertheimer and Kompert, an article by Graetz appeared in 1863 upon the rejuvenation of the Jewish race. The idea is developed that there are mortal and immortal races; the immortal races are those which have within themselves the capability and power of becoming young again, and the Jewish race is especially endowed with this power, of which it has given actual proof in various periods as, for instance, in the Babylonian exile. Graetz sketches in their main outlines the conditions and tendencies of the Jews in Babylonia, and at the same time shows how, in the midst of the most dire ruin, a seedling was deposited, which began the process of rejuvenation that led to the re-establishment of the Jewish nation. Among the small group it was the prophet now commonly called Isaiah II, the man of God, who awakened fresh life in the moribund Jewish race. Graetz goes on to indicate the main ideas in the speeches of the prophet and emphasizes chapter fifty-three, which he takes to refer to the people of Israel, the people with the Messianic mission. An anti-Semitic editor denounced the article to the State's attorney, who felt called upon to bring in a complaint against Kompert for having reviled, derided and dishonored the Messianic doctrine of the Synagogue. I cannot go into the details of this extremely interesting trial. It is not the political but the religious aspect which is of especial importance to us. Both Kompert and the well-known preacher, Mannheimer, who was summoned as an expert, absolutely protested against the assumption that Judaism is divided into sects. There are, said Mannheimer, among the Jews, as among all other men, some that are lax in their views, some that are strict, some that are liberal minded, some that are bigoted, some that are guided by the spirit of the law, some that adhere strictly to its letter. But all Jews who call themselves such equally accept Judaism, its doctrines and its entire foundation. In regard to the doctrine of the Messiah, Mannheimer said that it would not be wrong to maintain that an interpretation of the passage in Isaiah as *not* referring to a personal Messiah might still not involve a denial of belief in the Messiah. Rabbi Lazar Horwitz, the rabbi of Vienna, a

well-known Talmudist whose opinion as an expert was
also asked, said that every Jew believes in a personal
Messiah, but the way and manner in which the
Messiah will appear is a matter of private opinion.
The testimony of Mannheimer and Horwitz aroused
great indignation in many circles. The Neo-Orthodox,
led by men like Samson Raphael Hirsch and Israel
Hildesheimer, energetically protested against the idea
of unity in Judaism as proclaimed by the Viennese
rabbis. Reformers à la Geiger and Philippson were
very much dissatisfied with the dogma formulated by
Horwitz; in fact, the assertions of the Viennese rabbis
offered many a vulnerable spot difficult to defend.
Nevertheless, this historic conception of Judaism,
which lays great stress upon its unity, could not fail to
win Weiss over to its cause. Consequently, when the
Orthodox, under the leadership of Hildesheimer, issued
a protest against Horwitz and Mannheimer signed by
seventy rabbis, Weiss wrote his brilliant defense of the
Viennese rabbis under the title *Nezah Yisrael* (Vienna,
1864).

In this pamphlet of only twenty-one pages Weiss
gives in condensed but clear and precise form his
opinion concerning the two burning questions: Does
rabbinical Judaism recognize the existence of sects?
Does a denial of certain dogmatic principles of belief
as, for instance, belief in a personal Messiah, bring the
author of the denial without the pale of Judaism?

Although Weiss wholly embraced the orthodox
principles of faith or, to be exact, just because he was
still rooted in the old Rabbinism, he had to guard

himself resolutely against an admission that Judaism
is identical with a dogmatic religion. He explains,
then, the relation of Rabbinism to Sadduceism and
Karaism, and shows how the leaders of Rabbinism did
not expel even their most bitter opponents from the
Jewish communion. The pamphlet also contains a
sharp criticism of Reform, to which Weiss denies the
name of sect because it is absolutely negative, and the
essence of a thing must be positive.

A work against Weiss by Rabbi Nisan Schidlow of
Kollin appeared in the same year. It bore the name
Neshek Bar and defended the attitude of the rabbis
who had signed the protest.

The year 1864 was in another respect, too, a turning-
point in the life of Weiss. In that year he was appointed lector at the *Bet ha-Midrash* founded in Vienna
by Jellinek.

The old Bet ha-Midrash was not only the spiritual
and intellectual center for old and young, but it was
also a democratic institution in the best sense; it gave
the poor and humble an opportunity to show their
mental superiority, and so force the recognition of the
great and the mighty. Jellinek possessed more modern
culture than all the small minds put together that let
loose their tirades against "Oriental Judaism" in bad
German or in worse English; and yet he knew very
well that changed times demanded a change in the old
Bet ha-Midrash—a change, but not destruction. In
establishing his Bet ha-Midrash, the first purpose that
Jellinek had in view was to provide an opportunity for
further study to the many Jewish students in Vienna,

among them some who had come there from Eastern
Europe equipped with excellent talmudic learning. In
addition, the Bet ha-Midrash was to constitute a
center for the Jewish intelligence of Vienna, so that no
division in its forces should occur. Weiss and Meir
Friedmann were appointed lectors, and Szanto, the
Feingeist, also delivered lectures there. Weiss was
active in the Bet ha-Midrash for nearly forty years,
and only recently his colleague, Friedmann, took
charge of his courses because the former's age prevented him from being active as a teacher. The success
of the Bet ha-Midrash is proved by the fact that men
like Nehemias Bruell and Solomon Schechter have
gone forth from it.

Relieved of care concerning his daily bread, Weiss
could devote himself entirely to his studies, and the
first fruit of his new labors was an edition of the
Mishnah Berakot (Vienna, 1864) for his lectures in the
Bet ha-Midrash. It was provided with a short statement of its contents and with the various readings in
the two Talmuds. This was followed the next year by
an important scientific achievement in his critical
edition of the *Mekilta*, the tannaitic Midrash on
Exodus, which he provided with a valuable commentary and notes. His introduction upon the historic
development of the Halakah and the Haggadah in the
time of the Tannaim, won recognition even from
Geiger. In the same year Weiss started a Hebrew
monthly for the history and science of Judaism. After
four issues it went out of existence, although among
its collaborators were men like the two Bruells, father

and son, Friedmann and Reifmann. Two years later (Vienna, 1867) appeared the *Mishpat Leshon ha-Mishnah* of Weiss, studies in the language of the Mishnah. But the work that made Weiss a father of Jewish science did not appear until he was fifty-six years old. It was not until 1871 that he decided to have the first part of his *Dor Dor we-Doreshaw* printed. The fifth and last part appeared exactly twenty years later. But these years were not devoted exclusively to his *magnum opus*. In 1880, in conjunction with his colleague of the Bet ha-Midrash, M. Friedmann, he founded the Hebrew monthly for Talmud and Rabbinics, *Bet Talmud*, which in its five volumes contains a large number of important articles from the pen of Weiss, among which I will mention only the following three masterly biographies, published also separately: Maimonides (Vienna, 1881), Rashi (Vienna, 1882), and Rabbenu Tam (Vienna, 1883); and in the same year in which he completed his great work he published a new edition of the "Methodology of the Talmud," by R. Isaac Campanton, to which he prefaced an introduction. His biography of Saadia, published in the Hebrew year book *Ha-Asif* (1883), was followed by the biography of another Gaon, Hai, in 1893, along with an edition of the didactic poem *Musar Haskel* ascribed to the Gaon. On the occasion of his eightieth birthday Weiss wrote his reminiscences (*Zikronotai*, Warsaw, 1895), which contain valuable material concerning the spiritual condition of the Jews in the second third of the nineteenth century. With the brush of a master Weiss paints the portraits of the founders of the science of Judaism—Krochmal, Rapoport, Zunz and Luzzatto—and his descriptions of them belong to the best that has been written about them. Nevertheless, the fact must not be concealed that the entirely false judgment pronounced by Weiss upon Rapoport evoked several works against his Reminiscences. The chief of these is the work of Abraham Epstein, called *Dibre Bikkoret* (Cracow, 1896), in which the author, without personal attacks upon Weiss, calls attention to his wrong opinion of Rapoport.

Despite the great respect that Weiss cherished for the scholars I mentioned, he was nevertheless the first —at least among the older generation—to acknowledge willingly that the real founder of historic criticism among the Jews was none of these men, but the Gaon, R. Elijah Wilna. This greatest critical genius to whom the Jews can point, whose portrait would be hanging in the assembly hall of every university had he chosen some other field for his activity than Jewish literature, this great genius for nearly a century, was passed over in silence in the presentation of Jewish history, while the description of an apostate, who in his verses scoffed at Jews and Judaism, fills many pages. And why? One is almost inclined to say the Gaon was known as the Hasid, the saint, and nowadays there is no room for saints. Here the historic objectivity of Weiss is seen most clearly. Although entirely modern in his views and sentiments, he still has a perception for classic phenomena in modern times, and he not only knows how to honor the full spiritual greatness of an

Elijah Wilna, a Mordecai Benet and a Moses Sofer, but he does justice also to their personalities.

Take, for instance, the last-mentioned scholar. R. Moses Sofer combined all the great virtues of the old Jewish scholar with fighting courage and determination, and therefore he was not only the head of a Yeshibah, but also the leader of a strong party, especially strong in Hungary, which opposed the new tendency in Judaism with success. It was not lack of comprehension of the new tendency that made Sofer its violent opponent; his keen vision gave him insight sooner than anyone else into the radicalism into which it would degenerate. And it was Weiss who, in his sketch of Sofer in the Hebrew monthly *Mi-Misrah umi-Ma'arab* (Vienna, 1896) meted out full justice to this great personality, although Weiss did not adopt Sofer's conception of Judaism as his own. Moreover, Weiss did not descend to the manner of the so-called historians who are incapable of appreciating a great personality or a spiritual movement in its totality, but lose themselves in details and designate as characteristic the most insignificant points if they are bizarre, and the most unessential minutiae if they are curious. They judge accordingly, and as a result we hear opinions of the Jewish past and of certain tendencies in Judaism which, if the same logic were applied to the interpretation of general history, would give something like the following: Aristotle was a fool; he believed that the heavenly spheres were animated. Kepler understood nothing at all of physics, because he did not know so much as the law of gravitation, which is now known to every school-boy. And the fathers of the Dutch Republic were mischievous reactionaries, for in their political program they did not adopt universal suffrage.

It is impossible to give even a brief characterization of the many-sided literary activities of Weiss within the limits of a magazine article. But in order to do fitting honor to this "grand old man" of Jewish learning, it is absolutely necessary to know something about his achievements as an historian of Jewish tradition, which includes both Haggadah and Halakah but mainly the latter. To him who keeps his eyes directed on the surface, the "four ells of the Halakah" seem an extremely narrow field without charm of any kind, and even in its narrowness, a formless, disconnected mass of petty precepts. Not so to him whose vision penetrates into the depths. To him the Halakah is the converging point of all the various spiritual tendencies in Judaism. One-sidedness is the earmark of genius, both in an individual and in a nation. Poetry, music, rhetoric and art, therefore, found expression in ancient Israel only in religion, which dominated everything. Judaism, however, is a religion of deeds; it wants to elevate through action and so strengthen man's likeness to God. Hence it was interwoven with the life of the nation and thus became the possession of all of its members.

The Halakah, the "conduct of life," then, is not a mere external form; on the contrary, it is the spiritualization of every-day life. Despite Paul, who in recent times has attracted even Jewish followers, it is a fact that religious natures found complete satisfaction in active religion, falsely called legalism. The prime function of active religion is to give form to the religious consciousness, to express or present the religious feeling or thought of man. It obviously met some of the deepest needs of human nature, and met them in a striking way, and for that human type which has attained sharply-defined characteristics in the course of a long historic process, nothing can take its place. In this respect, religion is like music. As musical sounds of one race are unmusical and therefore unintelligible to another, so also the forms in which religious feeling is expressed are not universal but racial. Regarded from this point of view, which is neither that of a Galician Hasid nor that of a Western professor, the "four ells of the Halakah" appear of unfathomable depth, requiring the investigation of a man like Weiss.

A danger which few historians escape in their works is that of becoming narrow, pedantic and trivial. History very often threatens to degenerate from a broad survey of great periods and movements of human societies into vast and countless accumulations of insignificant facts, sterile knowledge and frivolous antiquarianism, in which the spirit of epochs is lost and the direction, meaning and summary of the various causes of human history all disappear.

Weiss understood how to bring to light the spiritual currents that left their traces in the Haggadah and the Halakah; how to make clear the inner connection that exists among the separate facts and occurrences,

which often seem to have no relation to one another,
and how to sum up, in one all-comprehending gener-
alization, the manifold observations made during his
thorough sifting of the vast accumulations of material.
From this dominating point of view, each detail to be
considered falls into its proper place and order comes
into the confusion that one is accustomed to face when
one looks through the sources. And, indeed, what a
gigantic task was accomplished when this material,
lying in huge masses, layer upon layer, here, there and
everywhere, then gathered together and again heaped
up indiscriminately, was completely systematized and
made available for all purposes, and was so arranged
and disposed that the various features belonging to an
historical picture came into due prominence and assumed the proper relation to each other. To have
recognized these features, to have constructed of them
a portrait of the whole period treated, and to have
given them lifelike expression through clear and
elegant delineation, this was the strength of Weiss'
work which raises it to one of the most important
achievements of Jewish learning.

Weiss' nature cannot be said to be of the same
creative, stimulating kind as that of Krochmal and
Rapoport. Truth did not manifest itself to him in
lightning flashes, and he did not win his successes
without effort. His power lies in the harmonious
symmetry of his endowments. Feeling for language,
critical acumen, historic perception, religious sentiment, all are present in a high degree, but none in such
excess as to detract aught from the other. A result of

these qualities is the sureness of method that distinguishes his "History of Tradition[7];" completeness of material to the limits of the possible; calm presentation; circumspect research and objectivity and impartiality of judgment. Not that in honoring Weiss I would go to the length of declaring him infallible, but I will make so bold as to avail myself in modified form of Wilhelm von Humboldt's opinion of the Kantian philosophy: There are some things that Weiss has shattered which will never be restored; some that he has founded which will never be destroyed, and he has pointed out the way along which the history of Judaism will have to move.

This opinion of Weiss' achievements must not prevent us from recognizing the fact that impartial critics find much to rectify and much to supplement in the most important chapters of "The History of Tradition." Especially, Isaac Halevy, in his *Dorot ha-Rishonim*, has offered us such valuable results that it would not be in the spirit of the master whose day of honor we are celebrating to maintain that he laid the foundations of the history of the Halakah and perfected its structure as well. Nevertheless, the importance of his great work is not impaired in the least by such criticism. Criticism has rather invested each chapter and each sentence that Weiss wrote, not only with peculiar charm, but also with imperishable value.

But Weiss' great work has still another characteristic which makes it a popular book for the Jewish people in the best sense of the word popular. It is the one work of dominating importance in modern Hebrew, and this fact gives it influence over thousands, even millions, of Jews who draw knowledge and counsel only from Hebrew books. Weiss' activity, therefore, is not only that of a scholar, but also that of a leader of his people. His ninetieth birthday is in the truest sense a festival of the Jewish people.

X

SOLOMON SCHECHTER

"Before the destruction of the Temple, new souls descended from Heaven to earth; after the destruction of the Temple, old souls only came down to Israel." Divested of its mystical garb, this passage, quoted from the great depository of mysticism, the Zohar,[1] may be paraphrased in the words of a famous English critic: Genius living at a time of national glow of life and thought finds his elements ready at hand; his work consists in giving expression to the ideas of his time; and such a genius is, to speak with the mystics, a new soul. Genius living at the time of national decline or decay finds a sort of equivalent, if not a complete one, for the nationally diffused life and thought in the treasures of the past. The national literature enables the man of genius to reconstruct in his mind the national life and thought in which he may live and work. To speak with the mystics, the soul of such a man is an old one reborn.

The tragedy of the Jews in modern times is not that they did not receive their full share of new souls, but that the new ones are not Jewish and the Jewish are not new. There is hardly any branch of human progress in modern times to which the Jews did not contribute their share, yea, more than their share, except in the field of Judaism. "They made me the

keeper of the vineyards, but mine own vineyard have
I not kept."

But truly the Lord forsaketh not His people. He
gave us, when the need was greatest, Solomon Schechter.[2] His was a new soul, permeated with the best
of modern thought, yet deeply rooted in the Jewish
past. To grasp the phenomenal achievements of Dr.
Schechter in the field of Jewish thought, to understand
his position among the fathers of Jewish learning, one
must start with a proper appreciation of his big
Jewish soul. Wisdom, remarked a Jewish sage, two
thousand years ago, does not enter into a heart which
is not pure.[3] This truth was restated by a modern
philosopher in the words: "Great thoughts originate
in the heart." A tenacious memory, a quick perception, and other mental equipments, do enable men to
acquire information; but to be a scholar or. to use the
Hebrew term, Hakam, "sage," who with creative
power interprets the information acquired in his own
way, one must be in possession of a great soul.

Dr. Schechter combined with great intellectual powers a disdain for conventionality, a temper imperious
and resolute, along with a most touching gentleness
and sweetness and a singleness of heart and purpose.
The key to Dr. Schechter the Scholar is Solomon
Schechter the Man. Criticism, he remarks somewhere,
is for him nothing more than the expression of conscience and he could as little dispense with it in
literature as with common honesty in dealing with his
fellow men. But his honesty compelled him to apply
criticism also to criticism and this brought him in

opposition to the idols of the day, the hypercritics for whom permanent doubt is the only certainty. Gentle as he was, he could admire enthusiastically any greatness of action and character, however remote it was from his own sphere, but his own subject, Jewish life and thought, was the absorbing interest of his life.

The love which he lavished in sketching the portrait of the founder of Hasidism is only equal to that which he expended in drawing the picture of the Gaon, Rabbi Elijah of Wilna, the deadliest enemy of Hasidism. His soul was so deeply Jewish that everything Jewish found an echo in it. Catholic Israel was with him more than a happy phrase—it reflected his soul. Hence the marvellously wide range of his contribution to Jewish learning. It is no exaggeration to say that there is hardly any branch of Jewish literature, the knowledge of which was not enriched, hardly any period of Jewish history upon which new light was not thrown by Dr. Schechter's studies and discoveries. We owe him gratitude for both, for the original way of interpreting the old, as well as the discovery of new facts. As in all empiric branches of human knowledge, so also in that of history the most important condition of progress is the discovery of new facts. But it is only he who masters the old that will be led to discover the new.

Dr. Schechter, though long known to scholars, first became world-famous through his discovery of the Hebrew original of Ecclesiasticus.[4] He had recovered a priceless treasure that was lost for nearly a thousand years. But the discovery of the Hebrew Ben Sira means more than this. In his introduction to this publication, as well as in his Essay on "The Study of the Bible[5]," Dr. Schechter pointed out in his masterful, terse, lucid and convincing style the great significance of the discovery for biblical criticism. More than one house of cards erected by the higher critics tumbled down at one blow. The Hebrew original of Ben Sira revealed the fact that neither the Book of Job, nor that of Ecclesiastes, nor indeed any other part of the Hebrew Bible, could be ascribed to Maccabean times. Dr. Schechter showed us that even the higher critics must renounce their claim to infallibility, since their hypotheses are often more improbable than those they attempt to displace.

The veil which covers the history of the religious and social life of the Jew in Maccabean times is thick. We hear of the rise of parties, the Sadducean and the Pharisean, which divided the nation. Modern historians not burdened by any first-hand information about these parties are ready with their explanations. But the very clearness of their presentation of the character of the parties is the best proof of its insufficiency. The life of a people does not lie on the surface.

The discovery by Dr. Schechter of the Sectarian Document[6], composed about 100 before the common era, is still more important than that of the original of Ben Sira. Through it we came to know that Judaism at that age represented a picture rich in composition, varied in light and shade, the interpretation of which is highly important for the history of the development of later Judaism. We will always remain

Dr. Schechter's debtors, not only for the discovery of this document and its interpretation, but also for signalizing its importance for Jewish history, theology and law, as he did in his scholarly introduction to this publication. The future historian of the Halakah will have to take his starting point from the Halakah of the Documents, the binding link between biblical and rabbinical law.[7]

The student of the Halakah, this most important but neglected branch of Jewish literature, owes much to Dr. Schechter also for some other invaluable material. I refer to the fragments of the three lost tannaitic Midrashim,[8] *Mekilta* of Rabbi Simon, *Mekilta* to Deuteronomy, and *Sifre Zutta,* discovered by Dr. Schechter. The Mishnah, the oldest halakic work, is but an extract of many works now unfortunately lost. Scientific study of the Halakah is only possible by making proper use of the tannaitic commentaries on the Pentateuch.

In his critical edition of the haggadic collection, *Abot de Rabbi Nathan,* with introduction and commentary[9], Dr. Schechter set a model for the future editions of rabbinic texts. The truth which has since become a truism, that the study of history necessitates the collection and edition in reliable form of its sources and documents, was discovered by scholars of the seventeenth century, but among Hebrew scholars it had to be rediscovered in modern times. Dr. Schechter was the first to make use of all the manuscripts and first editions for his publication. A marvellous mastery of the Haggadah, talmudic, midrashic and rabbinic, is

displayed in the notes to this edition as well as in his
edition of the *Agadat Shir ha-Shirim* and the *Midrash
Haggadol*.[10]

The centuries between the final redaction of the
Talmud and the beginning of Jewish culture in the
West, Southern Italy and Northern Africa, is one of
the most obscure periods in the history of the Jews and
at the same time one of the most important.   Dr.
Schechter's discoveries revolutionized our views concerning the history of the geonic times in a way un-
dreamed of before.   The letter of Rabbi Hushiel[11]
dispelled with one stroke the legend of the four
captives, with which Jewish history in the West was
supposed to start. We know now, through Dr. Schechter's discovery, that Jewish life in Southern Italy,
as well as in Northern Africa, stood under the influence
of Egypt rather than under that of Babylonia.

Dr. Schechter made us revise thoroughly our views
about the importance of Palestine for the history of the
Jews during the geonic period.[12] We must admit now
that neither Christian love nor Mohammedan hatred
was able to destroy entirely the deeply rooted culture
of the Jew in his native land. A good deal of what the
Jew of Europe received from Egypt was of Palestinian
origin. The geonic period was rich in great movements;
Karaism, Mysticism, harmonization of Hellenism with
Judaism are products of that age.   An adequate
estimate of the powers at work is only possible now
in the light of Dr. Schechter's discoveries.

In his studies of Anan's book of Laws[13] and of
Saadia's writings, he gave us not only insight into the

life and activity of the two greatest personalities of the period, but also the means for the understanding of the movements for which Anan and Saadia stood. Anan's work is the best proof of the fact that opposition to authority means but desire for change of authority. Anan tried to displace the authority of the Talmud, the product of a historical process of thousands of years, and to set up instead of it his own authority. In Saadia, the great defender of Rabbinism, we see the man who draws his inspiration from the past, and who also understands how to reconcile us with the present and to prepare us for the future.

Dr. Schechter was fond of quoting the following words of Humboldt: "Through my intercourse with great men I early arrived at the conviction that without serious attention to detail all generalities and theories of the universe are mere phantasms." In my attempt to sketch Dr. Schechter the Scholar, I endeavored to show how Judaism became richer in historical points of view through his detailed work and great discoveries, how he has furnished us with sound material for a foundation upon which to build the structure of Jewish history. For this alone the name of Dr. Schechter deserves to be engraved with golden letters in the history of our greatest men. But Dr. Schechter was a creative nature, full of life and vigor. He did not find complete satisfaction in merely collecting material; his real occupation was to call the dead to life, to give a soul to the dry bones.

His portrayals of such men as Nahmanides, the Saints of Safed, the Gaon of Wilna, the founder of

Hasidism, Krochmal, and many others[14], are often described as popular, which is certainly a misnomer. It is true in these Essays one does not notice the scholarly scaffolding used by him in erecting his structure, but they are nevertheless the outcome of painstaking study and deep investigation. And if the Jewish people love and understand them, it is due to the fact that Dr. Schechter was not only an artisan in history, but also a great artist. The Dutch peasant of to-day admires and appreciates Rembrandt, not because this great painter tried to gain the popular appreciation, but because he has penetrated into the depth of the soul of his people, and in looking at a Rembrandt the Dutch people recognize themselves in it. In truly Rembrandtesque fashion, Dr. Schechter portrayed in the lives of his heroes the ideals of the Jewish people. He interpreted the Jewish people to themselves, and as long as these ideals have not entirely disappeared from among us, we will continue to study, love and admire Dr. Schechter's sketches of Jewish life and men.

If the history of the Jew is his soul, the soul of his soul is his religion. Dr. Schechter's great Jewish soul is best revealed to us in his work on Jewish theology. If it be permitted to put the label of a school on such an original man, we would best characterize him as the theologian of the historical school. A theological system cut after the pattern of historical philosophical standards undermines its own basis. A theological system which ignores philosophy and history must degenerate into mysticism and cant. Only a man whose intellect has been blended harmoniously with imagination can see the spiritual truth underlying the actual. Dr. Schechter, possessing this happy combination of a great mind and a great soul could see the actual truth as presented in history and the spiritual as seen in religion.

What we look for in history are facts, in religion life, and only our soul fathoms the depth of life. Dr. Schechter's big Jewish soul penetrated into the soul of the Synagogue; where others saw only forms and ceremonials, he saw spirit and life. His theology[15] is not only a restatement of the facts of the religious life of the Jew, but also a new appreciation of them. There are fashions in religion as there are fashions in other things, some one remarked, but Dr. Schechter's religious and scientific conscience was repelled by the attempt made in recent times to turn the eternal truths of Judaism into a fashionable religion, to squeeze out of it the last drop of faith and hope, and make it acceptable to all and dear to none. Therefore his continuous combat against natural theology, this artificial product abstracted from some philosophical system, and his insistence upon the building up of Jewish theology on history.

The material to be used for such a structure, he teaches us, is Jewish life as expressed in its main currents. The Synagogue alone in its development of thousands of years can decide what it considers to be genuinely Jewish and what as foreign to Judaism. Jewish theology which ignores the standard works of the Synagogue and overestimates the importance of those which the Synagogue has rejected, the pseud-Epigrapha, is indeed a pseudo-theology. It is primarily the rabbinic literature which must furnish us with the material for Jewish theology. At the same time it is still true that rabbinic literature wreaked its vengeance on those who scoffed at it by remaining a sealed book to them.

Even a correct translation of a rabbinic passage is often a monstrous misunderstanding of it. The platitudes about Jewish legalism, the heavy burden of the law, the lack of spirituality of rabbinic Judaism, are not always due to prejudice and malice, much of it is rather due to ignorance, but as the rabbis of old say, "Error due to lack of study is a sin." Dr. Schechter is not an apologist of Judaism, but a teacher of it. He shows us that the law, far from being a burden to the observant Jew, is his greatest joy, that law is one of the highest expressions of spirituality as proved by the lives of the great teachers of the law who were at the same time the great saints of the Synagogue, men full of love of God, His Law, His teaching and His people.

The rabbis in their picturesque language remarked, "God counts the tears wept for the loss of the pious, and puts them in His treasury."[16] Our grief for the departed master can indeed be turned into a heavenly treasure, if we attempt to lead the life and follow the ideals set to us by him. What was the life of Dr. Schechter but continuous labor in the vineyard of the Lord—Jewish learning? And what were the ideals set to us by him? In his first public address in this country he stated that the paramount duty of American Jewry is the emancipation of Jewish science. If the science of history is the pride and ornament of a people, it is Israel's weapon and shield, a bulwark against enemies, a stronghold against derogation and misrepresentation, but also the source of our rejuvenation, the spring from which we draw life and existence. If we continue the life work of Dr. Schechter, then we may well say, "He who has really lived, cannot really die, but will live on in us, not only his work, but himself."

XI

DAVID HOFFMANN

Commenting upon the passage in Zechariah where the four fasts in memory of the four great national disasters are enumerated, the sages of the Talmud remark, "The Fast of the Third of Tishri, that is, the Fast in memory of the death of Gedaliah, follows in Scripture immediately upon the fast of the Ninth of Ab, the day of the destruction of the Temple, to teach that the death of the righteous is as a severe a loss as the destruction of the House of God."[1] This remark of the Rabbis, though expressed in extravagant language, contains a very great truth. In the culture of the nation, and especially in its highest expression, religion, two factors only count: Institutions and great individuals. It is only organized religion that makes it possible for men of each age to face the problem of the present enriched by the spiritual wisdom of the past. Yet while institutional religion is the stable background, it is only through the reaction of powerful minds and strong religious wills upon it that it develops with the developing life of society. Hence the death of a great man may well be said to be no less a calamity than the loss of a powerful institution.

We are here assembled to commemorate the life and work of a man by whose spiritual influence the Judaism of our own day has been carried forward. David

Hoffmann, by his gigantic intellect and saintly soul, has enriched Judaism so much that the enormity of the loss we have suffered in his death makes us turn our minds for a moment from the great evils that have befallen the Jew in recent times to the severe blows that have stricken Judaism.

The life of David Hoffmann is briefly told.[2] He was born November 24, 1843 at Verbo, Hungary, now Czecho-Slovakia, as the son of Rabbi Moses Judah, the Dayyan of that place. A true prodigy, he was able to read the Pentateuch in Hebrew at the age of three, and when five years old he was introduced to the study of the Mishnah. His talmudic training he received from Rabbi Samuel Sommer, Rabbi of Verbo and later of Papa, from Rabbi Moses Schück, of St. Georgien, one of the most prominent disciples of Rabbi Moses Sofer, the famous head of the celebrated Yeshibah of Pressburg, and from the latter's son and successor, Rabbi Abraham Samuel Sofer.

He also attended for several years the Rabbinical School established by Doctor Israel Hildesheimer at Eisenstadt, Hungary, and we are safe in assuming that it was the influence of this very strong personality that led the young Hoffmann to devote part of his time to the study of secular learning. Thanks to his extraordinary talent and industry he was able, after a few years of preparation, to pass the final examinations at the German Gymnasium (College) of Pressburg. After graduating from College about the age of twenty, Hoffmann left this city for Vienna to take up the study of Oriental languages and History at the celebrated University of the Austrian Capital. He remained in Vienna three years and, after interrupting for some time his university studies, he continued them at the University of Berlin. He received the Doctor's Degree from the University of Tübingen in the year 1870.

Needless to remark that Hoffmann did not neglect his talmudic studies during his university years. The main object of his studies continued to be the Talmud and rabbinic literature which he was now in a position to carry on in a modern scientific way. After holding minor teaching positions for several years, first at the preparatory Teachers' College of Rabbi Wechsler at Höchberg, Bavaria, and then at the Jewish High School of Frankfort on the Main, at the head of which stood Samson Raphael Hirsch, he was appointed in 1873 Professor at the Rabbinical Seminary, founded in that year by Doctor Hildesheimer at Berlin for the training of rabbis for the Orthodox ministry. For almost half a century Hoffmann taught in this institution Talmud, Codes, and the Pentateuch. On the death of Dr. Hildesheimer, in 1890, he was made acting president of the Seminary and in 1902 he became president. His activity as teacher and head of the Seminary continued to the very day of his death in November 1921.

The bibliography of Dr. Hoffmann's books, essays, articles and editions given in the Jubilee Volume published on the occasion of his seventieth birthday,[3] extends over twenty-seven pages. It would therefore be futile to attempt within the limited time of a short address an adequate estimate of Dr. Hoffmann's learned productions, of his original contributions to the study of the Bible, of his epoch making researches into the origins of tannaitic literature and of his standard editions of classical works. My present endeavor will be of a very modest nature—to sketch briefly what is new and original in Dr. Hoffmann, the modern interpreter of strict and uncompromising orthodoxy.

The problem of the Jewish religion in modern times —not of Judaism, still less of the Jews—has been and to some extent still is, how to bridge the cleavage caused in the life of the Jew by his emerging into the nineteenth century straight out of the fifteenth. The Middle Ages, aptly remarks Zunz, did not terminate for the Jew until the end of the eighteenth century. The predominating religion in civilized countries had almost four hundred years, from the Renaissance to the rise of German philosophy, in which to prepare for the struggle between modern thought and ancient faith, while the Jew had to face the same battle either entirely unarmed or with antiquated weapons.

The first among the orthodox to grasp the problem was Samson Raphael Hirsch. But even he, though a religious genius of the first magnitude and a man of extraordinary mentality, did not comprehend the problem in all its depth and width. He was preëminently an esthetic nature, thoroughly imbued with the Greek ideal of humanism which alone gives man the sense of the harmony of life. The religious problem of the Jew accordingly presented itself to him mainly as

one of feeling, viz. how to satisfy the feelings of the
modern Jew by a life dominated by the Torah. His
mission in life was the teaching that not only are the
Jewish religion and the noblest forms of Greek culture
compatible, but that they complement one another.
In his one-sidedness he overlooked the obvious fact
that the Greek genius also taught humanity once for
all that what is must be comprehended as something
that has come to be, and hence no harmonization
between Judaism and modern thought is possible as
long as we neglect to understand Judaism as a historical process. Of history Hirsch knew little and
cared less. The great historical importance of Dr.
Hoffmann is that he was the first to insist upon a
critical understanding of orthodox Judaism which is
possible only on the basis of a critical investigation of
its authoritative sources, the Bible, the Mishnah and
the Talmud. To him Orthodox Judaism was not a
tottering structure which too bold a word may over-
throw but, to use a metaphor of the Rabbis, a tree
deeply rooted, which neither wind nor storm can
move from its place. He combated the uncritical
method of the study of the Talmud not only from the
point of view of a modern scholar but also as an orthodox Jew. The Synagogue never taught that ignorance
is bliss; on the contrary, one of its maxims is, "the
ignorant cannot be pious," and to deprive Jewish
studies of the benefits of true criticism is tantamount
to the acme of ignorance.

I think it was Renan who remarked that one who
wishes to write a history of religion should have once

believed but have ceased to believe. The second qualification is intended to represent the power of detaching oneself from one's subject. Yet the sympathy which comes from the first condition, that of belief, is surely the more important of the two. We Jews certainly have had enough of historians and writers who were detached from Judaism even to the point of hostility and we have good reason to be thankful for having had with us David Hoffmann, whose love of Judaism was the key to his understanding thereof.

It is not a mere coincidence that Hoffmann, the representative of uncompromising orthodoxy and the strong opponent of higher criticism, was almost the only Jewish scholar of our times who devoted a good deal of his time and extraordinary ability to this branch of study. He did not approve of the ostrich policy of ignoring the problems raised by the modern investigators of the Bible, nor was he satisfied to dispose of them by a clever aphorism. As the microscope serves to make the wonders of nature seem all the more wonderful, so the criticism of Scripture can not be too searching and minute if only it be carried on by a "critic" in the true sense of the word, that is, by a skilled and impartial judge and not by "a harsh examiner," a hostile fault finder. Hoffmann was prepared to receive and welcome the fullest light of the new learning, but he refused to be dragged at the wheels of those who would make of the work of God a book partly myth, partly dishonest legend, deliberate fabrications, containing history which is not history, and a code of laws made a thousand years after the time of Moses. Such criticism is the product of a shallow rationalism that makes of religion a mere poetic aspiration, a mere conception of the ideal. But religion is not that. It pertains—and necessarily so—to the supernatural. A supernatural religion that does not rest upon a supernatural foundation is not faith but superstition.

Hoffmann was not frightened by a parade of seeming inconsistencies and contradictions in the Bible. His biblical studies belong to the best that has been written against the Graf-Wellhausen construction of Jewish history. One cannot help admiring the acumen and independent mind displayed by Hoffmann in these studies, written at a time when the views they combat had fascinated by their novelty and daring the scholarly world, to the extent that they were proclaimed as "the assured results of the best and latest scholarship." To-day very few will be found who still have the courage to speak of them as probable, still less as assured results.

One of the weakest points of modern biblical scholarship is the entire disregard of the later development of Judaism. In his commentary on Leviticus[4] Hoffmann showed how much one might learn from the Halakah as found in the tannaitic literature for the correct understanding of the legal parts of the Bible. When this work of Hoffmann appeared, one of the greatest Orientalists of the day described it as the most profound contribution to the understanding of Leviticus since Rashi[5].

The most important contributions of David Hoffmann to Jewish learning and thought are, however, to be looked for in another field—in that of the history of tannaitic literature. Judaism always taught that the God who could not speak would not be rational, and the God who would not speak would not be moral, hence for the Jew the idea of a written revelation may be said to be logically involved in the notion of a living God. Scripture however lends itself to endless interpretation. One finds in the Bible what one seeks there. Rabbinical Judaism, while it insists upon the infallibility of the written word, teaches at the same time that the Synagogue is its divinely appointed custodian or, to use the familiar terms, the oral Torah is co-eval with the written and of the same authoritative character. Such a conception of Judaism if applied in an uncritical and indiscriminate manner, harbors the great danger of burying Judaism under the debris of the past.

David Hoffmann by his great mastery of the entire talmudic-rabbinic literature, his immense diligence, his critical acumen and his simple devotion to Orthodox Judaism, was the man to make a stand against the danger threatening Orthodoxy in Middle Europe from the neglect of Jewish learning.

One of Hoffmann's earliest writings, his treatise, *Die Zeit der Omer-Schwingung*, though merely an archaeological study without the slightest trace of apologetics, is nevertheless one of the best defenses of the Orthodox doctrine concerning the origin of the oral law. In this work the rabbinic tradition concern-

ing the day upon which Pentecost should be celebrated
is shown to conform to the data ascertainable about
the celebration of this festival in biblical times. Of a
similar character is his work, *Der Oberste Gerichts-
hof*[7], in which he brilliantly refutes the view held by
many modern scholars concerning the origin of the
great Sanhedrin. He not only defends the historicity
of the data found in rabbinic literature about the
nature of the Sanhedrin, but traces back the origin of
this institution to biblical times.

While in these two books and in similar ones we
meet Hoffmann as the champion of the doctrine of
the high antiquity of tradition, he appears in other
works in entirely different rôles. His two most
learned studies are: *Die Erste Mischnah*[8] and *Zur
Einleitung in die halachischen Midraschim*[9]. In both
of them the author with the great lucidity peculiar to
him introduces the student into the very workshop of
the Tannaim and shows him the Halakah in the
process of becoming. He shows us the gradual development of the Mishnah, the methods of study in the
different schools of the old masters, and the different
layers and strata in the old rabbinic literature. All of
which warns us to be on our guard against confusing
catholic truths and individual opinion, first principles
and the guesses of genius, all mingled in the same
works and demanding to be discriminated. These
books of Hoffmann are still to-day indispensable to
the student of halakic literature as they were at
the time of their appearance, forty and thirty-seven
years ago respectively.

A Jewish legend run as follows: Once the Roman Government sent some people to Mount Nebo to locate the grave of Moses. They failed, however, in their attempt, those who stood on the top of the Mount thought they saw the grave in the valley and to those in the valley it appeared to be high on the top of the mount[10]. Thus legend expresses in its quaint way the uniqueness of Moses; from whatever point of view one looks at Israel's greatest master, from the highest peaks of human intellect or from the unfathomable depths of the soul, his greatness is immeasurable.

The master for whom we mourn was a true disciple of Moses, combining a gigantic intellect with the sublime and pure soul of the saint, in such a manner that the personality of David Hoffmann may be described as unique in the annals of modern Jewish history.

Great in learning, great in saintliness, David Hoffmann was also great in leadership. Orthodox Jewry in Middle and Western Europe recognized him as its true leader, and Orthodox and non-Orthodox alike gladly admitted that his leadership was a blessing not only for a section of Jewry but for all Israel.

"Greater," say the sages, "are the righteous when dead than when alive[11]." By this the thought is expressed that sometimes the ideals for which the great and noble stand are realized by the people only after a great shock, when their loss arouses the people to a clear apprehension and appreciation of these ideals.

The last few years have witnessed not only the ruin of millions of Jews but also the destruction of Jewish

learning and culture in many lands, and in addition
death has taken from us great leaders in the world of
thought. American Jewry has responded and I am
sure will further respond liberally and generously to
the appeal made in behalf of the suffering Jew, but it
is not at all cognizant of the great danger threatening
Judaism. Judaism is not a hospital religion but
primarily a spiritual and intellectual power. American
Jewry is doomed to fail if in these days of great
suffering and distress of the Jew, it will overlook the
agony of Judaism.

We are here assembled to give public expression of
our grief for the loss Israel has suffered in the death of
David Hoffmann who spent his life in noble self-
sacrifice, in study, practice and love of the Torah and
in devotion to the interest and ideals of Israel. The
best way in which we can show our respect, honor and
veneration for David Hoffmann is by attempting to
realize here in America his great ideal—the cultivation
of Jewish learning. Then we may well say, "The
memory of the righteous is for a blessing."

NOTES

NOTES

I

THE JEWISH PRIMARY SCHOOL

Delivered in the Course of Public Lectures of the Jewish Theological Seminary of America, January 31, 1907.

[1] Nedarim 41a.

[2] 'Am ha-Arez, literally "people of the land," is used in rabbinic Hebrew in the sense of an ignorant and uncultured person. Comp. above pp. 11 and 57–58.

[3] Learned man.

[4] Ginzburg-Marek, *Ebhreskeya Narodni Piecni*, Nos. 60–62.

[5] Pesahim 49b.

[6] Bereshit R. 65.19.

[7] 39.1–11. The translation is that of Box, *The Book of Sirach*, in Taylor's, *The Apocrypha and Pseudepigrapha*, 1913.

[8] Soferim in tannaitic sources in the sense of scholars is a rhetorical archaism, comp. Bacher, *Terminologie* I, 134 note 4. The Baraita, Kiddushin 66a, a quotation from a historical source composed before the beginning of the common era, has חכמי ישראל which means, men versed in Jewish learning in opposition to חכמי אומות העולם, men learned in secular knowledge. See also ps.-Philo, *Bibl. Antiq.* 24C: *assimilabi sapientibus qui de te nascentur*; the Hebrew original very likely read: משל להחכמים אשר יצאו ממך.

[9] Baba Batra 21a.

[10] *Contra Apionem* II, 18; com. also Philo, *Legatio ad Gaium*, 16.115.

[11] Yerushalmi, Hagigah I, 7; Pesikta, ed. Buber, XV, 120b.

[12] On the cultural state of the Babylonian Jews in pre-amoraic times, comp. Halevy, דורות הראשונים IIa, 162–210, who for apologetical reasons maintains that they had reached a high state of development centuries before the amoraic period. His view

however is not acceptable, comp. Epstein, *Revue des Etudes Juives* XLIV, 45–62.

[13] Baba Batra 22a.

[14] Comp. Berakot 17a, Sotah 21a, Nedarim 55a; comp. also Funk, *Die Juden in Babylonien*, Berlin 1902, 79 ff.

[15] Berakot 47b.

[16] On the early history of the Jews in Poland, see Dubnow, *History of the Jews in Russia and Poland*, translated by Friedlaender, I, 40 ff.

[17] The author of this saying is not known.

[18] Responsa No. 95; comp. also Graetz, *Geschichte* (fourth edition) IX, 57 note 1.

[19] On Simon Günzburg, see Maggid ספר תולדות משפחות גינצבורג 1–8.

[20] R. Jacob Pollak; comp. *Jewish Encyclopedia* X, 114.

[21] On Loria, comp. Horodetzki כרם שלמה, Drohobitzsch, 1896.

[22] Comp. the remarks of the author in *Jewish Encyclopedia* III, 34 top.

[23] *Brantspiegel*, chap. 47.

[24] This regulation was first published by Güdemann, *Quellenschriften*, 232–236, and reprinted by Asaf, מקורות לתולדות החנוך, 99.

[25] Asaf, l. c.

[26] Abrahams, *Hebrew Ethical Wills*, 210.

[27] Responsa, No. 36; comp. also *Mordecai*, Baba Batra beginning and Asaf, 22–23, 180.

[28] Comp. The School Regulation of the Community of Cracow of the year 1595, and see also R. Moses Moraftschik in Asaf, 88, bottom, 98.

[29] Comp. the complaint against the teachers who waste the afternoon of the New Moon day, by R. Judah ben Loeb, אומר מיהודה, paragraph 12.

[30] School Regulation of Cracow in Asaf, 101.

[31] The description of this ceremony is found in different versions; that in the text follows ספר האסופות as extracted from its manuscript by Güdemann, *Geschichte d. Erziehungswesens* I, 50–54; comp. also the sources quoted by Asaf, 2–4 and 162. Whether the first lesson was given by the teacher, or the Rabbi of the

community, cannot be stated with certainty as הרב in the text is ambiguous.

³² On the "pedagogic Haggadah" see Ginzberg, *Legends of the Jews* V, 5–6, note 10.

³³ R. Abraham Hayyim Shor, תורת חיים, Sanhedrin 60b bottom.

³⁴ On Leviticus as the first book read in school, comp. Pesikta, ed. Buber, VI, 60b and parallel passages by the editor. See also Friedmann in the Introduction to his edition of the Mekilta 35.

³⁵ Comp. Note 24.

³⁶ See Asaf, Index s. v. כתות.

³⁷ R. Judah b. Loeb, אומר מיהודה 12. See also Moraftschik in Asaf, 94.

³⁸ Comp. Maybaum, *Abraham Jagel's Katechismus Lekach-tob*, Berlin 1892.

³⁹ Baba Mezla' 49a.

⁴⁰ Makkot 24a, comp. also שאלתות, No. 36.

⁴¹ Baba Mezia', 85a.

⁴² R. Isaac b. Elyakim לב טוב chapter IX. ed. Amsterdam 93d, bottom.

⁴³ *Brantspiegel* chapter 47.

⁴⁴ A small four-sided toy of the top kind like the tee-totum. Among the German Jews it is known by the name of *trendel*— also spelled *trändel* and *tränderl*; comp. Löw, *Lebensalter*, 288.

⁴⁵ Yebamot 109b.

II

THE DISCIPLE OF THE WISE

Delivered in the Course of Public Lectures of the Jewish Theological Seminary of America, February 23, 1905.

¹ Gittin 56a–56b. In Ekah R. I, 5 the interview between the Rabbi and the imperator (Vespasian) reads quite differently.

² Shir R. 8. 11.

³ Comp. Deutsch, *The Talmud*, p. 6.

⁴ Foucher de Careil, *Oeuvres de Leibnitz*, I, 24.

⁵ This is the usual spelling, whereas *Talmid Hakamim* is the only correct form as the plural *Talmide Hakamim* shows. The

mannuscripts of the Talmudim and Midrashim have in most cases preserved the correct form *Talmid Hakamim.*

[6] Yoma 86a.

[7] Shabbat 75a.

[8] Berakot 58b.

[9] Joseph Scaliger, *Opus de emendatione temporum,* 101.

[10] *Prol. ad Oseam,* ed. Migne, XXV, 820.

[11] Yerushalmi, Megillah I, 9; 71c, bottom.

[12] Megillah 9b; Bereshit R. 36.8 and parallel passages cited by Theodor.

[13] Comp. Brüll, *Fremdsprachliche Redensarten . . . . . . in den Talmuden und Midraschim,* Leipsic, 1869.

[14] On the importance of Ibn Koreish (flourished about 900–950) for the history of the study of comparative Semitic philology, comp. Eppenstein, *Monatsschrift,* XLIV, 486–507.

[15] Cicero, *De Oratore,* I, 44.

[16] Abot V, 22.

[17] Comp. Hebrew Ben Sira 51.23.

[18] Abot I, 4 in a saying by Yose ben Joeser who lived about 170 B. C. E.

[19] *Contra Apionem* XX, 38. A contemporary of Josephus, the author of II Baruch, likewise writes, "We have nothing now save the Mighty One and His Law (LXXXV, 3). R. Gershom, the "Light of the Diaspora," who lived about a thousand years after these two authors, uses almost the very same words in describing the importance of the Torah for the existence of Israel. Comp. his penitential prayer (Selihah) זכור ברית for Ne'ilah according to the Ashkenazic ritual.

[20] Comp. Sanhedrin 32b.

[21] Comp. Letter of R. Sherira, ed. Lewin 82 and Mann, *Jewish Quarterly Review* (New Series) VII, 467–470. The last Gaon (head) of the Academy of Pumbedita was R. Hezekiah who presided over it after the death of R. Hai in 1038; comp. R. Judah Albarceloni, ספר השטרות 87, top, and Mann *l. c.* 469–470.

[22] Abot R. Nathan 3 (beginning): The School of Shammai says, one should instruct only him who is wise, humble, of good family and rich, but the school of Hillel says, one should instruct any-

body who desires to learn. See also Berakot 28a, the very strict policy of Rabban Gamaliel with regard to admission to the Academy.

[23] Nedarim 81a.

[24] Berakot 28a; comp. also Yerushalmi, Berakot IV, 1 (end) where it is said that R. Joshua was a "maker of needles."

[25] Horayyot 13b, Kohelet R. II, 17. On R. Meir's activity as a scribe, comp. also 'Erubin 13a and Gittin 67a.

[26] Abot VI, 2.

[27] Derek Erez Zutta I. The name דרכן של תלמידי חכמים "Conduct —or way—of the wise" given to it by several authors of the Middle Ages is most appropriate; comp. the author's article in *Jewish Encyclopedia* IV, 528–529.

[28] Berakot 17a. R. Meir Abulafia in his commentary on Sanhedrin 50b takes מרגלא in the sense of "pearl" and hence the opening words of this passage read: A pearl in the mouth of the scholars of Jabneh. Comp. however the phrase תדירא בפומא occurring frequently in Yerushalmi, which shows that מרגלא in Babli must be derived from הרגל as Rashi and (ps?) Saadia *ad loc.* have it.

[29] Yerushalmi, Sotah I, 4 (16d), Wa-Yikra R. 9.9 and in many other places; comp. Gaster, *Exempla* p. 117 No. 146 (145).

[30] Yerushalmi, Sanhedrin II, end.

[31] Yerushalmi, Baba Batra V, end.

[32] Megillah 28a.

[33] Abot VI, 4 (קנין תורה).

[34] Yoma 35b.

[35] Nedarim 62a, Yerushalmi, Shebiit IV, 2; Kallah II, 5b, ed. Coronel. The version of the story given in the text follows Kallah.

[36] Abot IV, 5.

III

THE RABBINICAL STUDENT

Delivered in the Course of Public Lectures of the Jewish Theological Seminary of America, January 11, 1906.

[1] Mohammed uses this expression to describe Jews, Christians and Sabeites who base their religion on written sources.

² See Schechter, *Jewish Quarterly Review*, XI, 643-ff. Comp. also above p. 246.

³ Maimonides, יד, תלמוד תורה 3.10.

⁴ Comp. Asaf, מקורות לתולדות החנוך, Index, s. v. פלפול.

⁵ Comp. the Responsum by R. Hai Gaon (939–1038) quoted by R. Judah Albarceloni, ספר העתים, 256.

⁶ On non-Jewish students in mediaeval times, comp. the standard work by Rashdall, *Universities of Europe in the Middle Ages*.

⁷ On the Requirements for Admission to the Mediaeval University, comp. Rashdall, op. cit.

⁸ *Goetting. Gelehrt. Anz.* 1879, 1047.

⁹ מנהגי מהרי"ל, ed. Warsaw 1874, 56b. Comp. also Responsa of R. Meir of Rothenburg, ed. Cremona No. 108. This great Talmudist in the middle of the 13th century accommodated in his own house twenty-four students in twenty-four separate rooms.

¹⁰ R. Yozel, לקט יושר, I, 33 bottom, 35, 36, 51, 97.

¹¹ R. Yozel, 57, 107.

¹² Asaf, 81, 118, 120–121, 291; comp. also R. Yozel, 97.

¹³ R. Yozel, 103-104.

¹⁴ R. Yozel, 153. The word *Ketowes* is very likely of slavic origin, comp. J. A. Joffe, *Pinkos*, I, 129–134.

¹⁵ On this students' song, comp. Brüll, *Jahrbücher*, V. 102-105.

¹⁶ R. Yozel, II, 26.

¹⁷ Rashdall, op. cit.

¹⁸ מנהגי מהרי"ל, ed. Warsaw 1874, 86a (לקוטים at the end of the book).

¹⁹ Comp. Israel Davidson, *Parody in Jewish Literature*, New York 1907.

²⁰ I do not know of any reference to "the mock Rabbi" in early sources; it seems to be of comparatively recent origin. Comp. Asaf, 121.

²¹ מנהגי מהרי"ל, end of לקוטים.

²² R. Yozel, I, 35; comp. also ibid. 34, 43.

²³ מנהגי מהרי"ל, catchword הא לך מוסר הלכות היתר ואיסור (middle).

²⁴ מנהגי מהרי"ל, heading פדיון הבן.

²⁵ R. Yozel, I, 116.

[26] Berakot 7b, bottom.

[27] R. Yozel, I, 141.

[28] On R. Meir of Rothenburg, see the author's article in *Jewish Encyclopedia*, VII, 437–440; see also Zimmels, *Beiträge z. Geschichte d. Juden*, Vienna 1926.

[29] Wisdom I.4.

[30] Comp. above, p. 141.

[31] The salaried Rabbi is, comparatively speaking, of recent origin; comp. Asaf, לקורות הרבנות, 19–28.

[32] Nedarim, 37a.

[33] מנהגי מהרי״ל, heading נטין, beginning; on the great cost of divorce, comp. Asaf, לקורות הרבנות, 26.

[34] Asaf, לקורות הרבנות, 32.

IV

THE RELIGION OF THE PHARISEE

Delivered before the Harvard Divinity School, July 6, 1920.

[1] Yerushalmi, Sanhedrin, X, 29c.

[2] With Hillel and Shammai the period of the "Pairs" lasting for about two centuries (ca. 173–30) ends. Its history is still enveloped in darkness. This much however seems to be certain that the Pharisaism of that period while forming a united front against Sadduceeism, was far from being uniform, and hence the "Pairs" as its leaders, the one representing the right wing, the other the left.

[3] Shabbat, 31a; comp. Moore, Judaism, II, 85–88.

[4] Gal. 5. 4.

[5] ספר רזיאל, 20b, ed. Wilna 1888; comp. Ginzberg, *Legends* V, 3, Notes 3–4.

[6] *Das Wesen des Christentums* (many editions).

[7] Sifre, Num. 115.

[8] Shabbat 105b.

[9] Berakot 61b.

[10] Abot IV, 17.

[11] Mishnah Sotah, end.

[12] Mishnah Yoma, end.

[13] Yerushalmi, Berakot X, 13a, towards the end.

[14] Simeon b. Shatah, in Mishnah Ta'anit, III, 5.

[15] Hullin 7b; the Hebrew word is the same for small toe and small finger, hence perhaps the small toe is meant.

[16] Yerushalmi, Shebi'it IX, 38d; comp. Matthew 10–29, "And one of them (sparrows) shall not fall on the ground without your Father."

[17] Comp. Mekilta, Yitro 2, with regard to the righteous judge.

[18] Midrash Tehillim 86, 1.

[19] Sifre, Deut. 27. Philo expresses the same view in a somewhat different form; comp. Ginzberg, *Legends* V, 4, note 6.

[20] Mekilta, Shirah, 3, 37a; comp. Schechter, *Some Aspects of Rabbinic Theology* 199–201.

[21] Bereshit R. 24.7 and parallel passages by Theodor *ad loc.*

[22] *Some Aspects of Rabbinic Theology*, 117.

[23] Herford, *Pharisaism*, 66 (first edition).

[24] The second benediction (אהבת עולם) of *Shema'* for the evening.

[25] Hermann Cohen, *Jüdische Schriften* I, 18.

V

JEWISH THOUGHT AS REFLECTED IN THE HALAKAH

Second Zunz Lecture of the Menorah Society, delivered at the University of Chicago, December 29, 1920.

[1] Megillah 28b, bottom.

[2] Yerushalmi, Berakot V, 9d.

[3] Mishnah Bezah, beginning.

[4] Kiddushin 49b.

[5] Comp. the very pertinent remarks on this point by Moore, *Judaism* II, 287.

[6] R. Simlai, a Palestinian Amora about the middle of the third century is the first to mention these numbers, though it is quite possible that the computation originated with an earlier authority. The attempts of Halper, *Book of Precepts*, 1–5, to find traces of this computation in tannaitic sources are not successful. Midrash Hagadol I, 226 top, has it in a statement by the Tanna,

R. Eliezer b. R. Yose—this passage escaped Halper—but there is no telling whether the number תרי״ג is not a later interpolation. Comp. also Guttmann, בחינת המצוות, 24 ff.

[7] Yebamot 3b, bottom, ff. and in many other passages of both Talmudim. Comp. Guttmann, *Emléköny Bloch Moses* 1–20 (Hebrew section). I wish to call attention to the fact that the term used by the Tannaim is: מצות עשה קודמת ללא תעשה (comp. Mekilta Mishpatim 20) and not מ' ע' דוחה לא תעשה as in the amoraic terminology. Guttmann has no references to tannaitic sources.

[8] *Law As a Means to an End*, 209–211.

[9] D. 5. 3. 25. 11.

[10] A verbal promise to the poor is binding; comp. Baba Kama 36b, bottom; see also Baba Batra 148b.

[11] Baba Batra 133b.

[12] Jacob adopted two sons of Joseph, comp. Gen. 48. 5–6.

[13] Kiddushin 17b.

VI

THE GAON, RABBI ELIJAH WILNA

Delivered in Commemoration of the Two Hundredth Anniversary of his Birth at the Jewish Theological Seminary of America, April 11, 1920.

[1] Rabbi Abraham Wilna, סערת אליהו 18, ed. Wilna 1894.

[2] Hillel N. Steinschneider (Maggid), עיר ווילנא 9–10; Dembitzer, כלילת יופי 1, 71a. The head of the Yeshibah at Lemberg דוד בהגאון מהו' מרדכי אשכנזי mentioned by Dembitzer, 29b is perhaps identical with דוד אשכנזי, the father of R. Moses. On the epithet Ashkenazi used by the German emmigrants to Poland, see Dembitzer II, 111.

[3] R. Israel Yᵉfe אור ישראל, Introduction.

[4] R. Abraham Wilna 1. c. 18; comp. also Finn קריה נאמנה 99.

[5] Joshua H. Lewin, עליות אליהו 53, ed. Stettin, and more fully Steinschneider, 152–153, end of note 3.

[6] Foreword to באורי הגר״א, אורח חיים where, acccording to Lewin, 53 note 2, ת׳פ is to be read instead of תפ׳ב. The reason

given by him for this emendation is not intelligible to me, as
nothing is said there about Tuesday having been the first day of
Passover in the year of the Gaon's birth. In the foreword to
שנות אליהו (Lemberg 1799) it is stated that the Gaon was about
twenty in the year תקט״ו, which is quite impossible. With regard
to the birthplace of the Gaon, it is to be remarked that the
statement in foreword to באורי הגר׳א about his father's residence in Seltz does not warrant the generally accepted opinion
that the Gaon was born in that town. At the age of five we find
him in Wilna and it is likely that he was born there.

⁷ Foreword to אדרת אליהו ed. princeps.

⁸ Foreword to באורי הגר׳א, או׳ח.

⁹ R. Hayyim of Volozhin in foreword to ביאור על ספרא דצניעותא.

¹⁰ R. Israel of Minsk, פאת השלחן (Introduction) and comp. the
sources referred to in notes 6–7; comp. also foreword to ...ביאור.
על כל הזוהר Wilna 1810.

¹¹ R. Baruch of Shklow in the Introduction to his Hebrew
translation of Euclid.

¹² R. Abraham Simhah (in his letter to Kalmann Schulmann,
in the latter's מלחמות היהודים) quoting his uncle R. Hayyim of
Volozhin as authority for this statement.

¹³ About 1756 one of his daughters was to be married (comp.
Steinschneider, 152) and accordingly he must have married early
in life. The maternal great-grandfather of the author, R. Solomon
of Neustadt, author of בית אבות, was advised by the Gaon, his
granduncle, to marry at the age of eighteen; oral communication
by R. Solomon's daughter.

¹⁴ Lewin, 65; comp. also 75, note 75 and 84, note 106 as well as
R. Abraham Wilna, 12 which passages indicate that the Gaon
must have lived for some time in Kaidan. The statement, how-
ever, that the Gaon at the age of seven studied there under R.
Moses Margalit, the famous author of the commentary פני משה
on the Talmud of Jerusalem (died at Brody 12 Tebet 5541, comp.
Jahrbuch d. jüdisch-liter. Gesellschaft 1920, 132) is based solely on
Lewin's authority (55) which is open to question. The exact
date when the Gaon settled permanently in Wilna is not known;
Finn, 133 gives 745 (תק׳ח is a misprint for תק׳ה) and refers to

NOTES 275

the biographical sketch by the Gaon's sons in the foreword to
באורי הגר'א, או'ח as his source. Nothing however is found there
which has any bearing on this point, comp. also Finn, 124.

[15] Finn, 133. A granddaughter of R. Moses was the wife of R.
Elijah, the great-grandfather of the Gaon, comp. Finn, 96.

[16] Eybeschütz לוחת עדות 71a, ed. Altona. There is not the
slightest reason for doubting the genuineness of this letter, which
is also referred to in the foreword to שנות אליהו ed. Lemberg 1799.

[17] R. Abraham Wilna, 13. Comp. also the text of the memorial
tablet in Finn, 155, where it is explicitly stated that the Gaon
taught in the same place for forty years—to be accurate, thirty-
seven years and six months, comp. above page 131, end—and not
eighteen as Finn, 139, erroneously has it. The י'ח years mentioned in the foreword to באורי הגר'א, או'ח, if not a misprint
for ל'ח, cannot therefore refer to the establishing of the Bet
ha-Midrash. See also R. Hayyim of Volozhin's remarks in foreword (end) to the commentary on the Mishnah by the Gaon.

[18] See Baba Mezi'a, 33a and comp. also the stories about
Hillel, Rabban Johanan b. Zakkai, and Rabbi Akiba, Sifre, Deut.
357, 150a.

[19] R. Baer b. Tanhum, מעשה רב, Nos. 127, 162-164, 170, 175,
193, 195, 225, 227, 229.

[20] Comp. the sources quoted in notes 4–6 and 17.

[21] R. Abraham Danzig חכמת אדם 133, 24. On the considerably
large amounts of money placed by the community of Wilna with
the Gaon for charitable and educational purposes, see also
Steinschneider, 104 and 120, end of note 1. The fourteen hundred
guilders given annually to the Gaon (Bershadzki, Litowskie
Ebhrei 50) were of course for disbursement among the poor and
not for his own use. Harkavy (Comp. his letter in Schapiro
תולדות ר' חיים) is to be corrected accordingly.

[22] Finn, 138–146; Lewin, 88a–90.

[23] Published under the title הספד על הגר'א by Abraham
Katzenellenbogen שערי רחמים Wilna, 1871. See also the second
הספד by Danzig in צואת ר' .. יחזקאל Wilna, 1871, where thirty-
five of the Gaon's writings are said to have been on the Kabbalah.

[24] Foreword to פאת השלחן; comp. also his letter to the Ten

Tribes (printed several times) where he gives the number of the Gaon's works as seventy-two.

²⁵ Zedner's Catalogue contains almost a complete list of the works of the Gaon published before 1870; on the unpublished ones, comp. Nathan Coronel's רשימה, (London 1871), and Lewin, 94–116. Most of the manuscripts recorded by Coronel are in the Library of Baron Günzburg (comp. Steinschneider, 171, note 5), where also are to be found those formerly in possession of R. David Luria. No trace however has been found of the missing part of his commentary of the Mishnah of which only that to the Orders I. and VI. (of II. only that on Shabbat) is printed, while his son-in-law, the editor of שנות אליהו, possessed also that on Order V. In the foreword to באור על הזוהר 3a, ed. Wilna 1810, his son and grandson speak of his commentary on the entire Mishnah הפליא להעזר בפי׳ למשנה כולו.

²⁶ R. Israel of Minsk in the foreword to פאת השלחן.

²⁷ Only his commentary on Shulhan Aruk and his treatises on trigonometry איל משולש and parts of ביאור על אגדות were printed from his autograph manuscript. Comp. Lewin, 95 and 116 top.

²⁸ Comp. note 25.

²⁹ Foreword to באורי הגר׳א, או׳ח.

³⁰ For one who is acquainted with his commentary on the Shulhan Aruk, this statement does not need any further proof. Comp. also the high praise of the Pilpul in ביאור על כמה אגדות, heading אורזילא דימא and commentary on Proverbs 14.4.

³¹ Quoted by R. Hayyim of Volozhin, חוט המשולש, No. 9, p. 39.

³² The emendations of the text of the Talmud by R. Solomon Loria and R. Joel Sirkes are almost entirely based either on manuscript readings or upon old authorities.

³³ His works, especially the commentary on the Mishnah and that on the Shulhan Aruk, contain numerous explanations of the Talmud different from those given by the old authorities and not a few explanations of the Mishnah which differ from those offered by the Amoraim; comp. f. e., Berakot 4.1 and 7.3. The author of the book גביע גביע הכסף Shklow, 1894, a disciple of the Gaon, has on folio 25b, bottom, the very interesting remark; ושמעתי מאדוני מ׳ו הגאון זצ׳ל שהמשנה נידרש בפשט ודרש. In other words,

the Gaon was of the opinion that in explaining the Mishnah or other tannaitic sources, one is to follow his good sense and not authority. See also R. Manasseh b. Porat אלפי מנשה 38b and 73b on the original method applied by the Gaon in explaining the Bible and the postbiblical literature.

34 Commentary on Prov. 14.2, 22.5 and Is. 11.4. Comp. also the references in R. Samuel Malzan, אבן שלמה, Wilna, 1890, 9a.

35 Commentary on Prov. 24.31 and 25.4.

36 Commentary on Deut. 1.13 and Prov. 13.4.

37 Commentary on Prov. 11.17.

38 Commentary on Prov. 4.11 and 31.11.

39 R. Hayyim of Volozhin in his foreword to ביאור על כל הזוהר writes: אך בימי חכמי התלמוד עדיין היו רשאי' לחדש מד'ר (=מצוות דרבנן) כוון ו'ח (נר חנוכה)... וכן למזר גזירות כגון י'ח דבר וכאשר נסתם תלמוד הקד' אין לנו אלא לעשו' ולקיי' את כל דברי תלמוד ה' (=הקדוש) בכל פרטיו ודקדוקיו. There can be no doubt that R. Hayyim stated in these words the view of his master, the Gaon, on the unique position of the Talmud.

40 Quoted literally by R. Hayyim in one of his responsa. Comp. חוט המשולש No. 9 and—slightly censored by the editors!—שו'ת ר'– יום טוב מקאפוליא. The commentary of the Gaon on the Shulhan Aruk shows almost on every page that he strictly adhered to his principles.

41 Finn, 133.

42 Eybeschütz לוחת עדות 71b, ed. Altona.

43 Foreword to מעשה רב by R. Baer ben Tanhum.

44 Foreword to באורי הגר'א, או'ח.

45 R. Israel of Minsk, foreword to פאת השלחן.

46 R. Abraham Wilna, סערת אליהו, 12. It might not be out of place to note here that this little book containing very valuable material for the life story of the Gaon is not known at all to his biographers.

47 The Talmid Hakam is forbidden many things which are permitted to ordinary men; comp. f. e. Shabbat 142b-143a; Mo'ed Katan, 11b; Ketubot 52b.

VII

RABBI ISRAEL SALANTER

Delivered in the Course of Public Lectures of the Jewish
Theological Seminary of America, February 25, 1904.

¹ Midrash Tehillim, 92, 412 ed. Buber.

² Comp. Ahad Ha-Am, על פרשת דרכים I, 178 (3d edition).

³ Most of the material in this essay is based on oral communica-
tions which the author had received in his early youth from his
teachers R. Isaac Blaser, R. Naphtali of Shat and R. Loeb
Raschkes, three distinguished disciples of Salanter. Some
episodes given here have been told to the author by his father
who was well acquainted with Salanter. I add here a selected
list of the more important books, essays and articles on Salanter
and the moralist movement in Lithuania. Blaser, אור ישראל
Wilna, 1900 (the most important source for the life and teaching
of Salanter); Benjamin, *R. Israel Lipkin Salant*, 1899 (in German);
Feldberg, קדוש ישראל, 1884; Finn, כנסת ישראל 1886 (pp. 697–698);
Eliezer Elijah Friedman, ספר הזכרונות Tel-Abib 1926 and in
התור (Jerusalem) VI, nos. 10–12; Mark, גדולים פון אונזער צייט
1908 תולדות ישיבת היהודים בקורלאנד Obzinski, 1927 (pp. 97–104);
(pp. 56–63); Rosenfeld, ר' ישראל סלנטר 1910 (in Hebrew and
under the same title also in Yiddish); Steinschneider, עיר ווילנא
(pp. 128–133); Weinberg, רבנו ישראל ותורתו המוסרית in הלבנון ed.
Elbinger, Warsaw, 1912. See also דרשות ר' ישראל סלנט 1912
(mainly a reprint of אור ישראל).

⁴ On R. Zundel, comp. E. Rivlin ספר הצדיק ר' יוסף זונדל מסלאנט
ורבותיו Jerusalem, 1927.

⁵ Comp. R. Baer b. Tanhum מעשה רב no. 61; on the influence of
the Gaon on R. Zundel, comp. Rivlin, 4.

⁶ Blaser, 79.

⁷ On Lilienthal, see David Philipson, *Max Lilienthal*, New
York, 1915.

⁸ Shapiro was a disciple of the famous scholar R. Manasseh Ben
Porat and like his master had great independence of mind.

⁹ This witty remark by Shapiro is only a variant of the Midrashic statement, Bemidbar R. 5.2.

[10] Comp. Benjamin, 27–29.

[11] The name of this Maecenas was Lachman, but he insisted that his name be kept a secret.

[12] It was published under the title עץ פרי, Wilna, 1881.

[13] Sotah 3a.

[14] Makkot 24a.

[15] עץ פרי 26a–26b.

[16] Mishnah Yoma (end).

[17] This episode was told to me by my father who was present at the visit paid by Salanter to my grandfather, R. Asher Ginzberg, the president of the congregation, whom Salanter had publicly chided.

[18] Mark, 76, gives a somewhat different version of this incident, but the one given in this essay is on the authority of the author's uncle, R. Loeb Raschkes, whose reliability cannot be questioned, as he was a pupil of Salanter.

[19] This episode was told to the author by his father.

[20] This story was told to the author by his teacher, R. Isaac Blaser.

VIII

ZECHARIAH FRANKEL

Delivered in Commemoration of the Century of His Birth before the Ohole Shem Society, New York, October 6, 1901.

[1] Comp. above pp. 125–144.

[2] On R. Abraham Wilna, the son of the Gaon, see Kauffmann, *Monatsschrift* XXXIX, 136–137.

[3] Comp. Mordecai Plungian, בן פורת Wilna, 1858.

[4] Comp. Finn, כנסת ישראל, 301.

[5] His critical notes on the Midrash Rabbah show him to have been a scholar of great acumen.

[6] There is only one comprehensive biography of Frankel, that by Saul Phineas Rabbinowitz (שפ״ר): ר׳ זכריה פראנקעל, 1898; comp. also Brann, Zacharias Frankel, Breslau, 1901, a collection of articles and essays on Frankel by the editor and others.

⁷ Comp. Hirsch, Gesammelte Schriften VI, 368–434; Auerbach, הצופה על דרכי המשנה Frankfurt, 1861; Klein, מפני קשט and האמת והשלום אהבו Frankfurt, 1861; Fischer, in Hirsch 1. c. 322–367.

⁸ Kämpf סוד ממתיק Prague, 1861; Rappaport, דברי שלום ואמת Prague, 1861.

⁹ X, 159–160.

IX

ISAAC HIRSCH WEISS

Paper written on the occasion of the ninetieth anniversary of his birth for The Jewish Comment, Baltimore, February, 1905.

¹ His autobiography זכרונותי, Warsaw, 1895, contains most of the data found in this essay.

² He was the author of a very learned commentary on Arama's works עקידת יצחק and חזות קשה published with the text under the title, ספר עקידת יצחק. . ספחנו... חזות קשה. . ועוד בה. . פירוש מקור חיים Presburg, 1849.

³ Comp. R. Baruch Shklov in his preface to the Hebrew Translation of Euclid; see also above p. 129.

⁴ Comp. שו׳ת מהר״ץ No. 3.

⁵ Jüdische Zeitschrift für Wissenschaft und Leben, II, 64.

⁶ Ibid. IV, 99.

⁷ Schechter, Studies in Judaism I, 182–212, gives a masterful appreciation of this great work by Weiss.

X

SOLOMON SCHECHTER

Delivered at the Schechter Memorial Exercises of the Jewish Theological Seminary of America, January 3, 1916.

¹ Quoted from the Zohar in ילקוט ראובני beginning of בהר but not found in our texts.

² For biographical and bibliographical material on Schechter, comp. Adler, Solomon Schechter, A Biographical Sketch (from American Jewish Yearbook, 1917); Bloch, Professor Solomon Schechter (reprinted from Hebrew Union College Monthly, II

Nos. 4 and 5) and Marx, *Solomon Schechter* (reprinted from *Publications* of the *American Jewish Historical Society*, 1917). Comp. also, *Schechter Memorial, Students' Annual*, III, 1916.

[3] Wisdom 1.4.

[4] *The Wisdom of Ben Sirah*, Cambridge 1899. The first formal announcement of the discovery was made by Dr. Schechter in *The Expositor*, July, 1896.

[5] *Studies in Judaism*, II, 31–54.

[6] *Documents of Jewish Sectaries*, I, *Fragments of a Zadokite Work*, Cambridge 1910.

[7] Comp. the author's book, *Eine Unbekannte jüdische Sekte*, 1922, pp. 148–220.

[8] Mekilta, R. Simeon in *Jewish Quarterly Review* (New Series), 1904, 443–445; Mekilta on Deut. ibid, 446–452 and in *Lewy-Festschrift*, 187–192; Sifre Zutta, in *Jewish Quarterly Review*, VI, 656–663.

[9] *Aboth De Rabbi Nathan*, Vienna, 1887.

[10] *Agadath Shir ha-Shirim*, Cambridge, 1896; *Midrash Haggadol*, Cambridge, 1902.

[11] *Jewish Quarterly Review*, XI, 643 ff.

[12] See especially the fragment published in *Saadyana*, Cambridge 1903.

[13] *Documents of Jewish Sectaries*, II, *Book of the Commandments by Anan*, Cambridge, 1910.

[14] Comp. *Studies in Judaism*, I and II, Philadelphia, 1896 and 1908.

[15] See especially his work, *Some Aspects of Rabbinic Theology*, New York, 1909.

[16] Shabbat, 105b.

XI

DAVID HOFFMANN

Delivered at the Hoffmann Memorial Exercises of the Jewish Theological Seminary of America, January 22, 1922.

[1] Rosh ha-Shanah, 18b.

[2] For biographical material, comp. Barischanski and Libschitz

ראיות מכריעות נגד ולהוין מאת... הופמן... עם מאמר הערכה על אישיותו in
ועבודתו המדעית... מאת רא'מ ליפשיץ... בצרוף הקדמה והערות אליעזר
באר ישנסקי, Jerusalem 1928; Marx, *United Synagogue Recorder*,
II No. 1, Tschernowitz, החקופה XIII, 479–491; Jeschurun,
IX, 1–19.

[3] *Festschrift z. Siebzigsten Geburtstage David Hoffmann's*, Berlin,
1904.

[4] *Das Buch Leviticus übersetzt und erklärt*, Berlin 1905–06.

[5] Joseph Halévi, *Revue Sémitique*, XV, 114.

[6] In *Jahres-Bericht d. Rabbiner-Seminars für das orthodoxe
Judenthum*, Berlin, 1874.

[7] In *Jahres-Bericht*, Berlin, 1878.

[8] Berlin, 1882; a Hebrew translation by S. Grünberg was
published under the title המשנה הראשונה Berlin, 1913.

[9] Berlin, 1888.

[10] Sifre, Deut. 357, 150a.

[11] Hullin 7b.

INDEX

INDEX

THE JEWISH PUBLICATION SOCIETY OF AMERICA

The Jewish Publication Society of America was founded in 1888 as a non-profit educational organization for the publication and dissemination of books of Jewish content. Among the four hundred titles published by the Society during the seventy years of its existence are works of belles-lettres, fiction, history, philosophy, religion and every other area of Jewish cultural and religious interest, both for adults and for children.

One of the greatest contributions of the Society to American-Jewish life has been its translation of the Bible, prepared by a committee of outstanding Jewish scholars and published in 1917. At the present time, the Society is in the process of revising this translation so as to bring it in line with contemporary language and scholarship.

Another of the contributions performed by the Society has been its publication annually of the foremost volume of Jewish statistical information—*The American Jewish Year Book.*

The Society is a membership organization, with annual dues ranging from $5.00 to $100.00. In return, members have the privilege of selecting books published during the current or prior years.